LPA 1990–2015

LPA 1990-2015
Tide of Architectural Lighting Design

Kaoru Mende + Lighting Planners Associates

Book Design and Layout:
Masaaki Hiromura and Hokuto Fujii

Translation:
Glenn Rich, Rachel Nakayama

Editing Cooperation:
Mari Kubota, Reiko Kasai, Emiko Nagata, Motoyo Yano, Noriko Higashi, Misuzu Nakamura

First published in 2015 by Rikuyosha Co., Ltd.
2-1, Shinkiba 2-chome, Koto-ku, Tokyo, 136-0082 Japan
Phone: +81-3-5569-5491 Fax: +81-3-5569-5824
www.rikuyosha.co.jp/

Printing and Binding:
Tosho Printing Co., Ltd.

©2015 Lighting Planners Associates Inc.

Printed in Japan
ISBN978-4-89737-796-4

All rights reserved. No part of this book may be reproduced
in any form without written permission of the copyright owners.

LPA 1990 – 2015
Tide of
Architectural Lighting Design

Kaoru Mende +
Lighting Planners Associates

Contents

1990–2015 LPA and the Shifting Tide of Architectural Lighting —————— 006
Kaoru Mende

Phase 1 The Architectural Lighting Enlightenment 1990–1995 —————— 010

The Architectural Lighting Enlightenment:
The Contributions of Edison Price, Arata Isozaki, and Toyo Ito   Kaoru Mende
Consciousness Light   Erwin J. S. Viray

Tokyo Design Center | Opera House in Frankfurt Auditorium Ceiling | Hotel Poluinya | Panasonic Data & Communication Center | Shimosuwa Municipal Museum | Pachinko Parlor II | Center for Advanced Science and Technology, Hyogo | Tokyo Tatsumi International Swimming Center | Beppu Park | Shibuya PARCO Façade Lighting | Kyoto Concert Hall | Toyonokuni Libraries for Culture Resources | Osaka World Trade Center | Shinjuku I - LAND PATIO | World City Expo Tokyo '96

Phase 2 The Saga of Public Space 1996–2002 —————— 068

The Saga of Public Space:
Tokyo International Forum and Kyoto Station Building   Kaoru Mende
Public Space Light   Erwin J. S. Viray

Tokyo International Forum | Waterfront City Symbol Promenade | Chihiro Art Museum Azumino | Fukushima Lagoon Museum | Kyoto Station Building | Odate Jukai Dome Park | Queen's Square Yokohama | Fuji-Q Highland FUJIYAMA | Fukui Children's Science Center | Toyama International Conference Center | Nara Centennial Hall | Kaoru Mende + LPA Exhibition "A Manner in Architectural Lighting Design" | Iwate Museum of Art | Osaka Maritime Museum | Keyaki Hiroba | OASIS 21

Phase 3 A Manner in Architectural Lighting Design 2000–2005 —————— 136

A Manner in Architectural Lighting Design: From Sendai Mediatheque
to Nagasaki National Peace Memorial Hall for the Atomic Bomb Victims   Kaoru Mende
Social Light   Erwin J. S. Viray

Sendai Mediatheque | Sapporo Dome | National Museum of Emerging Science and Innovation (Miraikan) | Kani Public Arts Center | one-north Master Plan | Chihiro Art Museum Tokyo | Katta General Public Hospital | Nagasaki National Peace Memorial Hall for the Atomic Bomb Victims | Moerenuma Park Glass Pyramid | Roppongi Hills | Toki Messe Niigata Convention Center / Toki Messe Bandaijima Building | Hiroshima City Naka Incineration Plant | W Seoul Walkerhill | Shiodome SIO-SITE | Kagawa Prefectural Higashiyama Kaii Setouchi Art Museum | The Tokyo Club | Chino Cultural Complex | Kyoto State Guest House | The 39th Tokyo Motor Show 2005 Nissan Booth

Phase 4 Overseas to Asia 2005–2009 ——————————————————————————— 222

Overseas to Asia:
Learning from Singapore, China, and Hong Kong   Kaoru Mende
Expanding Terrain Light   Erwin J. S. Viray

One George Street | Supreme Court of Singapore | The Chedi Chiang Mai | National Museum of Singapore | Changi Airport Terminal 2 Upgrading | Lighting Masterplan for Singapore's City Centre | Midland Square | OMOTESANDO akarium | Nicolas G. Hayek Center | National Centre for the Performing Arts | Banyan Tree Phuket, Doublepool Villas | Akita International University, Nakajima Library | Hilton Niseko Village | International Commerce Centre | Swarovski Ginza | Alexandra Arch, Singapore | W Hong Kong | ION Orchard

Phase 5 Designing with Shadow 2008–2015 ——————————————————————— 290

Designing with Shadow:
New Lighting Values Taught in 2011   Kaoru Mende
Shadow's Light   Erwin J. S. Viray

Commemorating the 50th Anniversary of the Reconstruction of MEIJI JINGU [akarium] | Alila Villas Uluwatu | Aman New Delhi | Tang Plaza Façade Enhancement | OSAKA "City of Light" | Kanagawa Art Theatre and NHK Yokohama Broadcasting Station | St. Regis OSAKA | Louis Vuitton Singapore Marina Bay | Reflections at Keppel Bay | Waldorf Astoria Shanghai on the Bund | NUS Education Resource Centre | Sengukan Museum | China Central Television (CCTV) | Ocean Financial Centre | Preservation and Restoration of the Tokyo Station Marunouchi Building | The Star | Kaga Katayamazu City Spa | Gardens by the Bay, Bay South | PARKROYAL on Pickering | The Interlace | InterContinental Osaka | Basic Studies on Lighting Plan for Railroad Station | Proposal for A New Nightscape for Sumidagawa River | Victoria Theatre & Victoria Concert Hall | The Otemachi Tower | Aman Tokyo | d'Leedon | Oita Prefectural Art Museum | CapitaGreen | Minna no Mori Gifu Media Cosmos | National Gallery Singapore | Ping An Financial Centre | Jewel Changi Airport

Index / Photography Credits / Profiles ——————————————————————————— 417

Chronology —— Appendix

Explanatory notes of project

Keyword: A theme or an important word regarding the lighting design **Designer's comment:** A summary phrase from the project team based on the experience **Custom-made fixtures:** Lighting fixtures customized or a luminous plane **Main light source:** Main light source used very often among 6 types of lamp below IL=Incandescent lamp / Halogen lamp, FL=Fluorescent lamp, HID=High intensity discharge lamp such as Metal Halide lamp, LED, Neon, Xenon=Xenon lamp **Brightness contrast level:** Index with 5 degrees of brightness and contrast. As in the chart, small value are for a bright and low contrast space. **Design period:** Design period from the kick-off in LPA to a project completion

1990–2015
LPA and the Shifting Tide of Architectural Lighting

Kaoru Mende

This book is a chronological and comprehensive look at the work of LPA from 1990 to 2015. The profound shifts in the global economy and the increasingly rapid pace of technological innovation in the IT field that have occurred over this time greatly impacted the social environment of architecture and architectural lighting design. These developments have also directly affected the work we do, and we should expect the work of lighting design itself to have changed in certain ways. Over the 25 years that this book covers we have completed some 700 lighting design projects. We have selected about 100 projects from among them that seem particularly significant and organized them chronologically in this book with the idea of bringing into relief the general tide over this time.

While LPA's history of 25 years is quite short it is still enough time to elucidate the extraordinary forces that have driven it forward. We want to uncover the source of those forces. Is it because of a changing global environment and socio-economic conditions? Was it brought about by innovations in lighting technology? Or is it nothing more than our singular passion for our work? We hope to reveal the shifting tides of architectural lighting design by exploring these questions.

A decade-long period of development

I committed to becoming an architectural lighting designer in 1980. I was in my second year of work at a research lab for a lighting fixture manufacturer. My inspiration was meeting the brilliant architectural lighting designer Edison Price.

Price established a small lighting company in New York City in 1952 and was active as an architectural lighting design consultant from the 50s through the 70s. As a participant in architecture projects designed by such luminaries as Mies Van der Rohe, Louis Kahn, and Philip Johnson, he developed and set a new course for architectural lighting. It is impossible to talk about the quality of American modern architecture without Price. His stories about his ideas and accomplishments in architectural lighting held me in awe. Later, on Price introduced me to two of America's leading architectural lighting designers: Claude Engle and Paul Marantz. I received several opportunities to work with them, where I spent my days finely honing my architectural lighting design skills.

I spent the ten years starting in 1980 under the guidance of a number of pioneers, most notably Marantz, old friend Arata Isozaki, and kindred spirit Toyo Ito, with whom I collaborated on Tower of Winds project. This was a time that might be described as the formative period for architectural lighting design in Japan.

What is the occupational aim of architectural lighting design? Who are its clients? What should it impart to society? How much distance should there be between the work of architectural lighting and the architect? The ten years leading up to the founding of LPA in 1990 were a kind of prelude that set the scene for the performance to follow.

An event-filled quarter-century

Many significant events have occurred over the 25 years since the founding of LPA. The fall of the Berlin Wall, the Gulf War, the launch of the European Union, the return of Hong Kong to China, the Kyoto Protocol, the founding of Google, the September 11 terrorist attacks in the United States, and the global economic crisis, to name only a few. Over that time, Japan experienced the collapse of a bubble economy, the sarin gas subway attacks, the Kobe earthquake, and the Tohoku earthquake and tsunami. Japan has endured a number of terrible events indeed during the long malaise following the end of the era of high economic growth. These events and phenomena also affected the work of lighting design in myriad ways.

German reunification and the launch of the EU prompted a realignment of the lighting design industry in Europe, while the Gulf War and fears of an energy crisis triggered a corresponding reduction in lighting consumption. Global economic crises and the collapse of bubble economies demanded that lighting design adopt a facility management perspective and search for technical solutions to the problem of energy consumption. In the wake of Japan's earthquakes and the Fukushima nuclear accident attention turned to energy conservation and natural energy, and lighting design took a close look at sustainability and energy conservation.

Technological innovation in the field of lighting during this period was even more dramatic. To begin with, a number of new light sources indispensable to lighting design appeared on the scene. The halogen and krypton lamps that were the best of the incandescent lamps, and which had been in constant use since the 1980s, were replaced in the 1990s by compact fluorescent lamps, small-sized metal halide lamps, and other high-energy efficiency light sources. Fluorescent lamps and discharge lamps also became more compact and therefore easier to use. Then, with the development at last of blue LED in 1993, the use of LED spread rapidly and the technology has now established a dominating presence all over the world. When LED first appeared its only selling point was efficiency, so I took a somewhat skeptical wait-and-see attitude. Today, however, LED is not only efficient it has made great strides in quality, so there are less and less reasons to reject it. Lighting design has at last welcomed the inevitable arrival of the LED era.

Lighting design based on LED light sources wiped away past design concepts. Instead of lighting fixtures governed by reflectors, LED controls light distribution by means of lenses and films. Since LED is a point light source, several light sources can be lined up and translated onto a luminous plane surface. Moreover, extremely small LEDs can be embedded into sashes, glass, furniture, and building materials. This means its potential as a lighting fixture is virtually without limits. LED has revolutionized lighting design.

Moreover, and in connection with the development of LED, lighting control technology has made tremendous advances. With the digitalization of voltage control systems an entire lighting system can be controlled with a personal computer device. The control system regulates not only the amount of light but also color temperature (the color of light). For instance, a general office lighting system might significantly change the light environment between morning and afternoon. In the morning, light is bright and whitish while in the afternoon illumination is slightly reduced and the light has a warm color tone. This is the greatest advantage of digital lighting control systems. What's more, control equipment is becoming more and more compact and seems headed toward devices as small as smartphones.

25 years is not a very long time, but in the world of lighting it has been a span of time full of amazing developments.

The evolution of LPA: five phases x five years

In this book, I divide LPA's 25 year history into five phases. This does not mean that there is a clear break every five years, however. Instead, it helps us pinpoint major turning points, project completions, and other important events over that time. Erwin Viray and I offer commentary for each time period. We want the reader to forget specific years and instead look at events as they have developed over these five year time periods.

We begin with a broad overview of the five years from 1990 to 1995 in a chapter titled "The Architectural Lighting Enlightenment: The Contributions of Edison Price, Arata Isozaki, and Toyo Ito" 30 years had lapsed from the time when Edison Price first pioneered the field of architectural lighting to when it was introduced in Japan. The work of LPA in its early phase, therefore, had the role of enlightening Japanese society about architectural lighting. While this period is dotted with important LPA projects done in collaboration with Nikken Sekkei, Hiroshi Hara, and others, the projects led by Arata Isozaki and Toyo Ito stand out. From these two, especially, I felt a passion for exploring the genuine role of architectural lighting, and I became utterly convinced that within architecture there are novel forms of light waiting to be discovered.

"The Saga of Public Space: Tokyo International Forum and Kyoto Station Building" is the title for Phase 2 covering the years 1996 to 2002. The chapter chronicles the role of public facility lighting in freeing Japan from twentieth-century assumptions about light. We want to plainly demonstrate to a mass public a commitment to quality of light over quantity of light. The lighting designs of Tokyo International Forum and Kyoto Station Building are expressions of this philosophy. The light quality for both of these projects moves beyond the conceptual framework for public architecture in Japan at that time. These projects were novel simply because they do not employ uniform, bright lighting.

The shadow-rich light environment of Kyoto Station Building and the lighting of public space in Tokyo International Forum with illuminance of 50 lux are both examples of new ways of lighting that are certain to contribute to better light quality in future public space.

Phase 3 from 2000 to 2005 covers the period when the LPA design style became established. This style was presented in Kaoru Mende + LPA Exhibition "A Manner in Architectural Lighting Design," an exhibition shown in fall 1999 at TOTO GALLERY-MA in Tokyo. The chapter is titled "A Manner in Architectural Lighting Design: From Sendai Mediatheque to Nagasaki National Peace Memorial Hall for the Atomic Bomb Victims." In addition to these two projects, the chapter profiles Roppongi Hills, OASIS 21, Katta General Public Hospital, Chihiro Art Museum Tokyo, among other projects. Within all of these projects dwell many of the 10 concepts and 27 manners articulated at the "A Manner in Architectural Lighting Design" exhibition, and all are heavily tinged with LPA's interpretation of and distinctive approach to lighting design.

Phase 4 covering 2005 to 2009 is titled "Overseas to Asia: Learning from Singapore, China, and Hong Kong." In 2000 — and now in its tenth year as a prospering enterprise — LPA established a group company in Singapore and set out to experience international competition in an overseas environment. We commenced on projects in collaboration with accomplished building designers and clients from all over the world. We completed lighting design for the Supreme Court of Singapore and National Museum of Singapore and established LPA's presence in the city with our work on the Shingapore's City Centre Lighting Masterplan. Just being unable use Japanese is an inconvenience when working overseas. But the snags and difficulties we knew we would meet along the way have made us more resilient than we had first anticipated.

Phase 5 covering 2008 to 2015 brings us to the LPA of the present under the title "Designing with Shadow: New Lighting Values Taught in 2011." In 2010, LPA published a book titled "Designing with Shadow."

The following year Japan experienced the Tohoku Earthquake, and from every corner came calls to conserve power. Even as recovery from the nuclear power plant accident stalled light returned throughout Japan, but the disaster made people reflect on a past that thought of light only in terms of quantity. "Lighting design starts with darkness and restores beautiful shadow." This is what the world has told us in the starkest terms. The disaster has taught us the value of light.

The LPA exhibition "Nightscape 2050 — A Dialogue between Cities·Light·People in the Future" opens in August 2015. The exhibition will tour Berlin, Singapore, Hong Kong, and Tokyo and hold workshops and symposiums together with people in each region. The exhibition will also include light interactive exhibits and exhibits drawing lessons from nightscapes from around the world. The theme is "the life of light in the future/where do we go from here?"

The 25 years and 101 lighting design projects presented in this book form an archive for understanding the present and imagining the future. The world of lighting design is always changing, and it is our hope that in the years ahead it will evolve for the better.

Phase 1

The Architectural Lighting Enlightenment
1990–1995

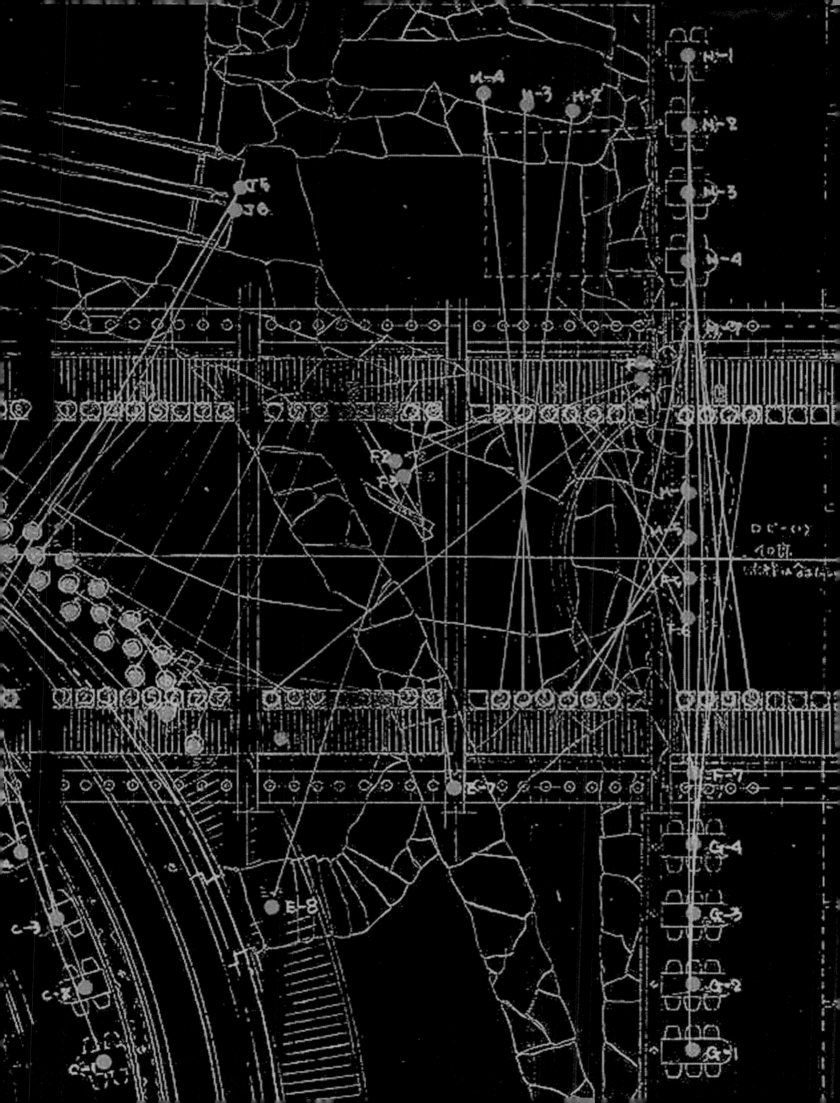

The Architectural Lighting Enlightenment:
The Contributions of Edison Price, Arata Isozaki, and Toyo Ito

Kaoru Mende

The idea of lighting design first took root in the 1950s on the east coast of the United States, mainly in New York City, where the lighting design genius Edison Price opened a small office along Manhattan's East River in 1952. Even though Price would be followed by such path-breaking lighting designers as Richard Kelly, Claude Engle, and Paul Marantz, the story cannot be told without the lighting fixtures such as, wall washers, and other downlight fixtures, or the multiple cross-section track light wiring systems, that Price developed.

Light is a material. A lighting fixture is a tool. The object of illumination is not the fixture but the architecture. This vocabulary of illumination was given concrete form as lighting design by these men. When we in Japan first studied lighting design around 1980, we were aware that we were 30 years behind the profession as it was practiced in America.

Of course, at that time a number of incandescent lamps were being developed, led by General Electric's shield beam lamp and including the halogen lamp and mini-krypton lamp. Blue LED was invented in 1993, though nobody understood its significance at the time. The low-voltage halogen lamp — which moved even closer to becoming a point light source with voltage lowered to 12V — was a cutting-edge light source that, together with advances in light distribution control technology, delivered on its potential for impeccably beautiful lighting effects.

The course of architectural design as it moved through modernists Le Corbusier, Frank Lloyd Wright, Eero Saarinen, and Louis Kahn has seen a complex intertwining of natural light and modern lighting technology, as exemplified in such works as Norman Forster's Hong Kong and Shanghai Bank Headquarters, I. M. Pei's Louvre Pyramid, and Jean Nouvel's Arab World Institute. In Japan, meanwhile, the field was pioneered by two architects: Arata Isozaki and Toyo Ito.

Arata Isozaki's collaborations with American architectural lighting designers on such projects as the Los Angeles Museum of Contemporary Art and the Palladium in New York City make him one of the most important figures in Japanese architectural lighting design. We completed the 1990s having collaborated with Isozaki on a series of projects: Art Tower Mito, Center for Advanced Science and Technology, Hyogo, Toyonokuni Libraries for Culture Resources, and Kyoto Concert Hall. As lighting designers, we were both giddy with excitement as well as resistant to Isozaki's unyielding design philosophy of extinguishing lighting fixtures from architectural space and that the architecture itself is an immense lighting fixture. For the Toyonokuni Library for Culture Resources project, Isozaki brought a 1/50 scale model to our office in order to passionately discuss the question of "how do we control and incorporate natural light into this building?" It is not an overstatement to say that without Arata Isozaki's passion and guidance our work as architectural lighting designers would not have become a socially established profession.

Toyo Ito's work has also been consistently profound and stimulating. These include Tower of Winds next to the west exit of Yokohama Station — a relatively early collaboration for me — followed by a number of projects completed in the 1990s, such as Opera House in Frankfurt, Hotel Poluinya, Shimosuwa Municipal Museum, Tokyo Frontier, and Odate Jukai Dome Park.

Ito has constantly sought to completely rethink light as a way to bring a new mood to architecture. The starting point for this quest was Tower of Winds, a cylindrical structure covered in perforated metal combining three different lighting systems that achieve infinite variation. Architect and lighting designer were both captivated by the idea for this project at the very same time. Can architectural lighting design so beautifully affect how we value architecture and bring about an enormous lighting fixture whose appearance completely reverses between day and night within a cold-hearted urban space? We could do nothing but marvel at the fruit of our labors standing before us. Possessing the drive and sensitivity of what we might aptly call an "architect of light," Toyo Ito is still radically transforming the dynamics of architectural lighting design.

The foundation of lighting design rests on the accomplishments of visionaries like Edison Price, Arata Isozaki, and Toyo Ito.

Consciousness Light

Erwin J. S. Viray

In the beginning, there is only light. How does light suddenly come to consciousness? How do we become aware of the potential of light? LPA's Kaoru Mende mentions how light consciousness emerges into being, beyond the light bulbs above our heads to the floodlighting of buildings, towards a potential that opens new horizons of day into night, light consciousness — a new consciousness that buildings and spaces exist not only in the day but also into the night. The collaborations with Arata Isozaki and Toyo Ito opened the potential of architectural consciousness of light.

My first encounter on the potential of light, how I gained consciousness is an encounter with the Dan Flavin Installation at Richmond Hall in the Menil Collection in Houston Texas. The initial encounter with the power of light, light itself creating space, sensing perspective, dimension, and providing direction to space gave an awakening on the existence of light.

Among LPA works, one strong encounter to awaken a consciousness of light is the Kent Vale Staff Housing. The first time I visited the place was at night. And I was surprised and in awe. I asked myself, is this faculty housing? Or am I in Bali? I tried to understand why that feeling of being in Bali is awakened. It was dark, but there were points of light floating and reflecting. These elements seemed to redefine the boundaries of space. They also seemed to redefine how I look at light as just something that gives beyond illumination. Light can actually awaken feelings. As I walked in the space, I could feel the wind, the breeze touching the skin, and the sounds of air in consonance with the combination of shadow and light. And so light consciousness is not just light, but the shadows that go with it. The space is very dramatic. Light and shadow provide a special quality given to an everyday space in the over-simplifying the architect's work living quarters of a university faculty. It gives an uplifting feeling, making one feel that one is in the magical land of Bali, possibly intimating the magical land of learning that is the nature of a university, a magical space in an everyday.

That encounter with light and space, how light and space provoked my sense of perception of space, how series of lights made perspective appear and gave a sense of direction to space, opened a consciousness of light.

In this phase, LPA and Kaoru Mende open our eyes to a consciousness of light.

Erwin J. S. Viray
Erwin Viray is Professor of Architecture and Design at the Kyoto Institute of Technology, Japan.
Erwin Viray was Assistant Professor in the Department of Architecture at the School of Design and Environment of the National University of Singapore (NUS) before taking up the position of Professor of Architecture and Design at the Kyoto Institute of Technology in July 2011. He was Head of the Graduate School of Architecture Design in 2012-2014, and now deputy University President. He is also Design Critic of Architecture at the Harvard University Graduate School of Design (GSD) in Cambridge, MA, USA.

Tokyo Design Center

1991 Tokyo, Japan
Design | Mario Bellini, Obayashi
Client | Sowa Estates

Keyword : An Italian Street Corner
Designer's comment : Arrival of Italian-style light and shadow
Custom-made fixtures : Elevator Slit Lighting
Main light source : IL
Brightness contrast level : 4
Design Period : 3 years

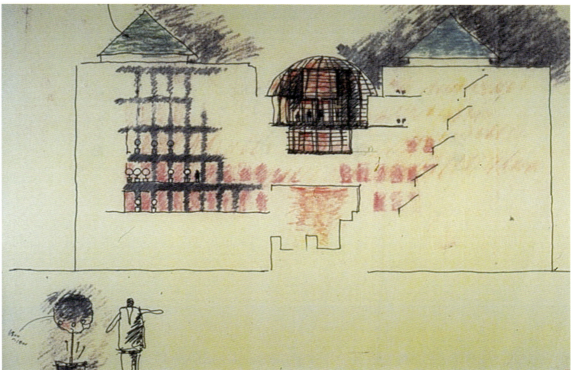

This building is a design center with showrooms, mini-galleries, an event hall, restaurants, conference rooms, and other facilities for companies in the interior design industry.

The building was designed by architect Mario Bellini. The centerpiece of his design is the large staircase climbing the five-floor galleria reminiscent of a street corner in an Italian town.

We focused on warm, soft light that seems to spill out from the massive walls on either side. We wanted the line of sight to naturally gravitate to the sculpture of the silver horse at the top of the stairs.

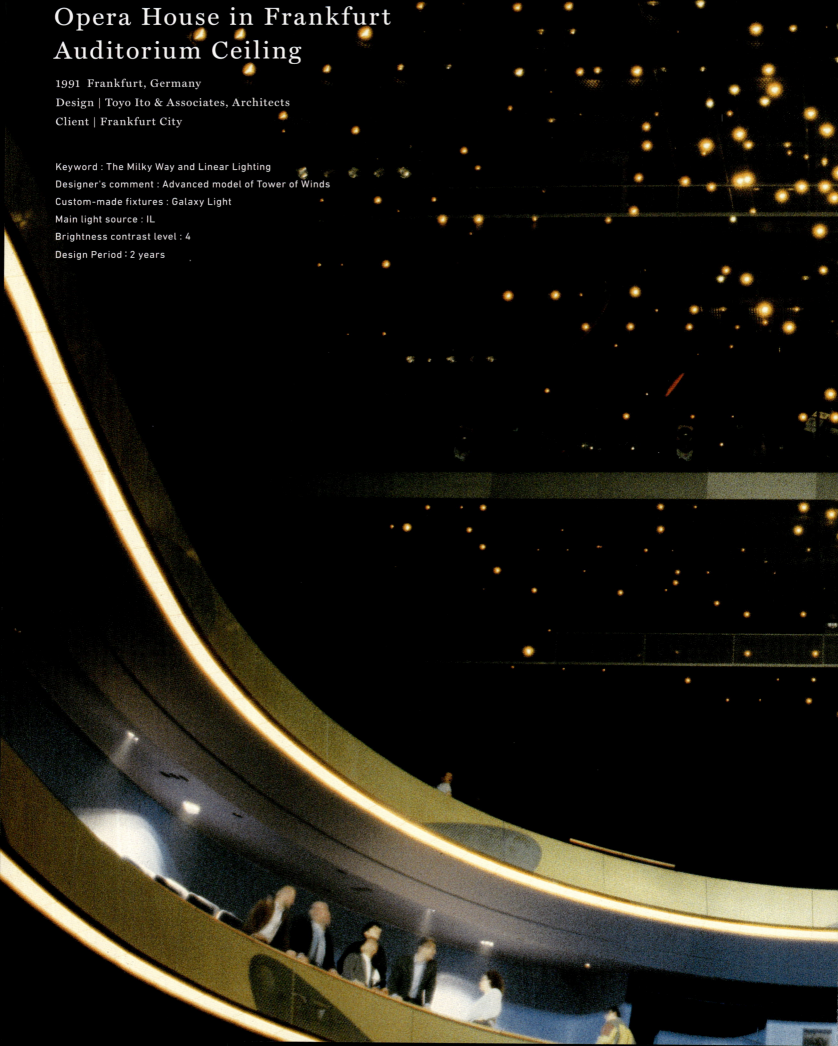

Opera House in Frankfurt
Auditorium Ceiling

1991 Frankfurt, Germany
Design | Toyo Ito & Associates, Architects
Client | Frankfurt City

Keyword : The Milky Way and Linear Lighting
Designer's comment : Advanced model of Tower of Winds
Custom-made fixtures : Galaxy Light
Main light source : IL
Brightness contrast level : 4
Design Period : 2 years

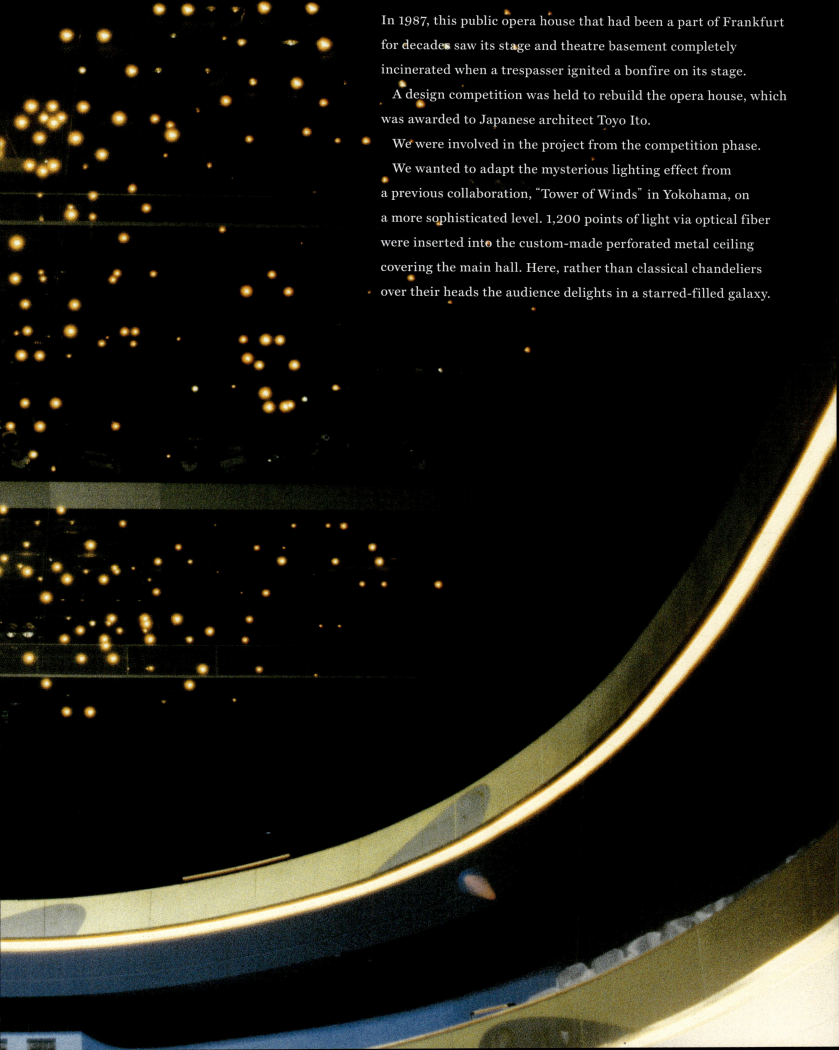

In 1987, this public opera house that had been a part of Frankfurt for decades saw its stage and theatre basement completely incinerated when a trespasser ignited a bonfire on its stage.

A design competition was held to rebuild the opera house, which was awarded to Japanese architect Toyo Ito.

We were involved in the project from the competition phase.

We wanted to adapt the mysterious lighting effect from a previous collaboration, "Tower of Winds" in Yokohama, on a more sophisticated level. 1,200 points of light via optical fiber were inserted into the custom-made perforated metal ceiling covering the main hall. Here, rather than classical chandeliers over their heads the audience delights in a starred-filled galaxy.

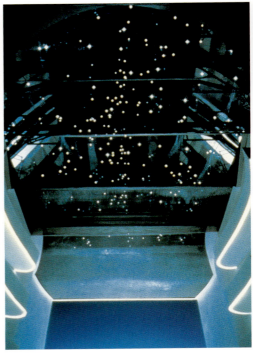
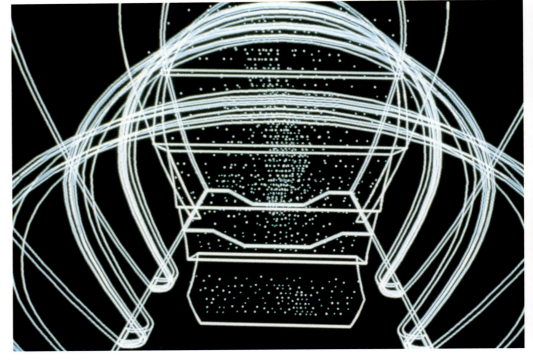

We were contacted by Toyo Ito soon after he had been invited to take part in the project, and from our very first meeting we had already spontaneously hit on the same lighting approach. Namely, a more sophisticated application in an indoor context of the "light concealed within perforated metal" technique that we had successfully used for our outdoor project, Tower of Winds in Yokohama.

For the competition presentation, we brought a model with lighting built to 1/25 scale, large enough for the clients to put their heads inside and experience the effect. The mayor and theatre representatives who attended Ito's presentation put their heads inside the model glittering with optical fiber and observed the lighting effect with great interest. Judging by their reaction and questions, we felt confident that Ito would be awarded the project.

The 1,200 light particles glowing through the perforated metal produce a subtle sparkling effect with just a small change in viewing point. The almost imperceptible effect that makes this possible could not have been achieved without an optical fiber lighting system. In addition, color conversion filters were manually installed in random places to give the galaxy asymmetry. Working behind the ceiling was exhausting but we nonetheless enjoyed the work immensely.

Hotel Poluinya

1992 Hokkaido, Japan
Design | Toyo Ito & Associates, Architects
Client | Nexus

Keyword : Minimal and Low Cost
Designer's comment : Grateful for the darkness of Hokkaido
Custom-made fixtures : Patrol Light

Main light source : IL, FL
Brightness contrast level : 4
Design Period : 2 years

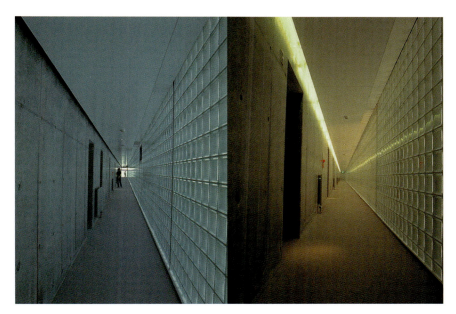

This quiet hotel sits at the foot of Mount Shari amid the beautiful Hokkaido landscape. Architect Toyo Ito was commissioned to design this low-cost yet deeply inviting hotel.

The lighting design is intended to bring out the landmark quality of the glass block wall in the guest room hallway, and the symbolic power of the entrance court with its thin layer of water. Above all, the change in appearance of the glass block guest room hallway from day to night is a clear statement of the dynamism of architectural lighting. This is a fine example of how simple details can be used to create the necessary and sufficient lighting effect.

Panasonic Data & Communication Center

1992 Tokyo, Japan
Design | Nikken Sekkei
Client | Panasonic (former Matsushita Electric Industrial)

Keyword : The Right Light in the Right Place
Designer's comment : Last minutes involvement but great results
Custom-made fixtures : 540,000cd Spot Light Reflector
Main light source : IL, HID
Brightness contrast level : 4
Design Period : 2 years

The building is a nine floor ecological office building with an immense atrium. The entrance lobby has a 40-meter high top-light that fills the space with natural light and gives it a pleasant semi-outdoor ambience.

We developed a high-efficiency, energy conserving lighting system that is also very easy to maintain. Low-voltage halogen lamps combined with anodized reflectors achieve ultra-narrow-angle light distribution while high-performance reflection mirrors installed in separate places in the ceiling sends light only to the specific points where it is needed. While the system may seem complicated at first glance, it is the logical outcome of working out the most practical method for achieving the goals of the design.

In the upper portion of the atrium, 100 mirrors, 500mm in diameter, were mounted along with spotlights shining down on the floor (P026, P027 top). Using 12V 100W spotlights with custom-made optical reflectors achieves an illuminance intensity of 540,000cd. (P027 bottom).

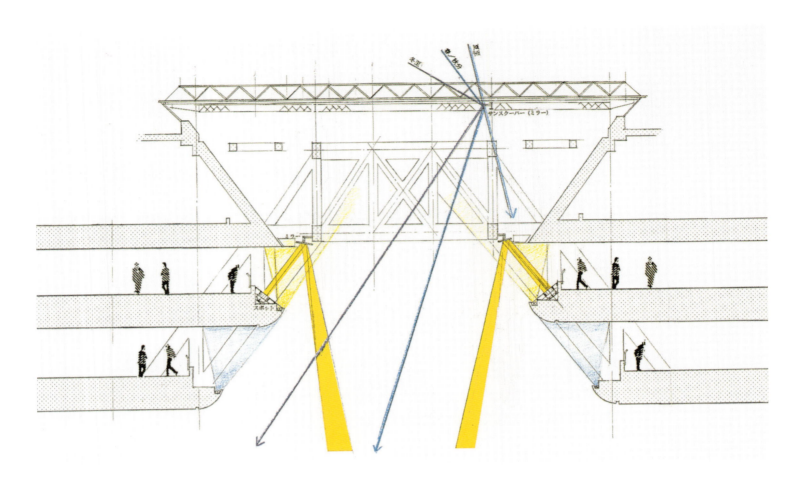

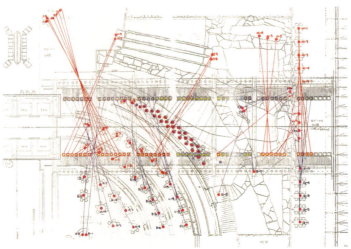

Realizing this unique lighting system required solving a number of difficult problems with unconventional ideas and technology.

To control the distribution of the super-narrow-angle light we used nearly point light source quality 12V 100W high-quality halogen lamps. Another crucial feature of the system is the use of optical reflection mirrors designed to enhance illuminance intensity. Providing 300 lux of illuminance to tables 40-meters beneath the light source requires illuminance intensity of 480,000 cd. Through trial and error experiment we arrived at an optical reflection mirror larger in size than the typical mirror that achieves 540,000 cd luminosity. This is an extremely high value for a standard 100W bulb.

We were also confronted with the problem of how to accurately direct this light to the tables 40-meters below. We built a system in which light from fixtures installed in the eighth-floor is reflected by φ500mm optical mirrors protruding from the atrium. To make this system work we had to constantly make minute angle adjustments, and we felt tremendous relief the moment when every light source originating from the 100 reflection mirrors installed at the top of the atrium was at last focused only on the spot it was supposed to illuminate. The mirror reflection system we developed creates a glare-free and pleasing light environment inside the atrium.

Shimosuwa Municipal Museum

1993 Nagano, Japan
Design | Toyo Ito & Associates, Architects
Client | Shimosuwa Town

Keyword : At a Distance
Designer's comment : The triumph of optical technology

Main light source : IL, HID
Brightness contrast level : 4

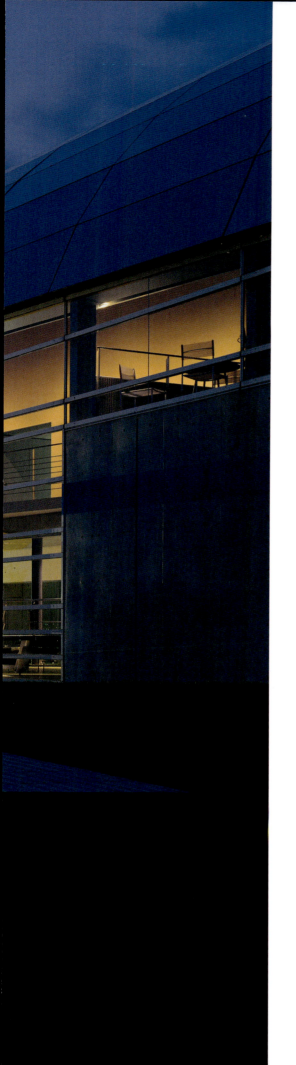

This museum with a gorgeous curved exterior on the shore of Lake Suwa exhibits traditional everyday items of the culture around the lake.

We wanted a lighting design that thoroughly conceals the presence of lighting fixtures and naturally highlights the architecture's carefree form. The exterior at twilight emphasizes the warm light radiating from the interior while a narrow angle spotlight 50-meters distant casts the curved roof in an elegant glow.

The ceiling of the exhibit room is a three-dimensional curved surface finished in 100mm-wide strip flooring with one of the strips serving as a slit within which fixed-point spotlights are installed.

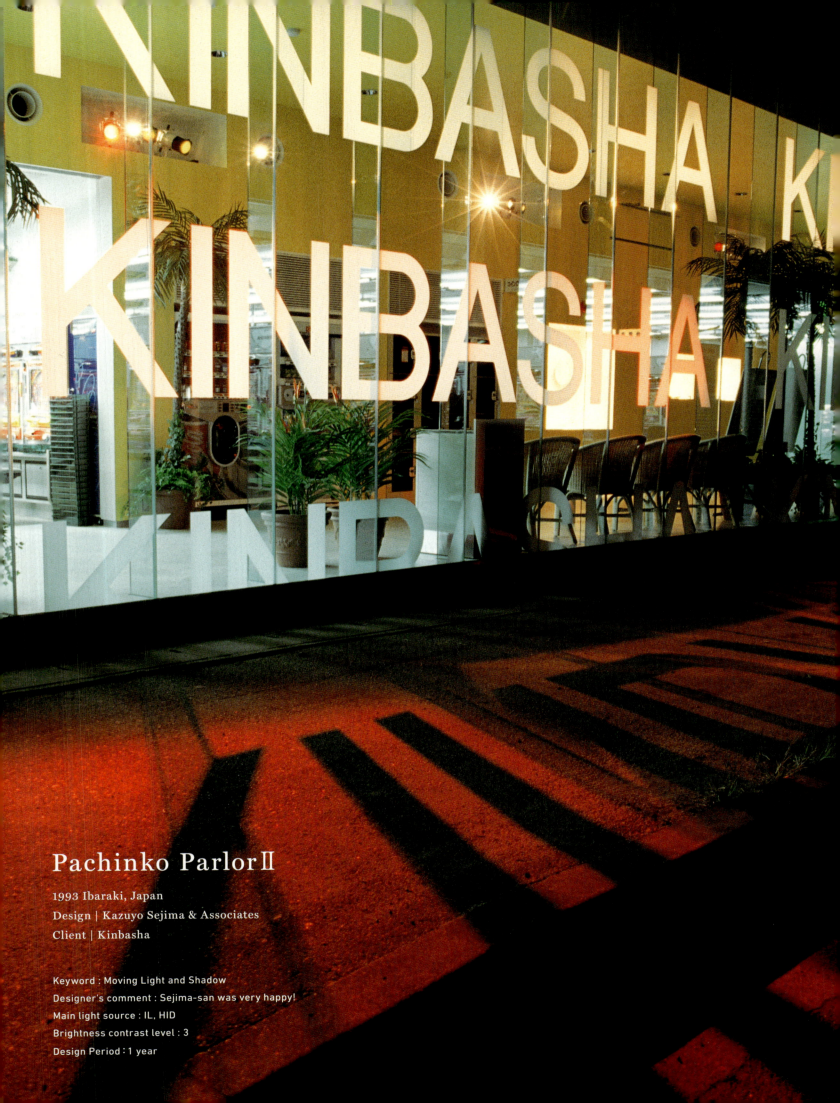

Pachinko Parlor II

1993 Ibaraki, Japan
Design | Kazuyo Sejima & Associates
Client | Kinbasha

Keyword : Moving Light and Shadow
Designer's comment : Sejima-san was very happy!
Main light source : IL, HID
Brightness contrast level : 3
Design Period : 1 year

Pachinko is one of Japan's most popular recreational arcade games. The client invited female architects to take part in a design competition with the idea of promoting pachinko as a more wholesome game.

We built light contrivances that exploit the materials of the building's 42.5 meter long rectangular glass façade facing the street and change its appearance in a variety of ways. The wall washer light cast on the yellow wall has a dimmer control that creates a light reservoir whose light flits quickly across the entire wall in-sync with the speed of cars passing by on the street. In addition, the "KINBASHA" logo affixed to the glass is highlighted with a variety of changing light effects that add an artistic flourish to the logo's advertising role.

Center for Advanced Science and Technology, Hyogo

1993 Hyogo, Japan
Design | Arata Isozaki & Associates, ADH Architects,
Peter Walker William Johnson and Partners
Client | Hyogo Prefecture

Keyword : Integration
Designer's comment : A great collaborative effort!
Custom-made fixtures : Super Lantern, Volcano Lighting
Main light source : IL, LED
Brightness contrast level : 4
Design Period : 2.5 years

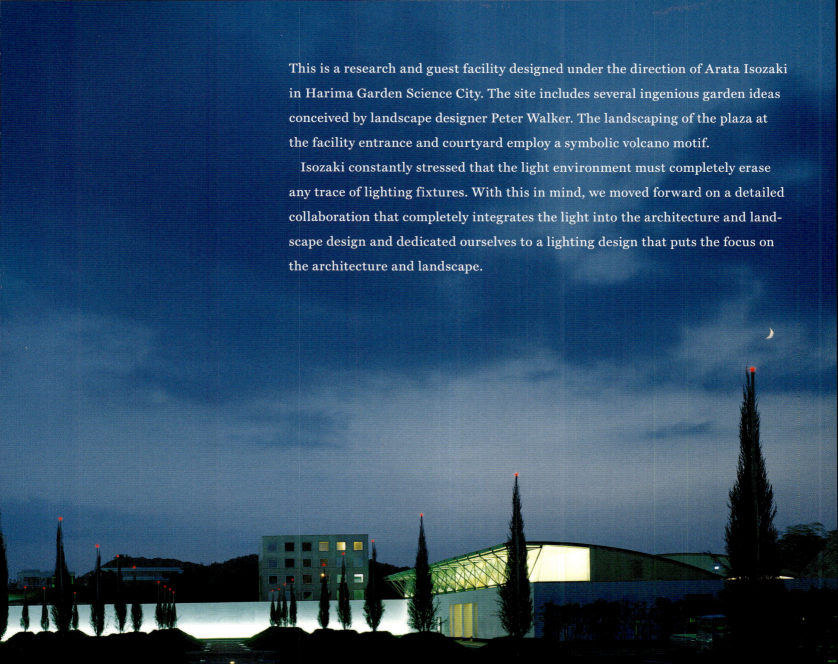

This is a research and guest facility designed under the direction of Arata Isozaki in Harima Garden Science City. The site includes several ingenious garden ideas conceived by landscape designer Peter Walker. The landscaping of the plaza at the facility entrance and courtyard employ a symbolic volcano motif.

Isozaki constantly stressed that the light environment must completely erase any trace of lighting fixtures. With this in mind, we moved forward on a detailed collaboration that completely integrates the light into the architecture and landscape design and dedicated ourselves to a lighting design that puts the focus on the architecture and landscape.

Landscape designer Peter Walker's design was conceived around a symbolic volcano motif. The entrance plaza has orderly rows of conically-shaped hills, each one topped by a single cypress tree. We installed red LED lamps at the tip of the trees that suggest the glow of volcanic magma. For the artificial hills and bamboo grove in the courtyard we employ a stage lighting approach that creates a nighttime scene completely different from its daytime appearance.

For the auditorium designed by Arata Isozaki, we created a space completely free of any ceiling lighting fixtures by using the ceiling plane as a large reflective panel.

For the guest rooms we designed floor stand fixtures dubbed "super andon" because of their resemblance to traditional paper lanterns. The lamps can be set to one of three lighting effects.

Tokyo Tatsumi International Swimming Center

1994 Tokyo, Japan
Design | Mitsuru Man Senda and Environment Design Institute
Client | Bureau of Port and Harbor, Tokyo Metropolitan Government

Keyword : Ceremonial and Everyday Lighting Environment
Designer's comment : Enjoy different scenarios of light
Main light source : HID, IL
Brightness contrast level : 2
Design Period : 3.5 years

This swimming facility operated by Tokyo Prefecture both hosts official competitions and serves as a public-use facility. The lighting design provides versatile program operation by combining ambient lighting that amply showcases the form of the Center's immense roof and a variety of functional lighting for meeting the facility's diverse lighting needs.

The functional lighting needed for illuminance, color temperature, and other lighting requirements of official swim competitions is installed in a catwalk suspended directly over the pool, while the curved ceiling that serves as its backdrop radiates soft ambient lighting.

The facility not only hosts international competitions just a few times a year it is open to the broader public at most other times, and we thought that providing a lighting environment appropriate to daily use was the more important priority. While competition lighting requires water surface illumination, uniformity ratio, and so on built to strict standards, a more relaxing light environment is needed when the pool is serving the public during normal operation.

In other words, the facility has two kinds of lighting: everyday lighting for normal use and ceremonial lighting for events. We used illuminance and color temperature to clearly distinguish the lighting for official competitions from the lighting that creates a relaxing ambience when the public uses the facility. In direct contrast to the high illuminance and color temperature required for events, we used restrained illuminance and low color temperature to create quiet, relaxed atmosphere when the pool is open to the public. Moreover, in contrast to the direct, high-efficiency downlights used during events, during normal operation soft, indirect lighting of the vaulted ceiling highlights the facility's architectural richness.

Beppu Park

1994 Oita, Japan
Client | Beppu City

Keyword : A Pyramid of Light
Designer's comment : Too bad that the park was vandalized after the opening
Custom-made fixtures : Movable Xenon Light
Main light source : Xenon, IL
Brightness contrast level : 5
Design Period : 2 years

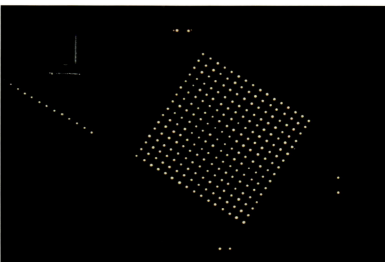

At night, this expansive 400-meter wide park and former Imperial property was illuminated only with security lighting and rarely visited. The mayor told us that he wanted "a park that was just as open and inviting to the public at night as during the day." Our design creates a park with a unique nighttime appeal and environment that is completely different from daytime and where thousands of citizens can mingle together.

  Our lighting design includes a "Light Pyramid" that functions as a clock, an "ocean of light" reminiscent of rolling waves, "firefly bamboo forest," and "metasequoia pond." We took advantage of the park's ample space to appoint a variety of creative light scenes for park visitors to encounter and enjoy.

The "Light Pyramid" originates from 4kw xenon floodlights positioned at each of the park's four corners. A computer program adjusts the free angle of the floodlights, which project traces of light high into sky for ten minute intervals only at the top of each hour and at an angle that enables visitors to tell the time by the height of the pyramid. Visible from the urban areas in the vicinity, the light pyramid also serves as a local landmark.

The "sea of light" is oriented at a 45° angle to the park and consists of 224 lighting fixtures embedded in the ground. A computer program modulates the brightness of the light array to create an effect that is like surf washing up on the shore. At "firefly bamboo grove" visitors encounter hundreds of artificial fireflies made from optical fiber and with motion sensors that make the lights flicker when people approach. Metasequoia pond is designed to illuminate the magnificent trees so that only their representation is cast on the pond.

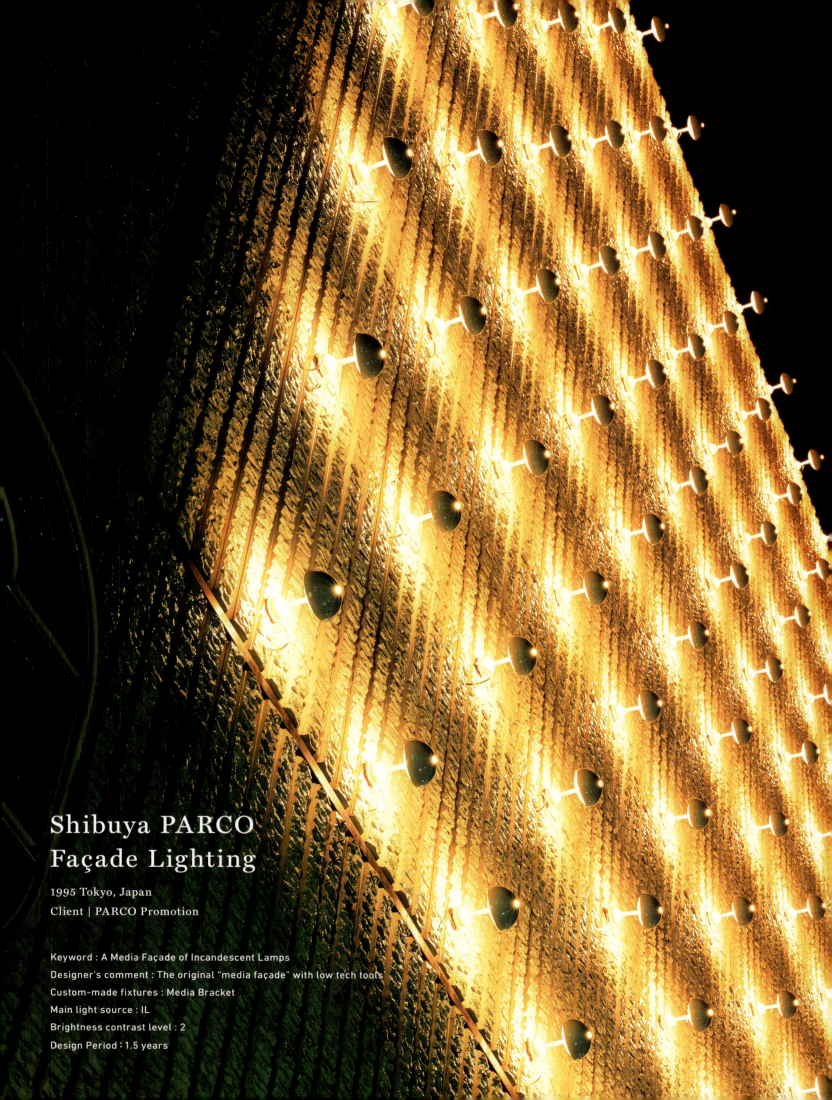

Shibuya PARCO Façade Lighting

1995 Tokyo, Japan
Client | PARCO Promotion

Keyword : A Media Façade of Incandescent Lamps
Designer's comment : The original "media façade" with low tech tools
Custom-made fixtures : Media Bracket
Main light source : IL
Brightness contrast level : 2
Design Period : 1.5 years

PARCO is an innovative multi-purpose fashion tenant building in Shibuya, one of Tokyo's main youth districts. At the time of the façade's renovation in 1995, LED lighting was nowhere to be found. The façade lighting we proposed manipulates a variety of graphical patterns to create an animation-like effect.

    All of the 152 wall-lighting fixtures installed on the façade are incandescent lamps.

    The skillful modulation of indirect and direct light creates a multihued appearance. Now that illuminating façades with LED is the dominant trend, it is all the more noteworthy how the warm light cast by this low-tech lighting system continues to enliven the street even today.

Kyoto Concert Hall

1995 Kyoto, Japan
Design | Arata Isozaki & Associates
Client | Kyoto City

Keyword : Lighting as a Part
Designer's comment : Highly detailed lighting!
Custom-made fixtures : Theatre Lanterns
Main light source : IL
Brightness contrast level : 3

This 22,412m² facility built by Kyoto city to commemorate the 1200th anniversary of the founding of the ancient capital is the home of the Kyoto Symphony Orchestra. It consists of a 1,839 seat shoebox-shaped large hall with pipe organ and a 514 seat small ensemble hall. The architect insisted throughout on a design that both mirrors the context of the city and integrates architecture and lighting.

The shoebox-shaped concert hall strives for a seamless unity between stage and audience, so we proposed finely contoured ceiling lighting that combines acoustic paneling and audience lighting. For the ensemble hall we developed a novel ceiling system that integrates to the greatest extreme possible stage and audience lighting.

We made a herculean effort to erase the presence of the concert hall's ceiling and stage lighting. The idea of an undulating ceiling followed logically from the function of the acoustical panels, so we proposed ceiling lighting that reflects and disperses light in a manner similar to the effect achieved in the interiors of Islamic architecture. This innovative ceiling system also functions to completely erase the presence of all stage lighting fixtures and general audience downlights.

Moreover, the walls on both sides open and close, concealing lighting fixtures, including stage side-lights, until they are needed. From the anticipation before the performance, and through the performance and intermission and to the finale, the hall's lighting system precisely fits each situation and stage of the program.

The ensemble hall avoids the uniform arrangement of audience downlights typical of most small halls in favor of four circular light modules that combine stage and audience lighting. Here, a luminous plane diffuses soft light while downlights installed along the outer periphery provide audience lighting.

Toyonokuni Libraries for Culture Resources

1995 Oita, Japan
Design | Arata Isozaki & Associates
Client | Oita Prefecture

Keyword : Super Ambient Lighting
Designer's comment : The mock-up experiment wins again
Custom-made fixtures : Indirect Light Above Beams
Main light source : FL, HID
Brightness contrast level : 1
Design Period : 3 years

This six floor, one underground floor building is a multi-purpose information facility with a library, museum, and public archive. The open-stack reading room recreates the "Hall of 100 Columns" found in ancient Roman and Babylonian architecture.

The columns are laid out in a 7.5 meter grid and the room is topped by a vaulted ceiling. Besides desktop illumination, the room's functional lighting needs include enhanced vertical illuminance when looking for materials on the bookshelves. Rather than rely on appliance lighting attached to bookshelves and ceiling downlights, we proposed securing horizontal and vertical illuminance by means of "super-ambient lighting" produced by light boldly reflected off the ceiling.

The "super-ambient lighting" challenge was met by attaching optical reflection mirrors to fluorescent lighting fixtures and installing them out of view on top of the beams that form the room's 7.5 meter grid and metal halide spotlights housed on top of poles rising from the floor that serve as air-conditioning vents. Uniform up-lighting of the vault ceiling casts light like that of the sky at midday, and reflected light alone produces 300 lux of horizontal and vertical illuminance throughout the room. In other words, the design achieves a completely shadow-less light environment.

"Super-ambient lighting" conceals lighting fixtures and essentially transforms the architectural space itself into an immense lighting fixture. Ensuring that this unique method was executed smoothly and without error required repeated lighting mock ups on site. At the site we built several 7.5 meter grid concrete structures in order to meticulously check lighting fixture placement, variations in reflection ratio among concrete materials, the resulting effective illuminance, and other details. The success of the library's lighting system has also been useful as a standard for subsequent library lighting design projects.

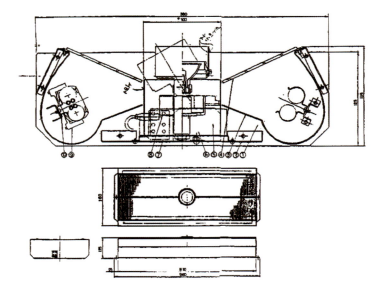

Osaka World Trade Center

1995 Osaka, Japan
Design | Nikken Sekkei, Mancini Duffy Associates
Client | Osaka World Trade Center Building

Keyword : A 21st Century Light House
Designer's comment : We handled the entire development.
Custom-made fixtures : Kinetic Lighting
Main light source : IL, FL, HID
Brightness contrast level : 2
Design Period : 4 years

   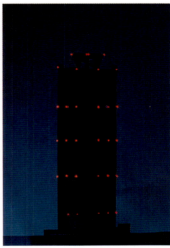

This high-rise office building located in the Nanko area of Osaka Bay is a landmark for ships sailing into the Bay as well as for places all over the city. Currently, it is a multi-purpose building owned by the Osaka Prefectural Government.

The lighting design was guided by a concept we called "21st-century lighthouse." The building's façade, exterior, and all public space inside are illuminated with "kinetic light," lighting with sensory qualities that go beyond functional lighting.

Above all, we invested considerable effort into the design of the aircraft warning lights that are a necessity for skyscrapers. The result is an illuminated building-top observation deck and a system that modulates light intensity at a rate equivalent to a heartbeat or deep breathing.

Shinjuku I - LAND PATIO

1995 Tokyo, Japan
Design | Housing & Urban Development , Nihon Sekkei
Client | Housing & Urban Development

Keyword : Sensory Design
Designer's comment : Be aware of functional changes.
Custom-made fixtures : Blue Tone Downlight
Main light source : HID
Brightness contrast level : 4
Design Period : 2.5 years

This patio is a tranquil 32-meter diameter sunken garden that sits alongside a 41-story skyscraper. Inside the patio stand four Japanese zelkovas marking the rhythm of the seasons and tables topped by sculpture-esque parasols where anyone can pass the time any time of the day.

The patio needed both tranquility and a cheerful atmosphere suited for the people who work in the office building. Seeking a public space that possesses a subtle yet ever-present sense of the passage of time, our concept became "design the sensation of time." But this palpable yet indescribable sensation, sometimes expressed in Japanese as *kehai*, depends not only on light: we also needed to design sound, smell, greenery, and environmental tools, so for this project we put together a multi-genre design team.

Kehai might be described as "a definite yet somehow indescribable sensation" — you are certain that you are feeling something but you are not quite sure just what it is. With that in mind, we asked "what if the five elements of light, sound, smell, greenery, and environmental tools subtly changed in step with the day and seasons?"

We combined the soundscape with the lighting design, designed furniture that changes with the seasons, coordinated the greenery to represent all four seasons, and even developed special fragrances to be occasionally carried by the wind.

We drew up a daily timetable and yearly calendar to chart the changes for each design element. This is because we felt that the rhythm of commerce is created by the moment-to-moment changes in the general environment. Many ideas worked and some never came to fruition. But, as we do with light, is it not the skillful design of sound, smell, wind, and everything else within a temporal framework that is the key to truly achieving comprehensive four-dimensional environmental design?

The central core of the patio is illuminated by timer-controlled 400W short-arc metal halide lamps installed on the apex of a 35-meter high obelisk and designed so that its light gradually transforms it into a space bathed in an enchanting blue.

World City Expo Tokyo '96

1995 Tokyo, Japan
Design | Toyo Ito & Associates, Architects , Akira Kuryu Architect & Associates,
Kazuhiro Ishii Architect & Associates, Riken Yamamoto & FIELDSHOP,
and others
Client | Tokyo Frontier Committee

Keyword : Temporary
Designer's comment : Still bitter that the Tokyo governor cancelled this project
Main light source : HID, IL, FL
Brightness contrast level : 3
Design Period : 2 years

Tokyo Frontier in Tokyo Waterfront City was scheduled to host the prestigious World City Expo over a 204 day period from March through October 1996. We were invited to do the lighting design as part of a design team that included urban planners and accomplished architects. Giving our imagination free rein, we developed a number of experimental approaches to urban lighting.

But the Expo coincided with the collapse of the bubble economy and the gut-wrenching decision was made to cancel the event just before it was to open. Guided by the theme "temporary," we had by this time developed several highly-transient lighting designs intended to endow the cityscape with a new look that even today retain their freshness and remain in our design stock.

1. Pylon Lights
An ordinary, but giant-size, construction-use pylon made of polyvinyl chloride was redesigned as a temporary street light.

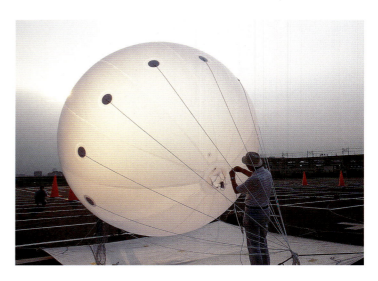

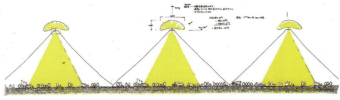

2. Balloon Light
This 10m × 5m giant balloon floated 20-30m in the air with power supplied from ground level.

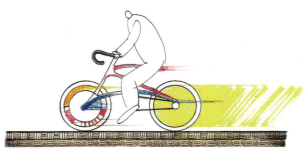

3. Electric Bicycle
A low-power illuminant as a light source is equipped with the combination of a small dynamo and battery glows brilliantly.

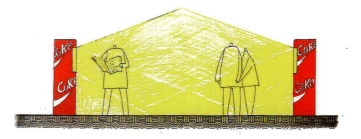

4. Vending Machines as City Lighting
The light radiating from vending machines is also an important lighting element, however the color temperature of all lamps used in the machines is unified to a warm tone.

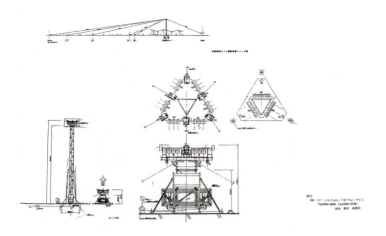
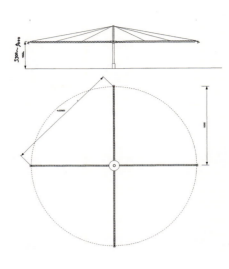

5. Automated Lift (Tomcat)

Lighting mounted on the Tomcat doubling as special effects and security lighting is visible at dusk as the lift slowly ascends to a position 30m above ground.

6. Large Span Pole Light

This lighting system supplied the necessary amount of light needed in a car park. The purpose was to reduce the number of poles and to change the way this typical landscape is viewed.

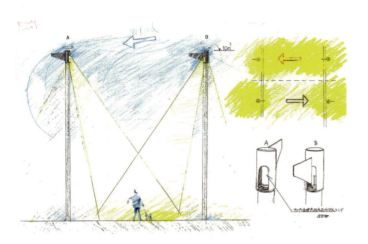
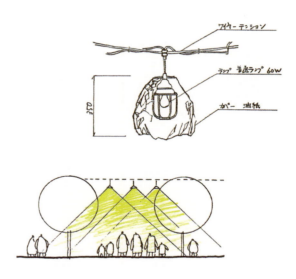

7. Weathervane Light

The focus of this pole lighting shifted moment to moment along with changes in the wind. The volume of light on the road surface also changed constantly.

8. Catenary Lighting in the Forest

Wire used to support greenery was used to mount catenary lighting. The use of oil paper lamp shades added a traditional Japanese touch.

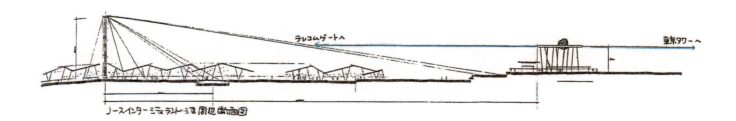

9. Urban Axis of Light

A xenon flood light mounted at the Aomi Zone 2 Daiba Gate created an axis of light between the Telecom Gate and Tokyo Tower.

10. Architecture as a Lighting Fixture
To provide the necessary light for the plaza, the architectural façade of the Ring, a 150m in diameter ring-shaped venue, was transformed into a luminous surface.

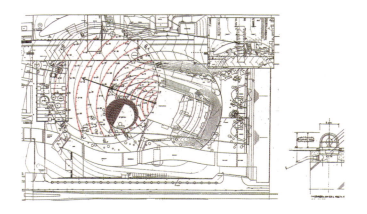
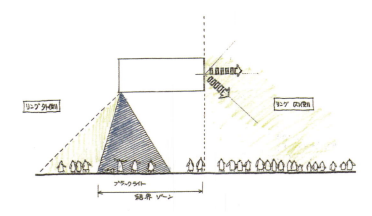

11. Lighting Ripple
Inside the Ring, indicator lights were embedded to light the ground, while the lighting operation simulated the motion of rippling water.

12. Space Barrier
The inside of the Ring is filled with light, while a dark zone with black lights acts as a barrier between the inside and outside of the Ring.

13. Rapidly Flashing Lights
Flash lamps installed along a 2km long east-west promenade aqueduct flash rapidly.

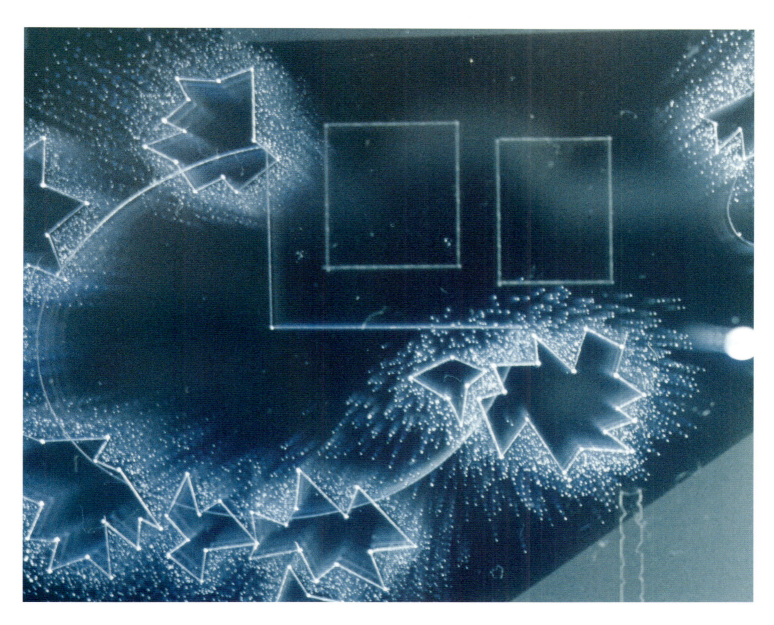

Temporary lighting design is a concept far removed from the world of architectural lighting with its many rules and requirements in that it allows one to conceive bold ideas considered somewhat outside the bounds of common-sense. The sole requirement when creating lighting design for the Expo was "keep the initial cost low." In other words, we were free to design without even having to take into account sustainability.

For instance, we were not compelled to work out designs that address the maintenance and management issues — "the need to use long-life lamps," "lighting fixture durability," "ease-of-maintenance," and so on — that are a fact of life in architectural lighting. Under the "temporary" banner we were free to indulge our designer egos through "experiments with new lighting technology," "designs that explore the extremes of shadow," and so on. We developed a number of lighting contrivances designed to spontaneously appear whenever it gets dark: Flashing lights that appear as streaks of light along the axis of the event site; 360° enclosed, donut-shaped light media; bare light bulbs that evoke the Asian city; lanterns for semi-outdoor open-air tea ceremony; balloons and airships that suspend light in the sky; an illuminated bicycle to ride around the Expo, and so on. It is only through the temporary that some dreams and truths are revealed.

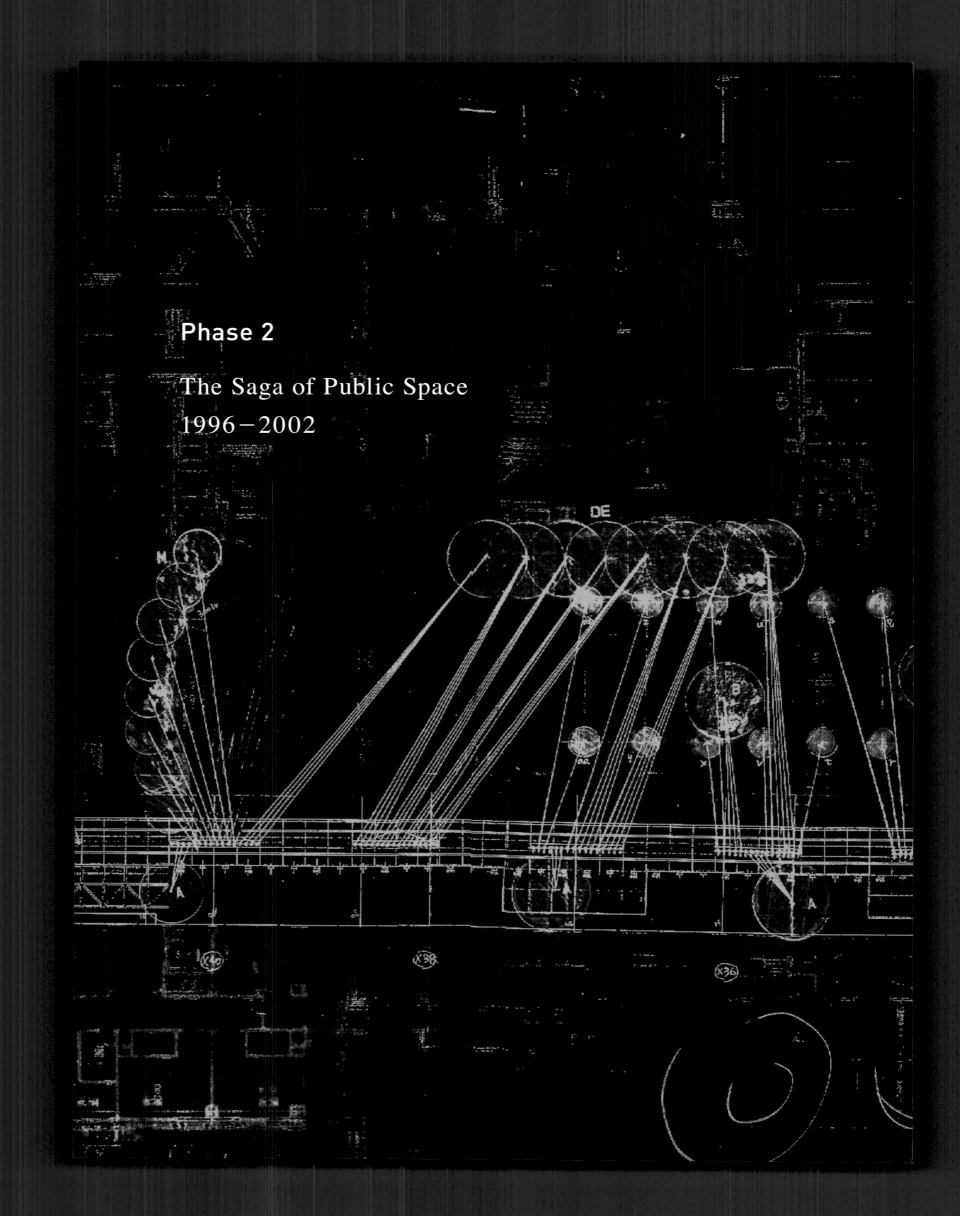

Phase 2

The Saga of Public Space
1996–2002

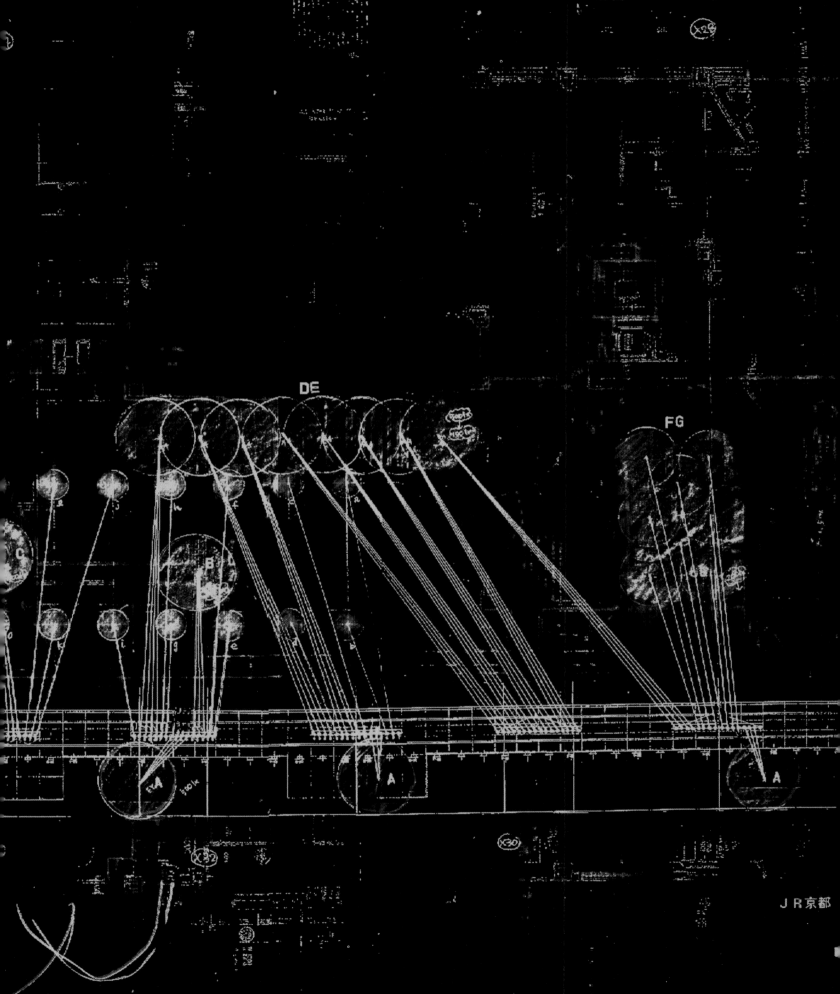

The Saga of Public Space:

Tokyo International Forum and Kyoto Station Building

Kaoru Mende

Japan possesses both technology of remarkable subtlety and unique modes of expression. It is a country whose accomplishments in art and design are admired around the world. These accomplishments extend into the realms of art, music, film, theatre, fashion, graphic design, interior design, architecture, and even to cuisine. Each of these has taken the best of foreign cultures and fused them with Japan's own ancient traditions. It is no exaggeration to say that Japanese digest everything the world has to offer, old and new, and are the world's most virtuosic arrangers.

Alas, this state of affairs has applied to everything but modern lighting. The Western rationalist approach of the "right light in the right place" failed to harmonize or find its place within Japanese tradition. Around a century ago daily life moved from torchlight to electric light, and in the 70 years since the end of World War II Japan's lighting culture has been in disarray. Before there was even time to heed the warning of Junichiro Tanizaki's masterpiece *In Praise of Shadows*, the fluorescent lamp had arrived, ushering in the era of brightness over all else. In Japanese society, light environments were governed by "Three Sacred Treasures," so to speak: brightness, white light, and uniform illumination. As if trying to outdo each other, roads and homes alike became bright environments. Brightness was an expression of affluence and happiness. This seemingly unstoppable trend had the unfortunate result of slowing the development of Japan's lighting culture by 30 years compared to America. While the quality of commercial lighting rapidly improved, the effects of this negative trend on residential and public lighting were all too clear.

In residential lighting, the appearance of the circular fluorescent lamps accelerated this trend. The image emerged of the nuclear family in thrall of "bright, white, uniform" lighting watching television together in silence. The same phenomenon was evident at government offices, train stations, underground shopping centers, and other public facilities. The theory took hold that space used by the general public needed to be safe above all else, which meant uniform illumination and shadow-less, bright lighting both day and night. Measuring illuminance level was the only important design technique, and, therefore, even as architecturally interesting buildings appeared among Japan's train stations and public facilities the lighting ruined the results. Since lighting was seen as just another piece of electrical equipment like air conditioning, there was no sense of lighting as design and no conception of a pleasant and comfortable public space.

A series of LPA projects completed in the period from 1996 through 2002 boldly overturned this state of affairs. Tokyo International Forum and Waterfront City Symbol Promenade were among projects in this vein completed in 1996, while projects completed in 1997 include Kyoto Station Building and Queen's Square Yokohama.

Unlike the "bright, white, uniform" light then the norm, the lighting environments of these newly completed public facilities were designed with an emphasis on "appropriate brightness, warm color light, and scenery with shadow." Tokyo International Forum is representative of this approach. For the building's glass hall lobby the Tokyo municipal government wanted uniform illumination of 300 lux but was convinced — after lengthy persuasion — that 50 lux is the appropriate level. When securing vertical luminance in a public space for pedestrian traffic, even floor illumination of just 50 lux produces a comfortable light environment. Tokyo International Forum is an excellent example that personifies and demonstrates this fact.

The lighting design for Kyoto Station Building concourse rigorously applied the design principle of "the right light in the right place" guided by the "in praise of shadows" philosophy and convincingly shows that asymmetry is the way to create a natural and comfortable environment. Illuminating only spots on the floor that need light with narrow-angle light has created space rich in shadow and also contributed to reduced energy consumption by 62%. This light environment upended the single-minded pursuit of uniform lighting, the exiling of shadow, that until then had been the norm for station buildings. After this project appeared the quality of transportation facility architectural lighting design changed radically.

In recognition of the lighting of these two public facilities, in 1997 LPA was honored with a Mainichi Design Award for "public space light design."

Public Space Light

Erwin J. S. Viray

A consciousness of the potential of light also opened a consciousness that we are not alone in feeling light but that we share it with others. By highlighting specific conditions, we actually realize that we enjoy light not in solitude but dwell on it in the company of others. It is not just in the solitary sphere but also plays a wide role in the public sphere. LPA's Kaoru Mende highlights this task of light, luminance rather than mere illumination. The works of LPA bring us to an experience of touching light gaining consciousness of things we have taken for granted.

Olafur Eliasson's Weather Project at the Tate Modern, awakened the power of light, the power of the sun, and the idea of the sustenance of life. As we live, we ask: "what is sustainability?" In our everyday life, we use things, we use oil or gas to create energy in order to sustain us, we create waste, we consume. In these little habits, an accumulation happens that makes things unsustainable. Weather Project at the Tate Modern also provoked the questions on what we can do individually and also collectively to deal with issues like climate change. This act makes us enter a public space. The sight of people laying down on the floor to watch the artificial sun created by Olafur Eliasson in the Turbine Hall of Tate Modern left an impression and led us to ask the question "what do we do to contribute to a better environment?" The expansive space of the Turbine Hall of the Tate Modern is similar to the public space in Kyoto Station Building and Tokyo International Forum, expansive and accommodating a huge number of people. Crafting a play of light in such immense space is always a challenge.

LPA offers some answers by consciously exploring methods of producing light that are environmentally friendly, energy conscious, and socially responsible. Each place is given specific qualities through the creation of light conditions responding to the place. Each light in Kyoto Station Building and Tokyo International Forum elicits a response as I have experienced in the sun at Weather Project at the Tate Modern. Light become a catalyst in the recognition of the social and being a part of a public sphere.

In this phase, LPA and Kaoru Mende take us to see our environment in new light, creating conciousness of public space through light.

Tokyo International Forum

1996 Tokyo, Japan
Design | Rafael Vinoly Architects
Client | Tokyo Metropolitan Government

Keyword : An Urban Lantern
Designer's comment : The very best architectural lighting possible
Custom-made fixtures : Luminous Floor, Buried Wall Washer
Main light source : IL, FL
Brightness contrast level : 3
Design Period : 6.5 years

This multiplex cultural facility has seven halls of various sizes, including 5,000 seat Hall A, an exhibition hall, and 34 conference rooms. The facility also has a glass hall featuring a spaceship-like structure suspended in an immense atrium and a 7.5 meter wide light floor that traverses the site. The lighting design has been singled out as an example of dynamic and comfortable architectural lighting that moves beyond the overbearing illumination typical of most public lighting.

From schematic design to final completion, the lighting design took six-and-a-half years. Especially noteworthy is the glass hall lighting, which has added a new icon to the Tokyo nightscape by illuminating only the unique structure suspended within it with pinpoint lighting from narrow angle spotlights.

1996 (after completion)

Nineteen years has passed since the completion of this project, and a visitor to the site today is aware of the gradual changes in the light environment that have occurred over that time. The glass hall's first underground floor lobby has a colorfully designed information booth and newly installed low-height light poles next to the benches. For the exterior, which was designed to be a low-stress public space, new guide signs are accompanied by a jumble of intense lighting.

Japanese zelkovas that had grown too large have all been replaced by younger trees and the lighting embedded in the pavement has been updated to LED. This kind of additional lighting can only mean that someone among the facility's users wanted brighter light.

People perceive brightness differently depending on age, gender, and many other attributes. It is impossible to have a level of brightness that agrees with everyone. Nonetheless, the reaction to the alteration of a comfortable light environment that had been achieved only after repeated experiments by the indiscriminate installation of vending machines and brightly lit signs can only be disappointment.

The replacement of the halogen lamps used when the project was first designed with high-energy efficiency small metal halide lamps and LED is entirely reasonable. But such changes should also include carefully thought out design changes that preserve the pleasant light environment at the same time that they improve efficiency. Changing the light environment is caught up in a number of thorny issues, including lighting design sustainability and lighting designer intellectual property rights.

The light environment at time of completion and as it appears today are shown on the left and right.

2014

1996 (after completion)

1996 (after completion)

Praise for this project as an outstanding example of a public building light environment has been due more than anything else to its steadfast pursuit of "visual clarity." Upon entering the site, one encounters surfaces radiating soft light at every turn. This is the result of maximizing the concept of vertical illumination by reflecting light off vertical planes that coexist with soft light emanating from radiant surfaces like luminous floors, walls, and ceilings.

For instance, the slanted wood wall that rises from the glass hall's first underground floor lobby is illuminated with an array of uplight wallwashers embedded in the floor. In contrast to the slavish use of 300 lux of illumination typical of public building lighting up to that time, the public space lighting here softens illumination to 50 lux. The design is evidence that a visually clear space loses none of its sense of brightness when the floor has a low illuminance level.

The glass hall's immense roof framework is sharply etched in the night sky by 600 small spotlights installed 32.5 meters above ground. Precise lighting sheared of all excess of the structure's keel section is the key to this visual effect.

The fundamental principle governing this dynamic architectural lighting is "glare-free." This project clearly shows just how important eliminating glare from light sources and the lighting fixtures themselves is to achieving a gentle and comfortable environment.

2014

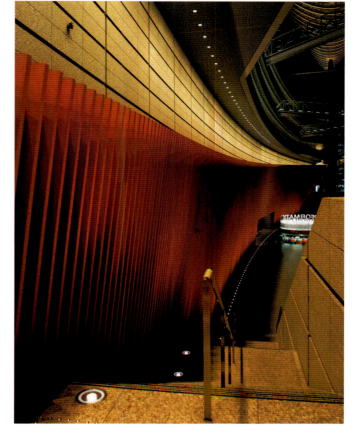

Waterfront City Symbol Promenade

1996 Tokyo, Japan
Design | Nikken Sekkei
Client | Tokyo Waterfront Sub-center Construction

Keyword : Low Positioned Lighting
Designer's comment : A bold, new promenade concept
Custom-made fixtures : Street Washer, Fiber Optic Strip Light
Main light source : HID, LED
Brightness contrast level : 4
Design Period : 2.5 years

Tokyo Waterfront City is a 442 hectare development on reclaimed land in Tokyo Bay. We proposed the development's light infrastructure, with a focus on road and plaza lighting and how it will look twenty years in the future. Our basic approach for the lighting design took into account "ecological lighting," "lighting on a human scale," "picturesque streets," "choreographed transitions," and "integrated street lighting design," among other themes. The use of high-color rendering sodium lamps and the color temperature unity of the overall development proved especially effective. Lighting along the Symbol Promenade pedestrian route linking Aomi, Ariake, and Daiba employs a number of low-positioned light sources, including bollard street washers, cylinder type garden lamps, and pavement-embedded linear light markings.

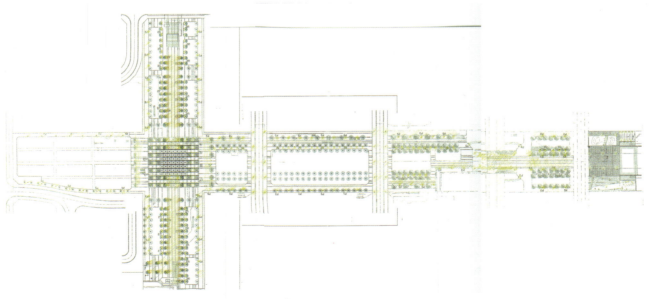

To create an ambience for a pleasant, leisurely stroll the design established three "low" light rules. Namely, low illuminance, low position, and low color temperature. Light that is not too bright and originating from places close to the ground is given overall coherence with warm light colors — a must for an environment intended as a dating spot.

To avoid functional pole lights, which cast uniform illumination on pavement, we designed glare-less bollards no higher than one meter called "street washers" with the idea of creating a gorgeous light environment that can be aptly described as a "luminous runway." For intersections, we proposed pavement embedded optical fiber and LED lighting that delights passersby with a slowly changing presentation. The promenade around the Hotel Nikko lined with 3m low-position pole lights on both sides creates a pedestrian-friendly rhythm of light and shadow.

The overall design uses three different heights — ground level, 1m, and 3m — to create light on a human scale.

Chihiro Art Museum Azumino

1997 Nagano, Japan
Design | Naito Architect & Associates
Client | Chihiro Iwasaki Memorial Foundation

Keyword : A Light-filled Art Museum
Designer's comment : Beautiful museum in a beautiful place
Custom-made fixtures : Multi-functional Line Bracket

Main light source : IL, FL
Brightness contrast level : 1
Design Period : 3 years

This art museum exhibits sketches and watercolors of picture book artist Chihiro Iwasaki as well as picture books and illustrations by artists from around the world. The museum stands in Shinshu Azumino in a rich natural setting that spans all four seasons and with majestic mountains in the distance.

Our design concept was "a bright and uplifting art museum fused with nature." The goal was an art museum open to the outdoors and a place where families can come for a visit and relax. We wanted a bright light environment that values ample natural light and a space where not only children but adults and the elderly can feel at ease. To take advantage of the building design, we designed a flexible lighting system that is both simple and functional.

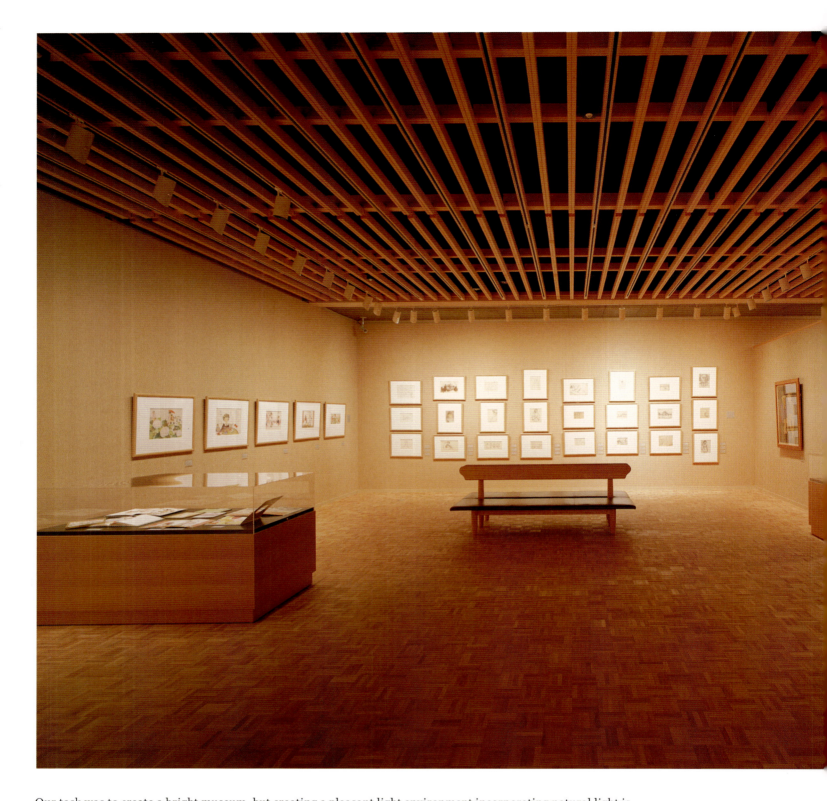

Our task was to create a bright museum, but creating a pleasant light environment incorporating natural light is by no means easy. The design also must take into account artwork preservation and viewer comfort. Most importantly, original picture book illustrations are often watercolors, which have a high damage coefficient and are therefore extremely sensitive to bright light. Our solution was to separate the art museum into an inner section of exhibit rooms with completely controlled lighting and a bright outer section encompassing circulation space.

Exhibit room walls are uniformly illuminated at 60 to 100 lux to preserve the pictures. When a room is empty of visitors, the system automatically reduces light to 30% of its normal level. Sculptures and other artwork with a low damage coefficient are exhibited in spaces that integrate the natural light of the café and shop.

The wood ceiling is illuminated with incandescent color fluorescent lamps, a method that obscures the beautiful ceiling with dark and heavy shadow during the day. This serves to harmonize the museum's interior all the more with the nature of Azumino.

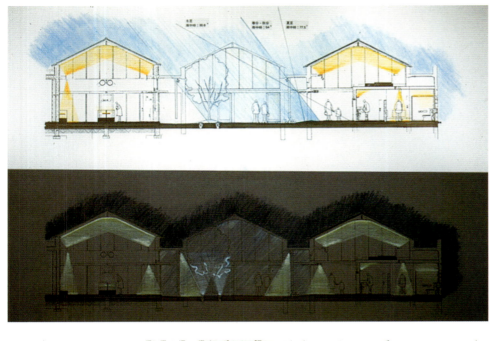
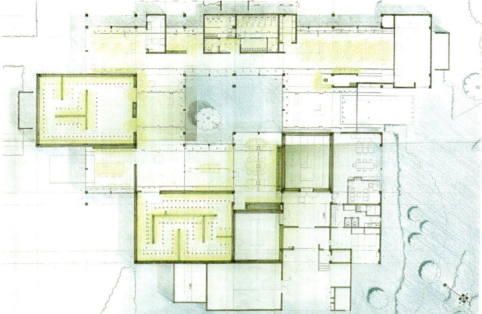
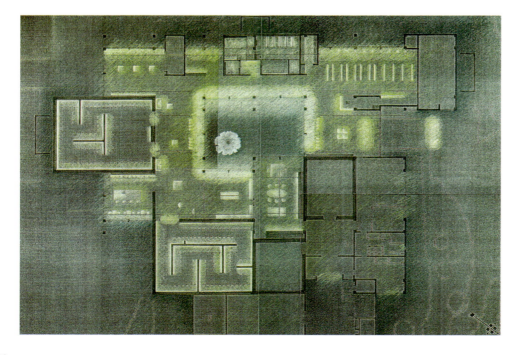

During the concept phase we drew day and night lighting sketches. Our image was of an interior filled with natural light by day, and then transformed into lantern at night, with light spilling out into the darkness (P090). Starting with the Pacovska Garden, the Azumino Chihiro Park is an area rich in nature with memorable scenes of those relaxing in the sun and children running and splashing in the fountain (P091).

Fukushima Lagoon Museum

1997 Niigata, Japan
Design | Jun Aoki & Associates
Client | Niigata City (Former Toyosaka City)

Keyword : Reversal
Designer's comment : Captivated by the beauty of the night
Main light source : IL
Brightness contrast level : 4
Design Period : 2 years

This museum dedicated to the ecology of Fukushima Lagoon is an upside down cone whose 16 meter diameter base expands to 28 meters at its seventh floor summit. A spiral staircase connects the first floor entrance to the top floor, with the spiral slope from the fourth to seventh floors serving as an exhibit gallery with a 360-degree view for appreciating the surrounding lagoon through the glass wall.

During the day, the space absorbs more than enough natural light and provides a sweeping view of the lagoon, while at night light from the interior floods into the surroundings as if releasing the energy taken in during the day. This is the kind of beautiful landmark we wanted the museum to become. The museum's shimmering reflection in the jet black lagoon is like a ship in space.

Kyoto Station Building

1997 Kyoto, Japan
Design | Hiroshi Hara + Atelier φ
Client | West Japan Railway, Kyoto Station Building Development

Keyword : In Praise of Shadows
Designer's comment : A darkness found only in Kyoto
Custom-made fixtures : Wall-embedded Up Lights
Main light source : HID
Brightness contrast level : 5
Design Period : 5 years

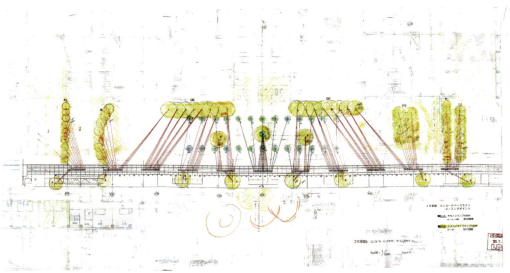

Kyoto's history and patina as Japan's ancient capital dates back more than 12 centuries. Kyoto Station Building is enclosed in an immense 470 meter long, 60 meter high atrium. The station's predecessor had a shadow-poor light environment due to materials that were almost entirely white and a lighting system designed for uniform high-illuminance lighting. At Kyoto Station Building, in contrast, a lighting design for the black granite flooring guided by "in praise of shadows" philosophy restores beautiful shadow and also contributes to more efficient energy use. Primary lighting is provided by elevated 150W narrow angle metal halide spotlights. These lights are sparingly used in spots only where needed, proving that an economical approach gives birth to meaningful shadow.

In Praise of Shadows written by the novelist Junichiro Tanizaki and published in 1933 is an exploration of the shadow aesthetic cherished by ancient Japanese tradition. Translated into numerous languages and a favorite book around the world, *In Praise of Shadows* is greatly valued outside Japan as a definitive statement of the Japanese aesthetic. Expressing disdain for glossy materials, the modality of light, Tanizaki argues that the essence of the ancient Japanese aesthetic resides in soft, diffused, faint light and in shadow.

After World War II, however, Japanese sought a lifestyle contrary to this aesthetic. Shadow-less light environments emphasizing volume of light became the norm. This was so for the home, for public space, and, above all, for train station buildings.

For Kyoto Station Building, we wanted to overturn the postwar light environment norm of bright, shadow-less station buildings: pleasant non-uniform light rather than uniform light, the calming effect of dim spaces with restrained light, and no light at all in places that do not need functional lighting. Here, a lighting design approach following these principles reduced unnecessary energy use by 62%.

Odate Jukai Dome Park

1997 Akita, Japan
Design | Toyo Ito & Associates, Architects
Clent | Odate City

Keyword : Luciferase
Designer's comment : My compliments to Ito-san's karaoke skills
Main light source : HID, FL
Brightness contrast level : 2
Design Period : 3 years

This beautiful, sleek, all-white dome appears unexpectedly amid pristine nature. The building — which is Japan's largest wooden dome — was built using 25,000 Akita cedars, all of which are at least 60 years old. The 52 meter high building has a 178 meter long-side diameter and a seating capacity of 5,040. Used primarily for baseball, soccer, and other sporting events, the dome is a multi-purpose facility that also hosts concerts and other events.

With the idea of making the dome's nighttime exterior a local landmark, we performed a series of lighting experiments on the dome's high-transmittance double-layer teflon plane and then designed lighting that produces luminance of 5cd/m² on the plane. The angle of the floodlights that light up the stadium are carefully calibrated, achieving exterior lighting that is both economical and very efficient.

Queen's Square Yokohama

1997 Kanagawa, Japan
Design | Nikken Sekkei, Mitsubishi Estate Architectural & Engineering
Client | T·R·Y 90 Associates, Mitsubishi Estate,
Urban Renaissance Agency, JGC

Keyword : A Carpet of Light
Designer's comment : Substantial time and money invested in the presentation
Custom-made fixtures : Rectangular Light Distribution Downlight
Main light source : HID, FL
Brightness contrast level : 3
Design Period : 5 years

This is a large multi-functional complex on a 44,000 square meter area. Three high-rise towers connected by a natural light-filled commercial mall extend a total length of 300 meters. A 40 meter high atrium leading directly to the subway station gate is in the center.

During the day, the dynamic presence of natural light creates a uniform and bright environment. At night — and in contrast to the typical commercial facility — floor illumination deliberately set at low levels and subtle light and shadow imbalances create an eye-catching scene for the store fronts and interiors along the mall. To set the scene, all lighting follows a detailed lighting schedule.

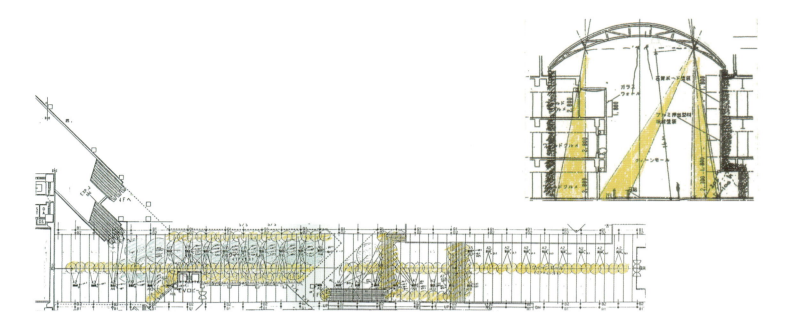

The lighting plan creates a variety of changing scenes throughout the day along the mall's entire 300 meter length: bright natural sunlight, dusk, night scene 1, night scene 2, and so on. 200W halogen lamps and 150W small metal halide lamp spotlights installed in slits built in the vault ceiling choreograph a variety of scenes. Based on the idea of a non-uniform and rhythmically changing "carpet of light" on the mall floor, starting at dusk a "carpet of light" changing ceremony is performed accompanied by ambient music during the last five minutes of every hour. When the ceremony begins the lighting system puts on a show to announce the start and then gradually settles down to a set scene by the end. Observing the scene closely, one will see that people either consciously walk on the "carpet of light" or avoid it altogether. In contrast to the mostly uniform daytime light, at night deliberately unbalanced light becomes entertainment.

Fuji-Q Highland FUJIYAMA

1997 Yamanashi, Japan
Design | Kitayama & Company
Clent | Fujikyu Highland

Keyword : An 80 sec. Drama of Light
Designer's comment : Terrifying!
Main light source : IL, LED
Brightness contrast level : 3
Design Period : 1.5 years

FUJIYAMA jet coaster holds three Guinness Book records: maximum height, maximum drop, and maximum speed. The jet coaster's 80 second ride is an adventure from start to finish. During the day the ride has an uninterrupted view of Mount Fuji, while at night riders encounter a variety of light set against the nocturnal background. Five light events add to the excitement of embarking on the ride at night and to the unique thrill it offers. This "active lighting" is integrated with the coaster's beautifully illuminated railing, further heightening the crowd appeal of the Fuji-Q Highland symbol.

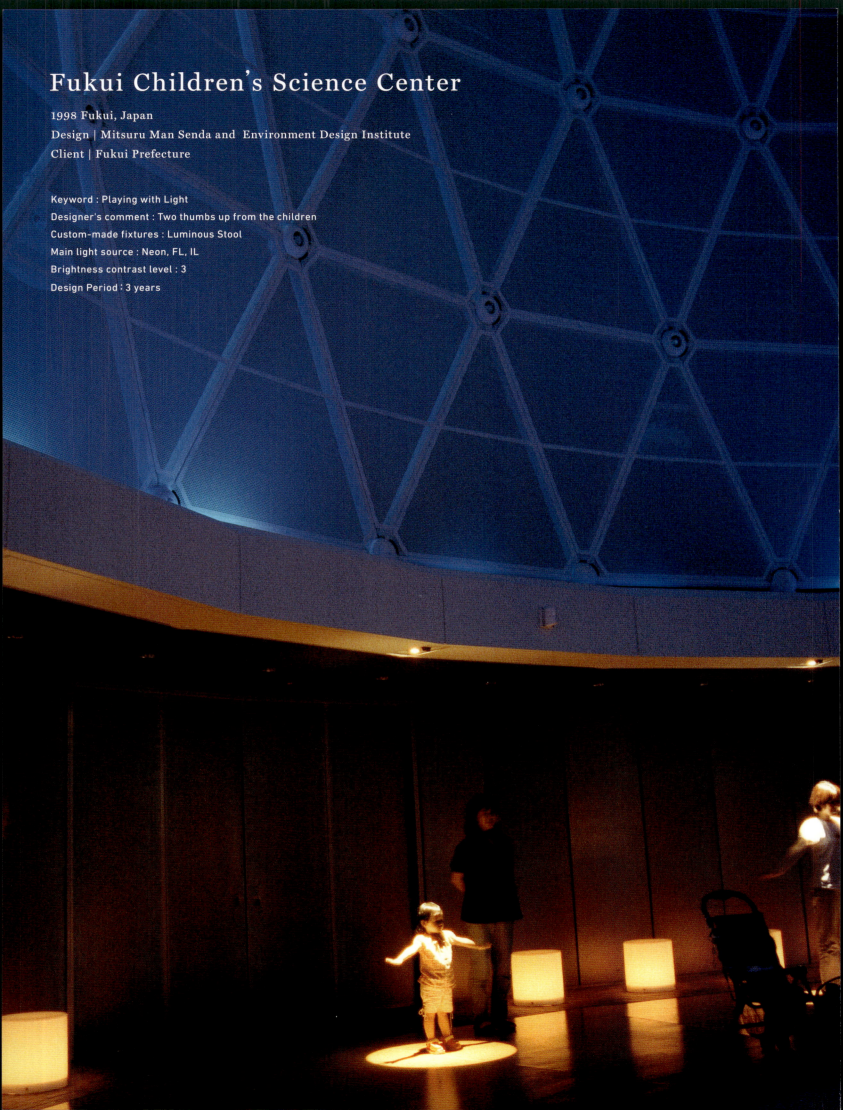

Fukui Children's Science Center

1998 Fukui, Japan
Design | Mitsuru Man Senda and Environment Design Institute
Client | Fukui Prefecture

Keyword : Playing with Light
Designer's comment : Two thumbs up from the children
Custom-made fixtures : Luminous Stool
Main light source : Neon, FL, IL
Brightness contrast level : 3
Design Period : 3 years

This facility is designed to make learning about science fun for children. Besides a space theater topped by a 23 meter in diameter dome-shaped screen, the center has a variety of fun attractions that explore the riddles of space and science, an interactive zone where children directly experience the workings of nature, a discovery zone for learning about human ingenuity, and a number of other learning areas. Relying on natural light during normal operation, the space theater also has a lights-out interactive light show that completely reverses the space.

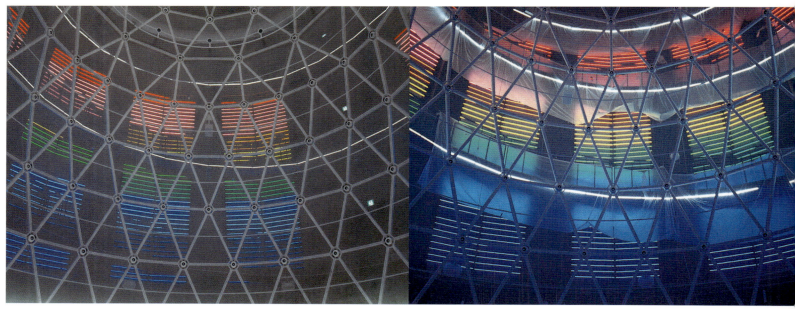

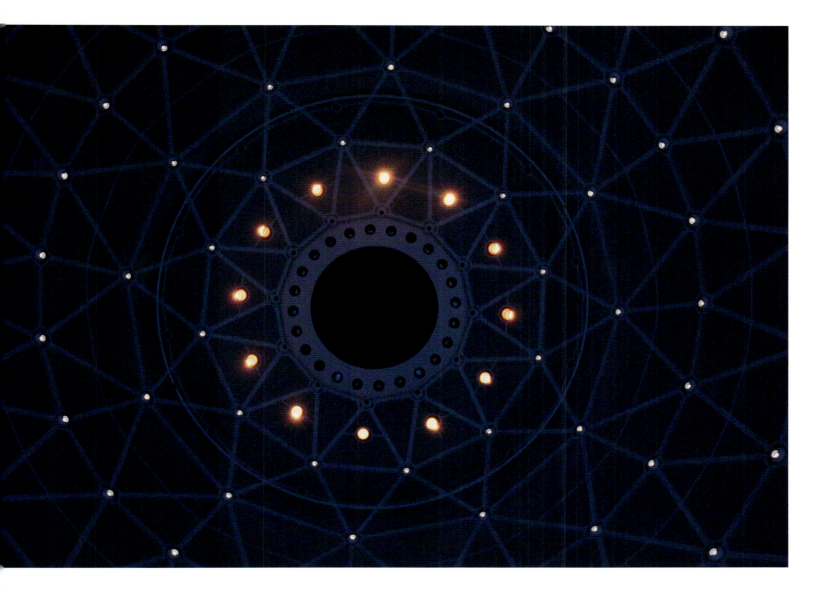

At a place where children learn science through play, the light also needs a highly interactive design that stimulates child curiosity. With this in mind, we made prominent use of the special exhibit room called the "space theater."

Topped by a high domed ceiling with a toplight, the space theater is filled with sunlight during normal operation, but at showtime the lights go out and the children are captivated by an elaborate light show. Audio, lighting, computer control specialists and production directors have collaborated on programming a light experiment show using the entire space.

The dome surface is covered with perforated metal, and whenever a show starts countless neon tubes and spotlights concealed behind it flash in response to the audio and change into a variety of different colors. Moreover, the space has numerous contrivances that play with light: shimmering fluorescent materials inlaid in the floor radiate ultraviolet light, light chairs flash when children touch them, a light wheel with a harp of light plays when a child steps into it, and more. Playing with light that appears in all sorts of unexpected ways never fails to nurture a child's emotions and creativity.

Toyama International Conference Center

1999 Toyama, Japan
Design | Maki and Associates
Client | Urban Renewal of Otemachi District, Toyama

Keyword : Spilling over with Light
Designer's comment : A large stock of special custom-made sample fixtures
Custom-made fixtures : Ellipsoidal Mirror Downlight, Fiber Optic Linear Light
Main light source : IL, FL
Brightness contrast level : 4
Design Period : 3 years

This facility containing all the functions of a convention center stands in a district next to Joshi Park in Toyama City. Along with the hotel enclosing a large mall opposite it, the facility is a redevelopment that forms a cultural district welcoming visitors to the region. The clean cut exterior features a welcoming wood lattice screen behind a transparent glass curtain wall. These two layers preserve the exterior's transparency while also providing the interior with an appropriate level of privacy and a relaxed atmosphere. At night, light radiating from the interior silhouettes the movement of people inside and outlines the volume of the main hall deep inside the foyer.

This building enclosed in a transparent glass curtain wall and facing Joshi Park and a large mall projects a welcoming presence within the town. The foyer, conference room, and other space inside are covered in places by a wood lattice screen. Anticipating that the facility would be very active at night, we made every effort to create a gentle, natural nightscape by radiating light through the two layers.

We felt that the third floor foyer enclosing the main hall is an important space for human interaction, so the light environment allows one to clearly see the faces of other people in the foyer while not sending unwanted light into the areas around it. In addition, the main hall's aluminum corrugated panel exterior wall, the red travertine feature wall, and other elements are fastidiously illuminated so as to draw the gaze of passersby toward the interior. The main hall is enclosed by white-ribbed walls with acrylic pillars between them. The distinctive rib walls are illuminated with light discretely originating from small holes in the walls directly facing them, while the gold lines in the acrylic pillars shine elegantly in the light. To accommodate the halls many different performance contexts, the acrylic pillars have optical fibers that emit light to accentuate the space as the occasion demands.

This project is also noteworthy for lighting fixtures that are almost all custom-made and processed in order to reduce details to a minimum.

Nara Centennial Hall

1999 Nara, Japan
Design | Arata Isozaki & Associates
Client | Nara City

Keyword : Transformation
Designer's comment : The architecture glows and transforms.
Custom-made fixtures : Up Light Washer
Main light source : IL, LED
Brightness contrast level : 3
Design Period : 3.5 years

This facility built to commemorate the Nara city government centennial has a large, medium, and small hall. The 1,476 capacity large hall has multi-vision and movable seating that can change to one of eight stage plans. The medium hall designed for small ensemble classical music concerts is enclosed by special glass on the periphery and uses lighting to alter the visual perception of the spatial volume.

The exterior lighting design is also unique. When dusk approaches, LEDs embedded in the pavement flash and highlight the graphic on the grounds with shining dots and lines. At every turn, light gracefully melds into the building and landscape.

This project took on the challenge of "territorial change." Most notable in this regard is the 434 seat medium hall, which is enclosed by a double-layer ceramic print glass wall. Our design here uses changes in the wall's illumination to affect a change in how the territory within the space is visually perceived. To raise the audience's sense of anticipation we proposed installing two-millimeter silver ceramic dots only on the outer side of the glass. 12V50W halogen spotlights with diffusion lenses spaced at a 15cm pitch illuminate the glass wall with linear bands of light from above and below. Turning on the lights creates an enclosed space within the glass, while turning off the lights incorporates the domain outside the wall and visually enlarges the space.

When announcing that a performance is about to begin, the slow transformation of the light environment in the hall achieved by controlling the glass's illumination creates an atmosphere over a 30 second interval that directs attention toward the stage.

The foyer features two long light ducts that cross in midair and change into various colors (left). As twilight approaches, the plaza's embedded outdoor indicator lights start to flash.

In addition, the soft glow of low-level lighting installed around the circular building's exterior outlines the architecture's silhouette against the night sky (bottom).

Kaoru Mende + LPA Exhibition
"A Manner in Architectural Lighting Design"

1999 Tokyo, Japan
Organizer | TOTO GALLERY - MA

Keyword : Reflection and Diffusion
Designer's comment : I was very nervous about how visitors would react.
Custom-made fixtures : Fiber Optic Wall Surface
Main light source : IL, HID
Brightness contrast level : 4
Design Period : 1.5 years

We presented an architectural lighting exhibition over a two month period at the invitation of a gallery well-known for its exhibits on architectural design. Three different exhibit rooms presented the nature of lighting design and the working environment of the lighting designer.

Room 1 employed 1,200 optical fibers to create a changing, experiential space. Room 2 was an outdoor terrace accessed from Room 1 with aluminum electropolished optical reflection mirrors laid out on the floor. Room 3 completely changed the pace with an introduction to the work of lighting design. This exhibit featured 12 video monitors, architectural lighting models, lighting fixtures that demonstrate optical techniques, and a variety of sketches and drawings.

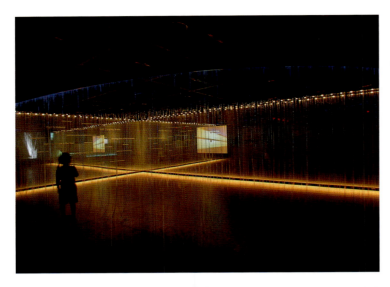

Room 1 | Gallery
1,200 fiber optics and a mirror create a 3minte 30 second "Metamorphose Space."

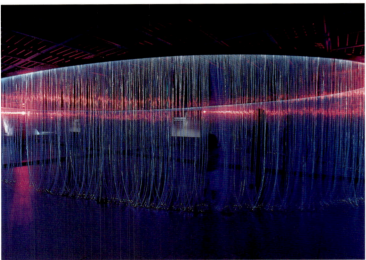

Room 2 | Outdoor Terrace
A lighting installation with xenon lights and aluminum mirrors spread over the entire floor.

Lighting enriches, enlivens, and enhances the comfort of architectural and urban space. We wanted visitors to the exhibit to physically experience the effect of lighting.

Mirrors were mounted on two sides of a gallery exhibit room and a wall of 1,200 optical fibers forming one-fourth of an ellipse was installed in the room. The shimmering optical fiber wall reflecting in the mirrors enveloped visitors in a virtual space forming a complete ellipse. The light slowly changed color and continuously changed from light to dark with a breathe-like rhythm. And, when the light suddenly extinguished, the elliptical space that until then had been assumed to exist also vanished and in an instant the space returned to reality with light radiating off the silk print lettering imprinted on the mirror.

The exhibit in the outdoor terrace featured a floor covered with 700mm square optical aluminum mirrors. When walking on the mirrors reflecting the midday sky, awareness of the ever-present clouds and movement of air produced a boundless floating sensation. At night, the mirrors were lit up by a 250W xenon spotlight, with the optical axis reflected off the mirrors creating a dramatic light effect.

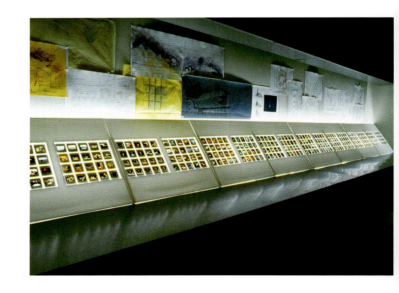

Room 3 | Reproduction of the LPA studio

The middle of the gallery featured a recreation of LPA's symbolic round meeting table.
　Drawings from past projects, lighting fixtures, and other work items recreated the atmosphere of a lighting design studio and gave visitors a look at the lighting design process.

Iwate Museum of Art

2000 Iwate, Japan
Design | Nihon Sekkei
Client | Iwate Prefecture

Keyword : Guiding Light
Designer's comment : Blue light was the key to the success.
Custom-made fixtures : Buried Wall Washer
Main light source : IL, FL
Brightness contrast level : 4
Design Period : 3 years

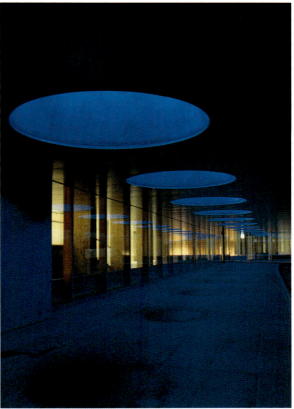

Located in a nature park, this art museum has a permanent exhibit hall featuring the work of local artists and a multi-use exhibit hall for various events. Conceived as a new kind of cultural facility, the museum sponsors not only art exhibits but lectures and workshops, concerts, and a variety of culturally related events.

Our design theme stressed contrasting day and night light environments with the idea that the museum should also be very active at night.

For the museum's unique circulation space, the all-important walls are highlighted to smoothly guide visitors through the exhibition space. To ensure the comfort of visitors, a glare-free philosophy permeates the entire design.

In addition, the presence of choreographed blue light at every turn creates a phantasmagoric nightscape at twilight time.

Osaka Maritime Museum

2000 Osaka, Japan
Design | Paul Andreu Architect, Port & Harbor Bureau, City of Osaka
Client | Port & Harbor Bureau, City of Osaka

Keyword : Reversal
Designer's comment : The dome's arrival by ship was a moment of joy.
Main light source : HID, IL
Brightness contrast level : 3
Design Period : 2.5 years

This building topped by a 70 meter in diameter dome in Osaka's bayside Nanko area is a museum dedicated to the city's maritime history. Visitors access the exhibition hall from the entrance building on the shore via a 60 meter long underwater tunnel, and when seen from the shore the building seems to float right on the water. Upon setting foot inside the dome, visitors first see a huge wooden ship and an open, four level, atrium-style exhibit space before their eyes. The dome shining with reflected sunlight during the day becomes increasingly transparent as the day shortens until the building's inner and outer light balance completely reverses. At night, the illuminated interior creates a futuristic scene, as if a spacecraft has landed on the sea.

The giant dome was moved in its present shape across the water to its location where it was painstakingly attached to its structural framework. Taking into account the solar radiation absorbed by the polyhedral dome, we employed four types of perforated metal with different apertures inserted between special glass and simulated daylight conditions inside the dome.

The dynamic day-night reversal of the dome's light environment was an important lighting design theme. The position of the special glass fixed by calculating sun elevation and rigorously and scientifically determined achieves an aesthetically pleasing nightscape. During the day the glass reflects sunlight so that the dome appears as a luminous solid, while at night it has enough transparency to radiate a soft glow originating from light inside the dome. Interior light visible through clear glass, light penetrating perforated metal of varying apertures: it is as if rational science has become one with vibrant artistic expression.

Keyaki Hiroba

2000 Saitama, Japan
Design | Ohtori Consultants Environmental Design Institute,
NTT Urban Development, Peter Walker and Partners
Client | Saitama Prefecture

Keyword : No Pole Lighting
Designer's comment : Heavy maintenance because of fallen leaves
Custom-made fixtures : Grating Light
Main light source : FL, HID
Brightness contrast level : 4
Design Period : 3 years

Saitama New Urban Center is a large-scale redevelopment project that includes a sports arena, art museum, offices, accommodations, and a hot spring. A plaza located in the center of the development, Keyaki Hiroba has 220 *keyaki* trees planted in a dense grid designed by innovative landscape designer Peter Walker. We worked out a detailed design that does everything possible to embed lighting design details into the landscape and building design.

This painstaking effort achieves a plaza completely free of public safety pole lighting, which was motivated by concern over unneeded light poles marring the beautiful daytime scene created by the rows of *keyaki* trees.

The plaza's lighting design is noteworthy for the complete absence of light poles. We wanted a daytime landscape free of unnecessary lighting fixtures. Providing enough light for public safety without light poles required embedding lighting equipment into the building and landscape.

Lights were installed in parts of the plaza's glass restaurant and in ventilation towers and other building equipment housing. Benches installed with lighting were placed in spots coordinated to the *keyaki* grid and lighting was embedded in the pavement grating in space not occupied by trees or benches. Although embedded pavement lighting does not provide regular street lighting it does have a visual role by amply contributing to the plaza's sense of brightness. The Forest Pavilion, the plaza's sole architectural structure, also plays a part in the plaza's lighting effect. The clear-glass staircases on the periphery are covered with striped diffusion sheets that radiate a soft, lantern-like glow.

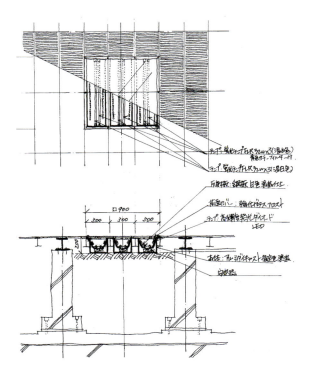
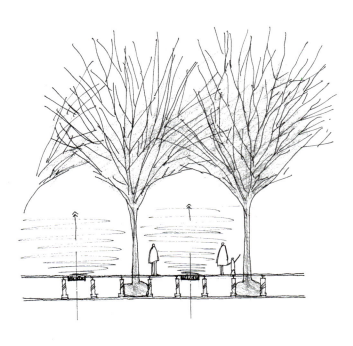

OASIS 21

2002 Aichi, Japan
Design | Obayashi
Client | Nagoya Urban Development Public, Sakae Park Promotion

Keyword : Luminous Spaceship
Designer's comment : Now, this is a city landmark, folks!
Custom-made fixtures : Handrail Lighting

Main light source : HID, FL
Brightness contrast level : 3
Design Period : 4 years

This city park adjacent to a shopping and entertainment district and cultural facilities is located at a major intersection of the city's urban network. An underground level combining shops and a bus terminal covered by sloping ground creates a scene like a painting inserted into the middle of the crowded city. Carved out in the center of the site is an elliptical hollow topped 14 meters above ground by an immense 106 meter long, 36 meter wide glass roof suspended in the air. Symbolically illuminated with color lighting, the large roof is a city landmark.

The center of the elliptical glass roof is filled with water. During the day, natural light penetrates the veil of water, outlining its contours on the underground plaza below. At night, dynamic lighting makes the roof look like a spaceship about to launch from amid its lively surroundings.

The color lighting of the glass spaceship changes in step with the seasons and time of day. The outer perimeter of the glass roof is an aerial walkway whose surface is illuminated with light in a variety of colors, creating a floor of light that reinforces the sense of being suspended in air for the people walking on it.

The ground level park area is completely free of the functional pole lighting typical of most parks. The park's public safety lighting is secured by means of lights installed in the surface of the gently sloping ground as well as by lighting built into benches, railing, public art, and other features, and by the reflection of light off structural members. The nighttime environment is a seamless fusion of the landscape design with light.

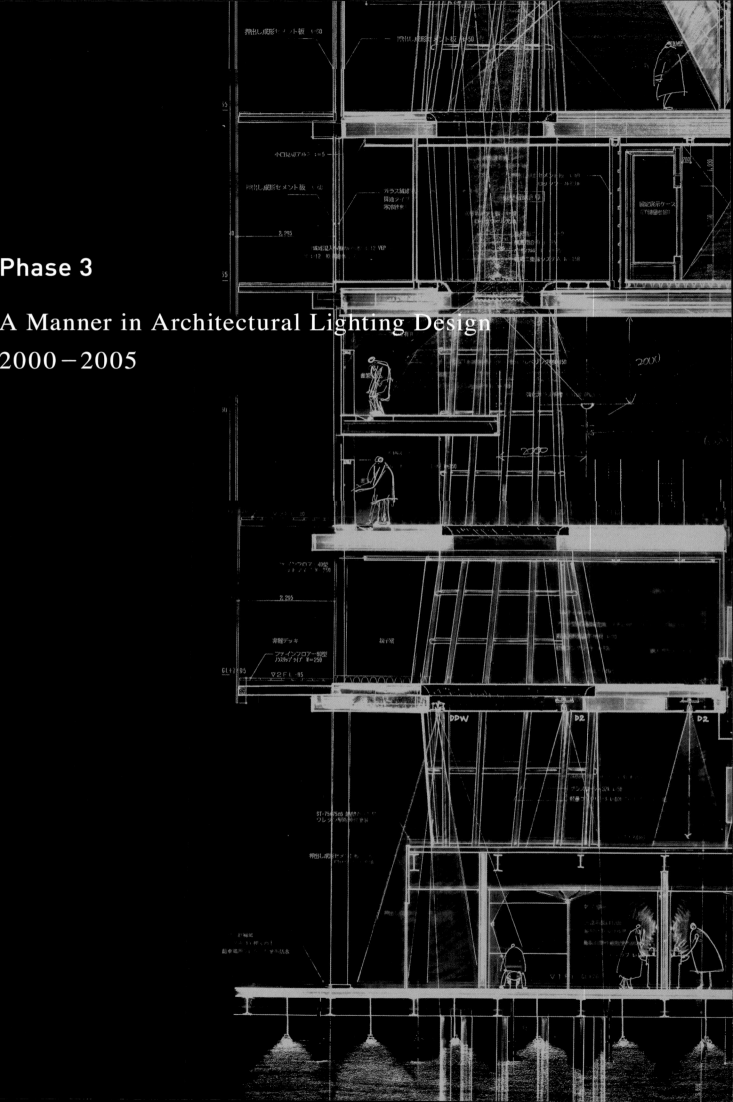

Phase 3

A Manner in Architectural Lighting Design
2000–2005

A Manner in Architectural Lighting Design:
From Sendai Mediatheque to Nagasaki National Peace Memorial Hall for the Atomic Bomb Victims

Kaoru Mende

Around the time that the concept of architectural lighting seemed to have taken root in Japanese society, I was approached by TOTO GALLERY-MA about doing an exhibition on architectural lighting design. Located in Tokyo's Minato Ward, TOTO GALLERY-MA is known for its unique exhibitions, lectures, and other activities mainly on the thought and work of architects. Lighting design is a field related to architectural design, so an exhibition about the work we do seemed deeply significant, and I pondered just what we should convey to the public at such an exhibition.

The product of our labor is not a "work" in the sense the word is used when referring to the creation of artists and architects. A light design project always takes form as a collaboration with the architect as well as many other professionals. The work we call lighting design does not produce something even close to an individually created and copyrightable piece of art. A lighting designer is rather a kind of artisan who creates remarkable architectural space by manipulating light and shadow. As we debated these points over and over, rather than an exhibition only of beautiful photographic images of lighting design projects, we ultimately decided on an exhibition that would both show what the actual work of architectural lighting design entails and give an idea of the outlook of the fully dedicated professional.

At the exhibition venue we recreated a studio in the image of our own workplace and exhibited design implements, light tools, all kinds of hand drawings, optical fiber intensive architectural lighting models, and the many other things that lighting designers use every day. This exhibition bringing together the thinking and design processes behind the lighting designer and whose work is the product of a back and forth collaboration between the architect, and client was titled "A Manner in Architectural Lighting Design." We organized writings expressing our long-held views on architectural lighting design and presented them from the perspective of 10 thoughts and 27 manners.

The 10 architectural lighting thoughts are: Light is a material, a lighting fixture is a tool, lighting should light people and architecture, the character of the light is defined by the space, light creates atmosphere beyond function, time is visualized by light, sequential design creates dynamism, learn from the rules in nature, lighting design must always be ecological, lighting = designing shadow.

The exhibition helped us to evolve into an organization of lighting designers sharing a clear vision. Clearly showing the skills and the type of work at which we are best narrows down our range of potential clients and the project requirements we can fulfill. With the exhibition, a dialogue gradually began about what we as lighting designers can and cannot do.

Projects completed after the exhibition and publication of the commemorative book clearly demonstrate this approach. Sendai Mediatheque, which was completed in 2000, undergoes a complete night-day transformation that visualizes the concepts of "Lighting should light architecture" and "the character of the light is defined by the space." The lighting design of Roppongi Hills completed in 2003 put into practice "learn from the rules in nature" by emphasizing, for example, low color-temperatures and low-positioned of light sources. The 70,000 optical fibers on the bottom of the water basin of Nagasaki National Peace Memorial Hall for the Atomic Bomb Victims articulate the concepts of "light is a material" and "light creates atmosphere beyond function." Other projects completed around this time such as Chino Cultural Complex and Kyoto State Guest House likewise manifest light environments that vividly demonstrate the "a manner in architectural lighting design."

Every field of design has its own particular theories and methodologies. The field of lighting design has a history and a design system unique to it going back centuries, if we only consider stage lighting, which dates back to an era when torchlight was the main lighting tool. The history of architectural lighting design, however, goes back only 50 or 60 years and is still evolving. We can therefore expect to see many different designers introduce new manners and methods of architectural lighting design in the years ahead.

Social Light

Erwin J. S. Viray

Since the beginning of 21st Century key words appear frequently that guide the creators of the environment. One of these is "sustainability," another is "social." In exploring these words and concepts we optimistically hope that they will bring new worlds of possibilities to the world we are now in. LPA seems very conscious of this, because this book is part of the exploration to find relevant issues and contribute significantly to the bettering the environment. Of course, LPA and Kaoru Mende deal with light, and so it is with light that they offer possibilities in terms of innovations and inventions.

One phenomenon that has always interested me in parallel with the social space consciousness of LPA is in the light exploration that happened in Sendai Mediatheque, a landmark project by Toyo Ito. Sendai Mediatheque redefined how we look at space and structure and function program distribution. A library is a public space, a gathering place while also accommodating the need for individual solitude. The web cage structures create a continuous space and at the same time show possibility of creating diversity in the continuous space, creating specific qualities in homogenous spaces. In these conditions, light plays an indispensable part. It elicits participation in the users in subtly guiding how spaces could be used and how the spaces could be navigated. As these internal spatial inventions define the quality of the spatial feeling in the building, the light quality too defines a presence in the city, in the environment it is located in. It is no longer just a lamp lit in a context but a defining element to give identity to a place. As one walks Jozenji Street, one can see the building and one is awakened to the ephemerality of light while at the same time impart the presence of light that redefine augmented habits of people when looking at the environment. Somehow the sentiments echo the ephemerality and feeling of solitude in life and the relation of solitude in the multitude, an individual, and a community. Through Toyo Ito's architecture we realized a consciousness of light.

In this phase, LPA and Kaoru Mende, offer to us, "Light is social, Light is life."

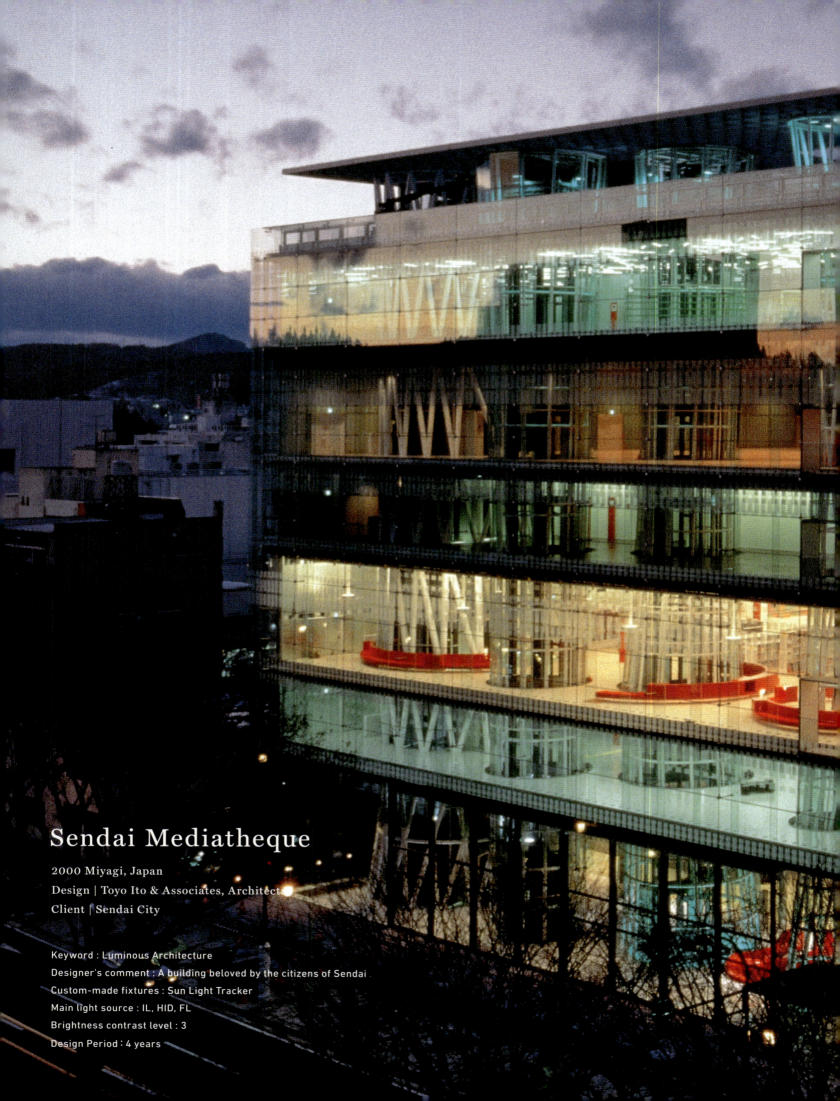

Sendai Mediatheque

2000 Miyagi, Japan
Design | Toyo Ito & Associates, Architects
Client | Sendai City

Keyword : Luminous Architecture
Designer's comment : A building beloved by the citizens of Sendai .
Custom-made fixtures : Sun Light Tracker
Main light source : IL, HID, FL
Brightness contrast level : 3
Design Period : 4 years

This seven level above ground floor glass building includes a public library, gallery, theatre and a workshop amd event space. The building serves as a multi-functional arts and cultural facility for community cultural activities. The building is composed of seven steel sandwich panels, a shaft of 13 steel-frame "tubes," and a double-layer glass facade.

The entire 50 square-meter exterior is glass, so that during the day the nature outside has a tangible presence inside the building while at night the activity inside can be observed outside. This exterior-interior unity also makes the building unique in terms of light.

"A different ceiling lighting system for every floor," "natural and artificial light transmitted through the tubes," "flexible light that adapts to spatial change," and "warm 3,000K color temperature light" are among the many lighting features that made this project a story of diverse concepts.

Glass architecture by its very nature must struggle with light. Buildings of transparent glass do more than simply allow in light: this same light can obstruct vision or be reflected and diffused within the space. When the glass façade is exposed to the mid-day sun, the view inside may be of the bright Sendai cityscape and roadside trees but outside the glass appears as nothing more than a screen mirroring the sky. But from dusk onward the phenomenon reverses, with the glass becoming mostly a mirror from inside while from outside the building shimmers like a multi-layered plate of light that enables one to appreciate the activity inside. This day-night reversal, especially, shows how dynamically the building interacts with light.

During the lighting design process we used a variety of light sketches and explanatory drawings to explain design concepts to third parties. These include lighting effect plans showing light intensity and color temperature, night exterior elevation drawings illustrating exterior lighting, reflected ceiling plans for working out lighting fixture placement, and so on. But for us the most important drawings and sketches of all are light cross-section drawings. Coloring in the lighting concept into architectural cross-section drawings together with schematic explanatory drawings is essential to explaining the intended effect and the method by which it is to be achieved.

At Sendai Mediatheque every floor — from the two basement levels to the seventh and top floor — is different and has its own unique functions. We therefore worked out and selected lighting methods specific to each floor, including the lighting employed around the thin, flat slabs. Being able to interpret all this from light cross-section drawings is the key to lighting design.

1F

The first floor is a broad, open space along Jozenji Dori. Beside a café and shop, it has an open square for hosting all kinds of events. Lighting is installed in round recesses in the ceiling plate. 150W metal halide lamps and 250W halogen lamps provide both general lighting and local lighting.

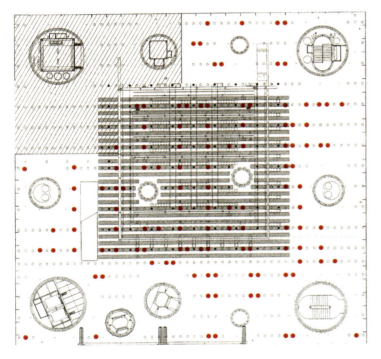

2F

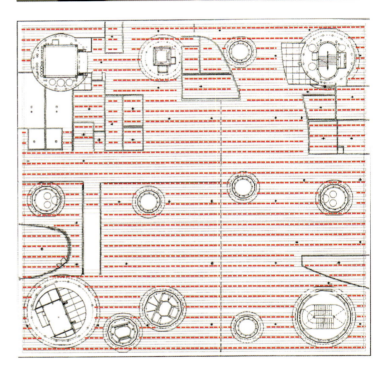

The second floor is a general information center organized around a reception and consultation counter. Lighting is provided by a linear array of high-efficiency seamless fluorescent lights with reflecting mirrors.

3F

The third and fourth floors are the library. These floors are bright, open, high-ceiling spaces suited for general open-stack shelves. In order to achieve the required illuminance of 400 lux with visually comfortable and soft ambient light alone, the design uses pendent indirect lighting fixtures. Light from metal halide lamps directed at the ceiling provide uniform lighting throughout the reading room and endow the space with unity and openness.

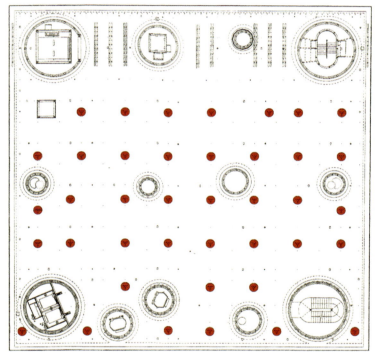

7F

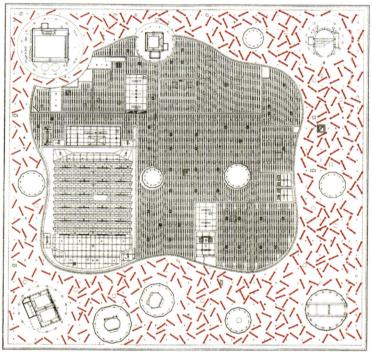

Called the "Studio," the seventh floor's functions include community services and space for building staff. At the time of completion, the seventh floor had only 3,000K 40W fluorescent lamps randomly positioned in the ceiling along with ballasts installed inside the ceiling (top). The ceiling collapsed during the March 2011 Tohoku Earthquake and the ceiling system was reevaluated, with the lighting converted to LED downlights (bottom).

Sapporo Dome

2001 Hokkaido, Japan
Design | Hiroshi Hara + Atelier φ, Atelier BNK
Client | Sapporo City

Keyword : Up Lighting
Designer's comment : A snowy construction site was very slippery.
Main light source : HID, FL
Brightness contrast level : 1
Design Period : 2.5 years

This all-weather, multi-purpose dome built in snowy Hokkaido has a light exterior reminiscent of a sailboat's billowing sail. The distinctive building form visible inside the immense arena is illuminated even when no events are taking place so that the crowds of people visiting the Dome's observation deck and arena restaurant can enjoy the atmosphere. In contrast to the arena's high-energy sports lighting, the concourse is bathed in soft ambient light originating from uplighting behind the steps, creating a place where people can gather and relax during events.

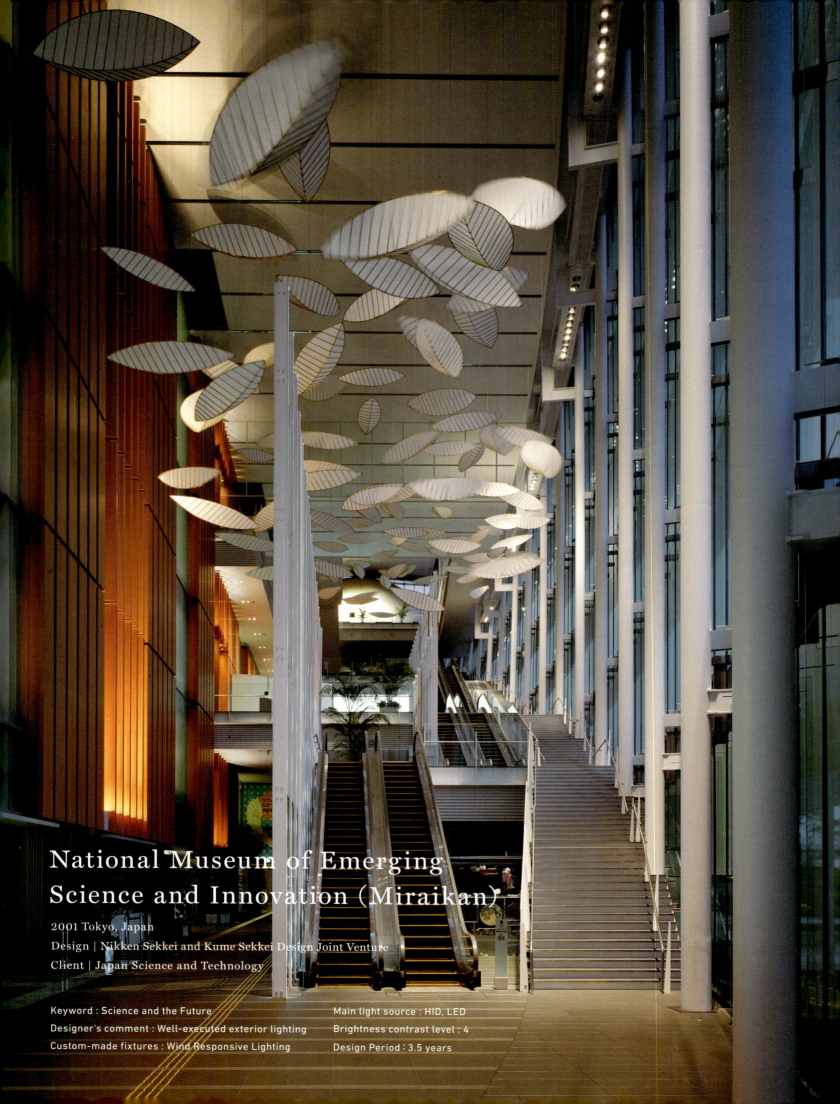

National Museum of Emerging Science and Innovation (Miraikan)

2001 Tokyo, Japan
Design | Nikken Sekkei and Kume Sekkei Design Joint Venture
Client | Japan Science and Technology

Keyword : Science and the Future
Designer's comment : Well-executed exterior lighting
Custom-made fixtures : Wind Responsive Lighting

Main light source : HID, LED
Brightness contrast level : 4
Design Period : 3.5 years

Visitors experience science and technology in real time and in a variety of dimensions at this museum, from simple everyday questions to the latest technology, the global environment, and space exploration.

We worked out the museum's lighting design around the concept "sun, wind, moon." The atrium light well on the north side is filled with warm light that after sundown further enriches the interior's appearance. White LEDs installed in the glass mullions on the top of the building have sensors that detect outdoor wind velocity and flicker organically in response.

Kani Public Arts Center

2002 Gifu, Japan
Design | Hisao Kohyama Atelier
Client | Kani City

Keyword : Vertical Luminance
Designer's comment : Forms and outlines reflected in the pond is a key detail.
Custom-made fixtures : Various Luminous Walls
Main light source : HID, FL, IL
Brightness contrast level : 4
Design Period : 2.5 years

This building was designed as a center for the cultural and creative activities of the local community. It includes a large and small theatre art gallery, a loft for all kinds of activities, workshop rooms, among other facilities. The building is an assemblage of block-shaped rooms covered by a large, flat roof. The walls of each of these volumes are illuminated and given a sense of brightness with a lighting method specific to each space.

The building's glass façade extends in an L-shape around the grass courtyard, and at night light radiating from the walls of each block reflects in the copper-panel ceiling, adding a dynamic quality to the activities going on inside.

To bring out the dynamism of architecture, it is often more effective to light up walls rather than floors. Consider this issue from the visual perspective of people using a facility: since the field of view includes a high proportion of vertical surfaces in the form of walls, it is walls that provide most of the visual cues and spatial orientation.

The light environment for this building is organized around wall luminance with this in mind. In addition, the luminance is designed to reflect off the distinctive copper panel ceiling that covers the whole building and off the water basin outside.

The design illuminates large, tile-covered walls with wallwashers, casts the distinctively textured hallway walls in ambient light, and transforms the large, light diffusing glass surfaces into luminous walls radiating light from the interior.

The glass wall was especially challenging with regard to the architectural dimensions, and in order to ensure uniform light we worked out various details — lighting fixture reflective mirror design, light reflecting backboard color, the film for enhancing glass diffusion, and so on — with mockup tests.

one-north Master Plan

2002 Singapore
Design | Zaha Hadid Architects
Client | JTC Corporation

Keyword : Evolving Lightscape
Designer's comment : A seemingly impossible plan to achieve
Main light source : HID, Xenon
Brightness contrast level : 2
Design Period : 2 years

The Singaporean government sponsored an international urban design competition for this 194 hectare area. The competition's winner, Zaha Hadid, proposed a streamlined cityscape of seemingly unachievable beauty. Landscape designers, lighting consultants, and other project participants struggled forward on the project, caught between the design draft's conceptual ideal and the client's need for a realistic approach. We put together a plan proposal envisioning the cityscape 20 years from now and embodying our "Evolving Lightscape" concept of a high-quality and flexible light environment.

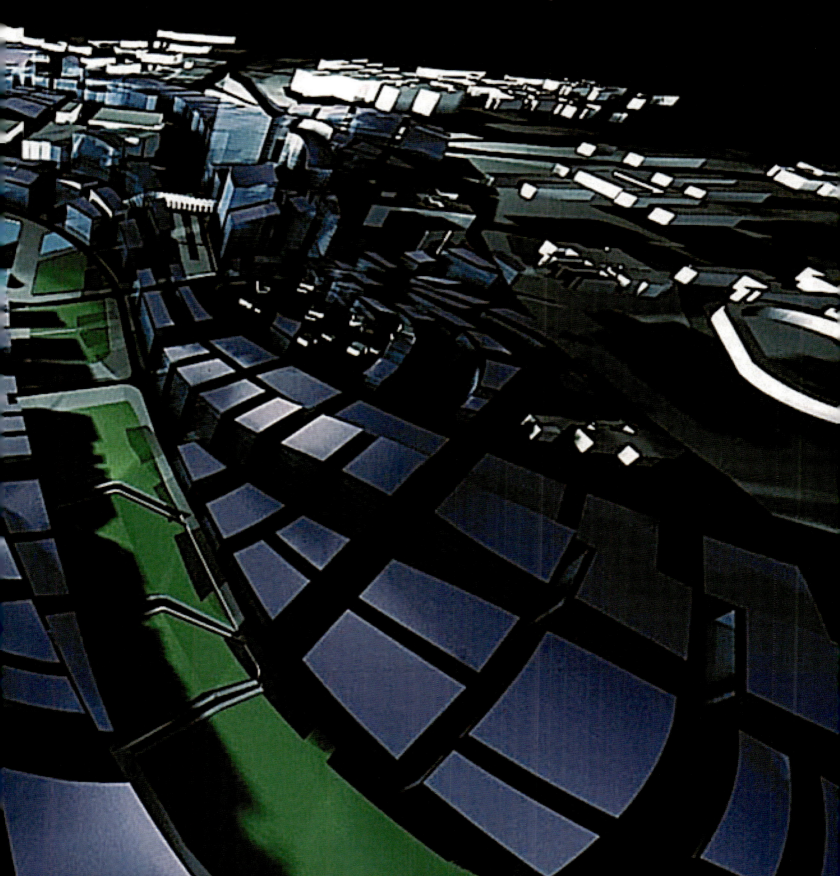

"Evolving Lightscape" refers to design that anticipates the urban growth process. As the city undergoes phased development, this concept suggests that its light, besides proliferating in phases, likewise constitutes a system always in motion and rich in variation. In other words, a city and its light constantly grow and evolve together.

We put the evolving lightscape concept into practice with the following five methods.

1. Flexible lighting system

An evolving lightscape lighting system possesses three kinds of flexibility: flexibility of light, of fixture, and of installation. "Light flexibility" refers to being able to freely select light sources and light distribution and to a system that can adjust illumination direction in line with actual conditions. "Fixture flexibility" refers to a system in which the various fixtures are compatible and interchangeable. For street lighting, for example, these might include poles, lamps, transformer boxes, banners, information boards, spotlight arms, and so on. And "installation flexibility" refers to an underground wiring system encompassing the entire site that enables a flexible approach to wiring, pole setting, and other installation work.

2. Lighting operation diagrams

Changes in city nightscape appearance are governed by four types of operation plans. "24 hour operation" begins with the daytime sunshade design and changes in step with 4 kinds of nighttime scenes. "One week/7 day operation" choreographs light according to a weekday-weekend schedule. "Four season operation" creates scenes with a seasonal ambience. And "holiday operation" refers to light operation reserved for various festive occasions and national holidays. These light diagrams also invigorate the urban environment and help reduce energy consumption.

3. Visualize and integrate urban functions

A city is a mixture of facilities with different functions, districts with their own character, and so on. The lighting system needs to visually represent these various functions and attributes at night. Night lighting guidelines that establish rules for illuminance, luminance, color temperature, light source height, glare index, light quality, and the like are very helpful in this regard. Light that visually integrates different functions together into a coherent whole is also very important. Light draws attention to building edges and façades and highlights the flowing lines etched on the nightscape by their rooftops. Light icons called "fireflies" located at various key points on the site also add unity and coherence.

4. Efficient use of sustainable energy

Wasteful consumption of light, as was the norm in the twentieth-century, is no longer acceptable. A lighting plan that uses limited energy resources efficiently and skillfully and harmonizes light and shadow is vital to the system's success. In addition, the lighting plan actively incorporates lighting equipment that uses solar energy, wind power, geothermal heat, and other clean energy sources.

5. Light = media = information

A lighting system does more than simply illuminate a city. Our lighting scheme consciously uses light to transmit information and appropriates it as a form of media on an urban scale. First, light guides the line of sight of people in the city. Secondly, light interactively represents and visualizes natural phenomena and local conditions, and, moreover, projects all kinds of visual information onto an immense environmental canvas.

Evolving Lightscape

Xchange

Lines

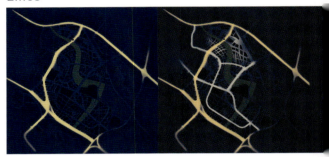

Park

Operation

Scene1 : Twilight Time   Scene2 : Dinner Time

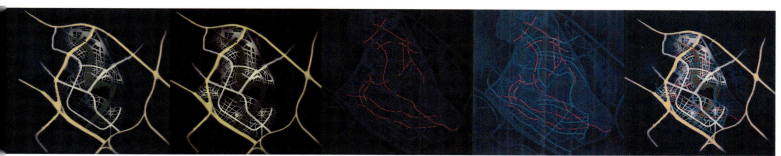

Illuminated Roof Lines Overall Urban Line

Firefly Forest Interactive Lighting

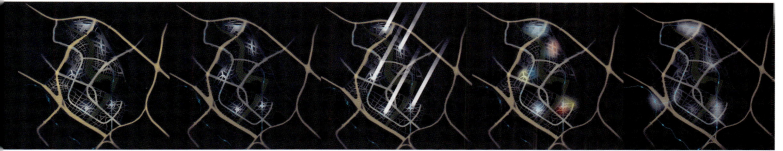

Scene3 : After Dinner Time   Scene4 : Midnight   Festive Operation A   Festive Operation B   Light at PMS Station

Xchange Lighting

Xchange Square
Artistic illumination of the deck that extends out from the station creates a distinctive nightscape for this relatively quiet area.

- FOREST COURT
- DECK
- LOCAL ROAD
- ARTERIAL

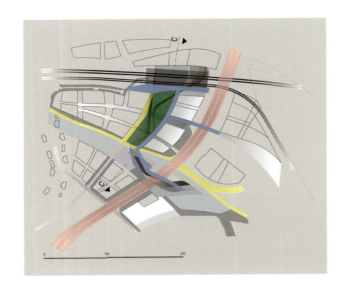

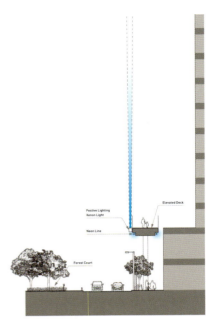

Central Xchange
The illumination scheme for the mall is of vital importance. We try to fit the whole lighting system in the mall's upper area.

- CANOPY
- CROSS POINT (XCHANGE)
- LOCAL ROAD
- PRIMARY ACCESS
- ARTERIAL
- CROSS POINT (GENERAL)

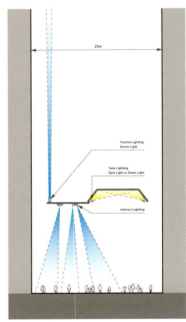

Life Xchange
Skywalk is a central and defining feature. The ceiling is illuminated and lights are installed on the sides.

- CANOPY
- CROSS POINT (XCHANGE)
- LOCAL ROAD
- PRIMARY ACCESS

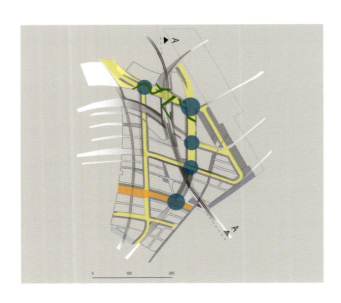

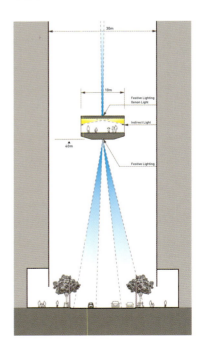

Operation Diagram

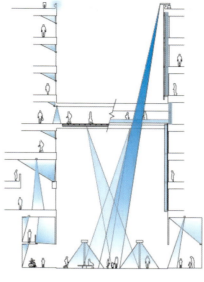
Scene 1 : Twilight Time

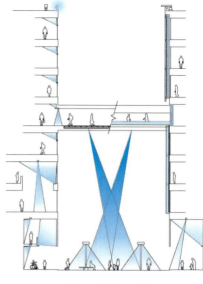
Scene 2 : Dinner Time

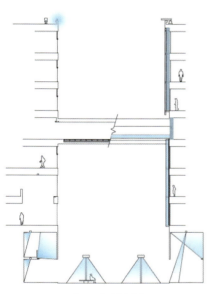
Scene 4 : Midnight

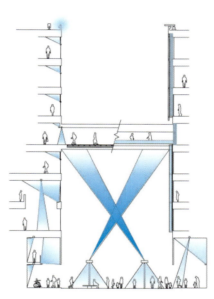
Weekend

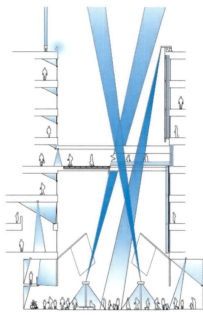
Festive Time

Standard Section

Based on the standard section plan for Xchange, we proposed a number of guidelines and detail recommendations for building façade and lower street area lighting.

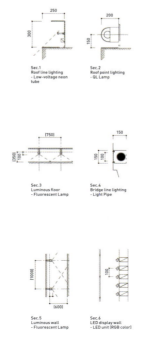

Sec.1 Roof line lighting - Low-voltage neon tube
Sec.2 Roof point lighting - QL Lamp
Sec.3 Luminous floor - Fluorescent Lamp
Sec.4 Bridge line lighting - Light Pipe
Sec.5 Luminous wall - Fluorescent Lamp
Sec.6 LED display wall - LED unit (RGB color)

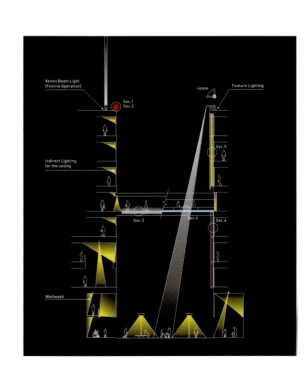

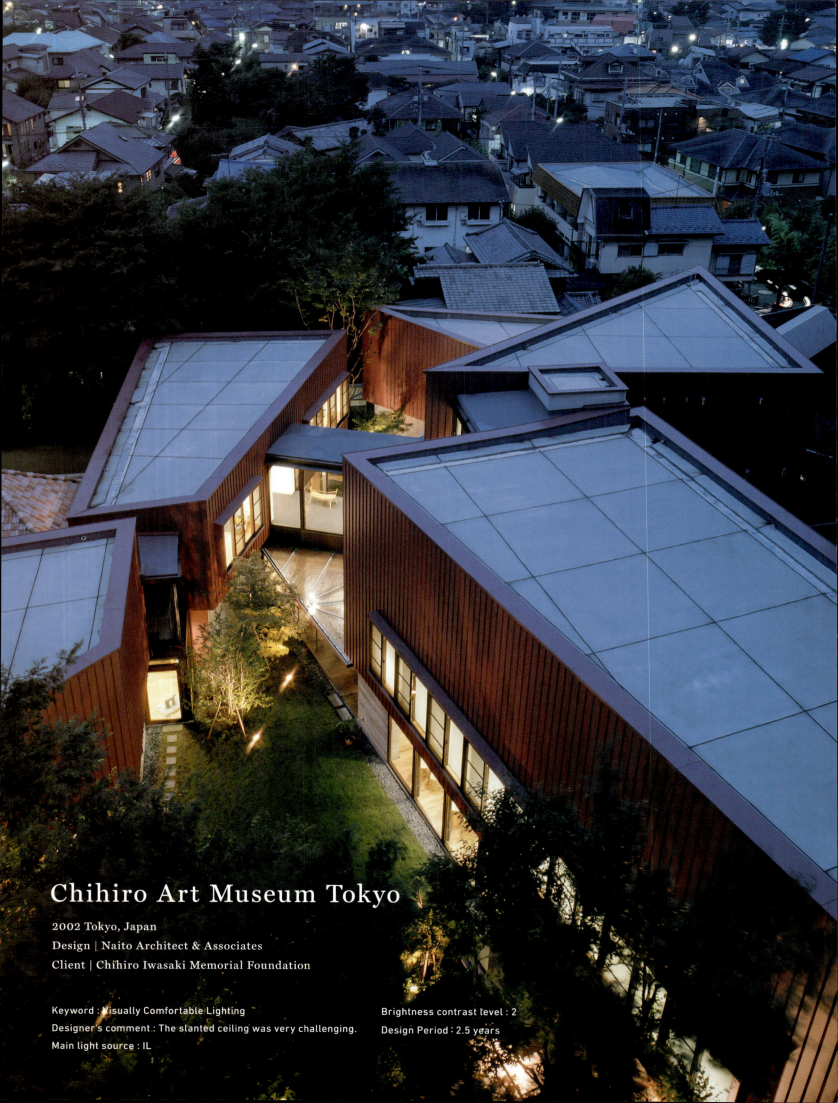

Chihiro Art Museum Tokyo

2002 Tokyo, Japan
Design | Naito Architect & Associates
Client | Chihiro Iwasaki Memorial Foundation

Keyword : Visually Comfortable Lighting
Designer's comment : The slanted ceiling was very challenging.
Main light source : IL

Brightness contrast level : 2
Design Period : 2.5 years

This picture book art museum was built on the site occupied by the home of picture book artist Chihiro Iwasaki during the artist's lifetime. Located in a typical high-density residential area, the site has an irregular shape, which the architecture exploits with a building segmented into four blocks and linked together by corridors.

Crucial to this layout is "a comfortable inward line-of-view" centered on the courtyard, where several lines of view cross one another. Light concentrated on the walls along the border of the site guide a person's gaze from the courtyard to the inside of the buildings. A light environment appointed with soft, low-color temperature lighting creates a relaxing art museum experience.

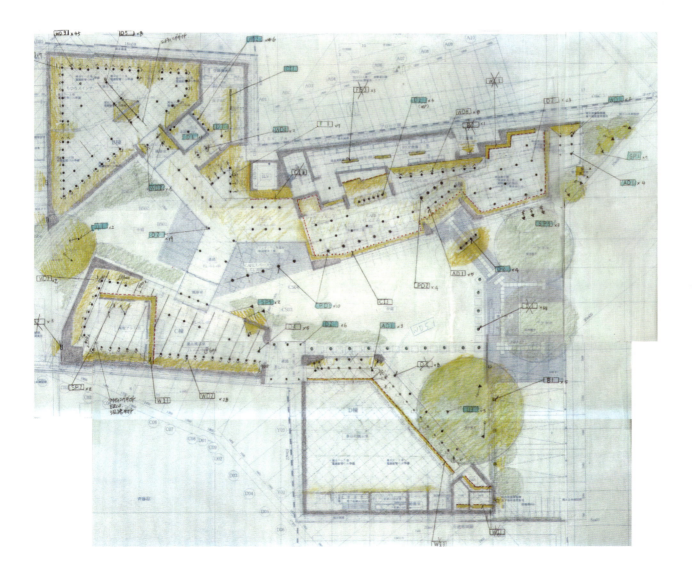

Katta General Public Hospital

2002 Miyagi, Japan
Design | Architects Collaborative (Taro Ashihara Architects,
Koh Kitayama + architecture WORKSHOP,
Hideto Horiike + URTOPIA)
Client | Shiroishi Hoka Nicho Association

Keyword : Patient-friendly Lighting
Designer's comment : Seeing things from the patient's perspective was vital.
Custom-made fixtures : Ceiling Ambient Light
Main light source : FL, HID, IL
Brightness contrast level : 2
Design Period : 3.5 years

This is an outstanding example of innovative public hospital architecture. This three-floor, 100×140 square-meter building has outpatient care facilities as well as various medical screening facilities and a full-range of hospital rooms for in-patient care specially designed to provide patients a stress-free visual environment.

The first floor is a large piloti space with the reception and outpatient waiting area, the second floor contains offices, and the third floor contains patient rooms and a rooftop garden. All patient rooms face the garden or the terrace — both filled with natural light — to make the entire ward the embodiment of a "healing space." Lighting design is without question assuming an increasingly important role in hospitals and treatment facilities.

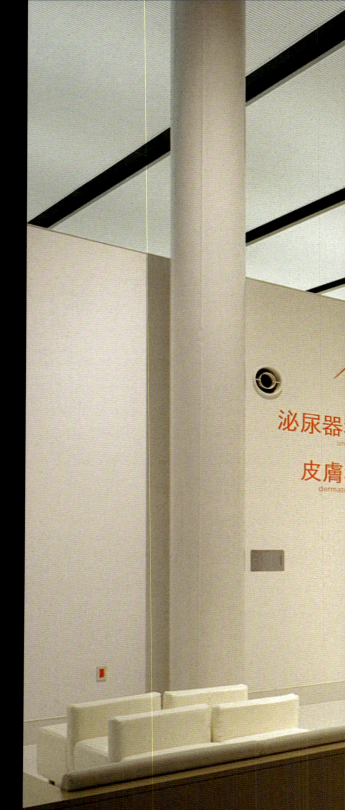

The person whose needs are the most important at a hospital is the patient. We began the design process by asking "how do we create a light environment for people recovering from illness?" We dedicated ourselves to achieving "patient-friendly light": lighting with an "at-home" ambience, ultra-simple lighting fixtures, the maximum use of natural light, views with greenery, and warm light colors that put the patient at ease.

The "patient-friendly lighting" concept inspired a number of lighting methods and design ideas. The lighting for the spacious, two-story atrium-style outpatient area is provided by two types of fluorescent lighting: daytime-color and incandescent-color. The white light brightly illuminates the ceiling during the day, while the warm incandescent light provides a soothing light environment at night. A daylight sensor automatically adjusts lighting to the appropriate setting. Patient room corridor lighting set to 50 to 300 lux creates a calming, rhythmical light environment that is also economical and functional.

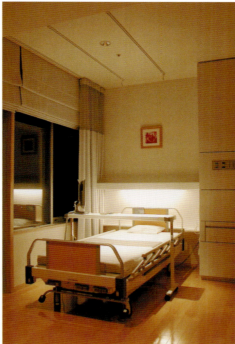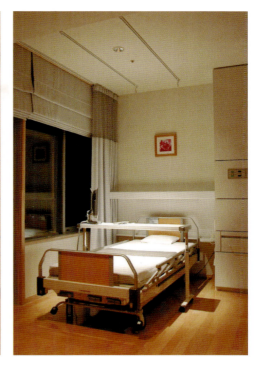

White light illuminates the ceiling during day (above left) and after dusk changes to warm, calming light (above middle). Ceiling downlights are turned on when treating patients (above right). All patient rooms face the inner garden and have picturesque views of the sky (bottom).

Nagasaki National Peace Memorial Hall for the Atomic Bomb Victims

2003 Nagasaki, Japan
Design | Kyushu Regional Development Bureau, Akira Kuryu Architect & Associates
Client | Ministry of Health, Labour and Welfare

Keyword : Healing Light
Designer's comment : A beauty that almost brings tears to my eyes
Custom-made fixtures : Fiber Optic Underwater Lighting
Main light source : FL, IL
Brightness contrast level : 5
Design Period : 3.5 years

At 11:02 in the morning on August 9, 1945, a plutonium implosion atomic bomb was detonated over Nagasaki, killing 70,000 people. This memorial is an expression of mourning for the atomic bomb victims and a prayer for everlasting peace on behalf of the nation and a place for fostering a deeper understanding among the people of the world of the horrors of the atomic bomb and a place that preserves the experience of atomic war for future generations.

While the memorial is mostly underground, the design includes a circular monumental water basin 29 meters in diameter. Reflecting the nation's wish to express the enormity of the destruction and the opinions of the local building committee, a light particle for each person who had died was placed on the bottom of the water basin. 70,000 light fiber particles swaying gently in the Nagasaki wind create a solemn nighttime scene for remembering the dead.

The memorial stands as an earnest plea to abolish all nuclear weapons from the earth.

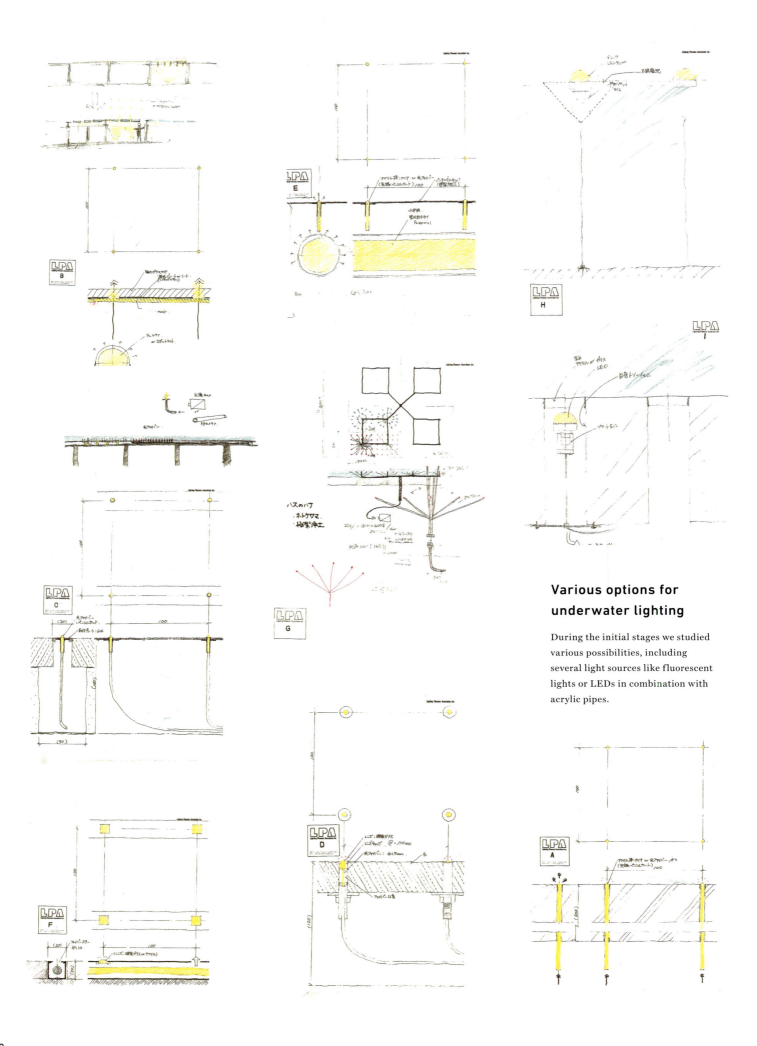

Various options for underwater lighting

During the initial stages we studied various possibilities, including several light sources like fluorescent lights or LEDs in combination with acrylic pipes.

When visiting the memorial at night, the first thing one encounters is the 70,000 light particles swaying in the circular water basin. Little light fiber tips peek out from tiny holes spaced at an 86 mm pitch on the floor of the black granite basin. These tiny, inorganic particles of white light swaying with the Nagasaki wind and the water comfort the hearts of the people standing at its side.

Embedding a grid of 70,000 light fibers in black granite was not as easy as we had expected. Any deviation among the straight lines of 3 mm holes hand bored at the same pitch is immediately obvious. We worked out how close to place the fiber tips from the surface with a series of water tank mockup tests.

After installation, there was also the issue of small bits of debris, dirt, and other impurities obstructing the little fiber tips. For the perfect execution of the intended lighting effect we are indebted to the technical skill and dedication of all the people involved in the installation. This project clearly reminds us that lighting design cannot be accomplished just with the ideas on the desk of the architect and the other designers.

Warm tone, indirect lighting softly envelopes the serene pathways (left). Indirect handrail lighting leading from the ground level entrance to the basement captures attention from the approaching stairway (below right and bottom). In the vaulted memorial space, white metal halide lamps illuminate rows of columns creating a symbolic place of prayer and remembrance (P175).

Moerenuma Park Glass Pyramid

2003 Hokkaido, Japan
Design | Architect 5 Partnership
Client | Sapporo City

Keyword : Shadow of the Structure
Designer's comment : Adjusting lighting angles required great effort
Custom-made fixtures : Buried Luminaire with super narrow light distribution

Main light source : IL
Brightness contrast level : 4
Design Period : 2 years

This symbolic building is the core structure in a park whose master plan was created by sculptor Isamu Noguchi. The building contains a public gallery, restaurant, and other facilities. The building is a 32 meter high glass pyramid with a 51 meter base supported by a beam string structure using precision parts to make it as transparent as possible.

  Our primary theme was how to illuminate the transparent glass. To achieve the proper effect, we carefully analyzed the light distribution, quantity, and installation position of fixtures at each point on the pyramid so that they align with the different beam sizes and lengths. We also built a heat evacuation space under the floor for each fixture that keeps cover glass surface temperature from rising.

Roppongi Hills

2003 Tokyo, Japan
Design | Kohn Pedersen Fox Associates, THE JERDE PARTNERSHIP,
Mori Building First Class Registered Architect Office, Maki and Associates,
Ohtori Consultants Environmental Design Institute, and others
Client | Roppongi 6-chome Area Redevelopment Association

Keyword : 24-hour City
Designer's comment : Adjustments seem to take forever for this massive development.
Custom-made fixtures : Buried LED Luminaire
Main light source : HID, FL, IL, LED
Brightness contrast level : 4
Design Period : 5 years

Roppongi in Tokyo's Minato Ward is well-known as a trendsetting neighborhood dotted with upscale commercial facilities, residences, office buildings, and cultural facilities. Roppongi Hills is a massive redevelopment that completely demolished and revitalized an 11.6 hectare parcel in this district. The development brings together a variety of urban functions, including a super high-rise office tower, art museum, commercial facilities, high-rise residences, a hotel, a television station, and gardens that has garnered attention as a model for twenty-first century redevelopment.

  The lighting plan was articulated around a number of key words: gentle light, beautifully presented light, elegant light, light visualizing time, light for special occasions as well as for ordinary occasions, and so on. Warm, glare-less 3,000K light unifies the entire development and every effort was made to employ low-position lighting

In terms of light quality, the project was especially particular about "low-color temperature + low-positioned light." Despite Minato Ward being a center of Tokyo's cultural scene, street lighting, building interior light, and so on use cool white - namely, high-color temperature, light. In contrast, our plan employs warm color temperatures throughout the entire site.

While the site uses a variety of light sources — metal halide lamps, fluorescent lamps, LED, and so on — as a rule they all share a 3,000K color temperature. This creates a peaceful and composed atmosphere throughout the site. In addition, with the exception of street lights, the position of outdoor lighting fixtures and light sources were kept as low as possible. Low positioned light such as ambient lighting beneath benches and pavement embedded LED have a symbolic function, while the garden lighting includes 3.5 meter high street lights and bollard lighting. Low-positioned light imparts human scale and creates a light environment encouraging leisurely strolls.

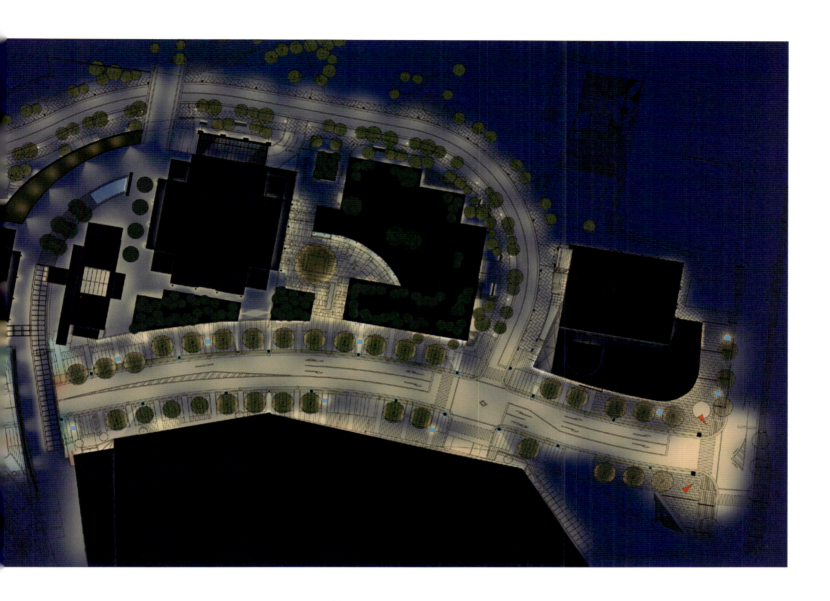

Roppongi Keyakizaka Dori is a 400 meter long shopping street traversing the expansive site north to south. Since the street is administered by the Ward, the government and public collaborated on the street environment design.

The ambience of this street lined with charming shops, restaurants, and bars embodies the high-quality that characterizes Roppongi Hills.

Street and pedestrian lighting was planned in consultation with Minato Ward. Lighting for streetlight banners and the installation of spotlights for lighting up the upper part of shops on each side of the street are among features that are a first for a public-private collaboration.

Most shopping streets at the time had high pavement illuminance and uniform, shadow-less lighting to create an energetic atmosphere. But we felt that this project was best served by subdued pavement illuminance and rhythmical light and shadow that naturally draw ones gaze to the inside of the shops along the street and creates appealing shop fronts. Accent lighting for the *keyaki* trees and flowers also contributes to a striking, shadow-rich nighttime streetscape.

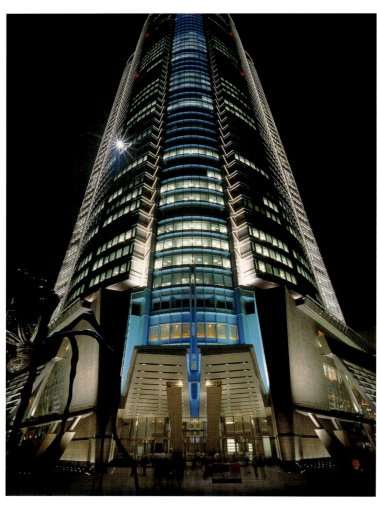

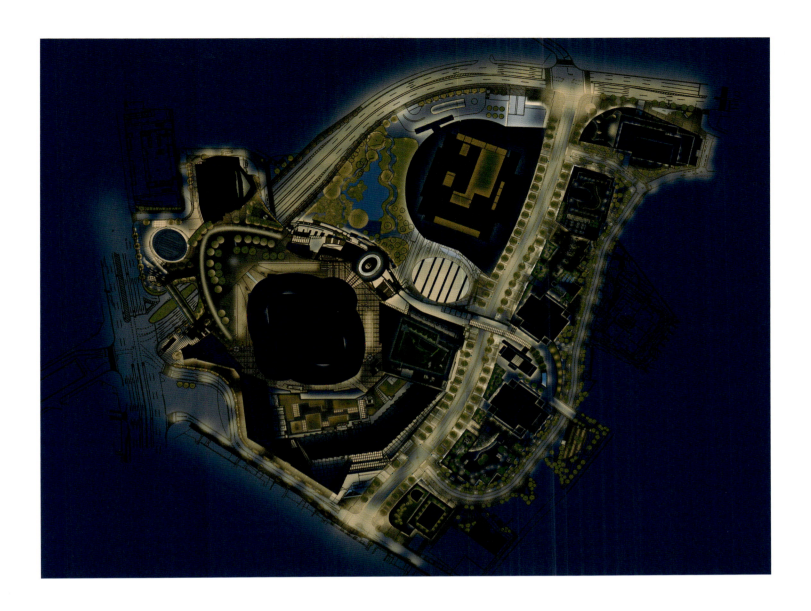

This project was completed by a team of 7 lighting design companies, including LPA, assembled from around the world. LPA's principle assignment was the design of the main outdoor public areas: the exterior around the tower, streets bordering the site, Roppongi Keyakizaka Dori, and the park and garden space.

Mende was appointed Lighting Masterplanner by the project operator. He started with selecting lighting designers and then produced a light master plan and coordinated the work of the project's talented lighting designers. Coordinating the work domains for a team of creative lighting designers from around the world was a difficult task. While it was vital to let the designers exercise their creativity, he also could not allow the finished light environment to lack cohesion.

In addition, since the site is so huge and has a complex spatial layout, it was difficult to accurately grasp the interconnections among designers in terms of the overall design until design details were checked with architectural models. The only solution was a series of dense mutually conducted workshops. The Lighting Masterplanner's responsibilities included simultaneously coordinating the activities of the client, builders, building designers, lighting designers, manufactures, and everyone else involved in the lighting design.

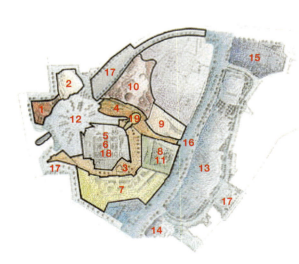

	Area	Lighting designer
1.	Station Plaza	
2.	Multi-use Tower	KPAL Kaplan Partners Architectural Lighting
3.	West Loop	
4.	East Loop	
5.	Office Building A (façade, lobby)	ISOMETRIX
6.	Office Building A (building crown)	MILD Motoko Ishii Lighting Design Inc.
7.	Hotel	FMS Fisher Marantz Stone
8.	Theatre (façade)	
9.	Main Plaza	UCLD Uchihara Creative Lighting Design Inc.
10.	Japanese Garden	
11.	Theatre (roof)	
12.	Entrance Plaza	
13.	Residential Towers A B C D	
14.	Office Building B	LPA Lighting Planners Associates Inc.
15.	Roppongi Hills Gate Tower	
16.	Street running east to west	
17.	Streets on the outer perimeters of the property boundary, but adjacent (Cirular Highway 3, TV Asashi Street, Sectional Highway 3)	
18.	Office Building A Driveway (loop apron)	
19.	Entranceway Structure (art museum)	KPO Kilt Plannning Office Inc.

Toki Messe Niigata Convention Center
Toki Messe Bandaijima Building

2003 Niigata, Japan
Design | Maki and Associates, KAJIMA DESIGN
Client | Niigata Prefecture, Niigata Bandaijima Building

Keyword : View from the Opposite Shore
Designer's comment : Cost adjustments and getting lux levels approved were a major headache!
Main light source : HID, FL
Brightness contrast level : 4
Design Period : 5 years

This multipurpose facility located on Bandaijima along the Shinanogawa river hosts international exhibitions and conferences. We worked out the light design around the theme of how to present from the view of the opposite shore the corridor shared by the international conference tower dramatically piercing the sky and the international exhibition hall, which extends out horizontally. The cylinder-shaped section protruding from the roof illuminated with faint light that complements the surrounding darkness and a common passage with illuminated walls along with functional lighting achieves façade lighting that highlights the building's beautiful horizontal lines.

Hiroshima City Naka Incineration Plant

2004 Hiroshima, Japan
Design | Taniguchi and Associates
Client | Hiroshima City

Keyword : Urban Axis
Designer's comment : Industrial Beauty
Custom-made fixtures : Buried Wall Washer
Main light source : FL, HID
Brightness contrast level : 3
Design Period : 1.5 years

This garbage processing plant built on a site facing the bay includes a reforested park. The central corridor cutting through the plant is a publically open route symbolizing the plant's public accessibility. Designed as a tunnel enclosed by glass on three sides, the corridor can be freely used by the public for field trips. Since the glass corridor serves as a place from which visitors can observe both sides of the plant, even piping and other plant equipment are illuminated with spotlights to create a more dynamic visual experience.

The tunnel-shaped central corridor passing through the plant stretches to Yoshijima-dori, a main Hiroshima thoroughfare that extends to the sea. The tunnel's separation of the garbage processing plant's functions into two distinct areas on the left and right also creates two sharply contrasting views of Hiroshima on one side and the vast blue ocean on the other.

The lighting we designed for the glass corridor is simple and straightforward. The glass section, which looks like a ceiling panel suspended in air, is illuminated with 50W glare-less downlights, while the shape of the tunnel's two sides naturally accommodate rows of ambient lighting installed in the floor. From the Ecorium, as the corridor has been named, visitors have an intimate view that gives them the full impact of this towering and gigantic plant. To convey the depth of this complicated and intricate facility, we installed lighting guided by repeated mockup and onsite experiments. Bathed in white light, the plant could be from a scene set in the not too distant future.

For the simple landscape along the shore, ground lights installed in the curb draw graceful curves of light against the backdrop of the softly illuminated exterior.

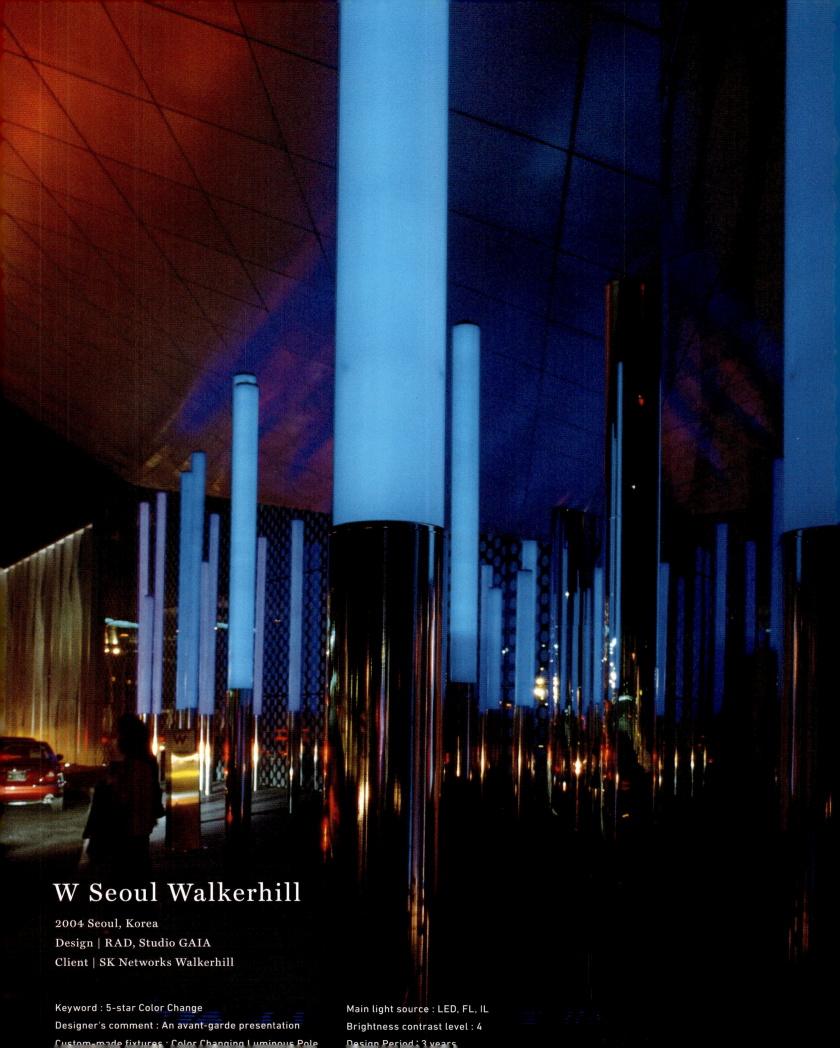

W Seoul Walkerhill

2004 Seoul, Korea
Design | RAD, Studio GAIA
Client | SK Networks Walkerhill

Keyword : 5-star Color Change
Designer's comment : An avant-garde presentation
Custom-made fixtures : Color Changing Luminous Pole

Main light source : LED, FL, IL
Brightness contrast level : 4
Design Period : 3 years

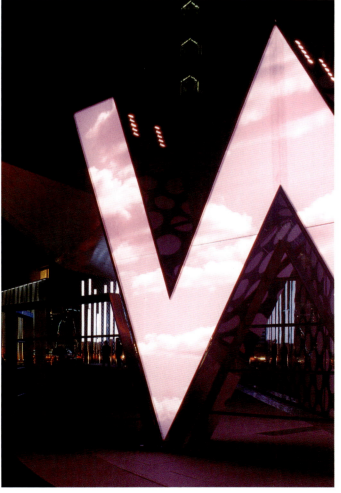

This hotel on Mount Acha overlooking the Han River is the first in Asia for the W hotel brand.

Guests luxuriate in a hotel with a whole new sensibility and exceptionally designed interiors filled with modern art. The lighting design likewise sought not only to enhance this 5-star hotel's pleasant ambience but to create an entertainment experience using the most advanced full-color LED available at the time. Following the avant-garde design of each distinctive space — the 253 guest rooms, lobby, spa, and more — has an avant-garde interior and lighting designed to appeal to sensibility and taste.

Ascending the mountain road on Mount Acha, one is met by the hotel's glass curtain wall exterior embellished with a cloud motif and a large metal canopy with striking sharp edges. Rows of light emitting poles slowly transform into a variety of colors, which are reflected in the metal canopy. Each of the 200mm light emitting poles have linear LED units attached on the pole's core structure and a light diffusion sheet encased in a two-layer milky-white acrylic pipe that together achieves highly uniform light and color-rich operation.

Guests then pass through the revolving door into a lounge called the "living room." The interior has different levels that afford excellent visibility and a large window through which guests can enjoy the view of the Han River at night. The floating-floor stage features floor lighting that adds to the lively nightlife atmosphere by changing color as if in step with the music flowing from the DJ booth.

Shiodome SIO-SITE

Keyword : Block Individuality and Unity
Designer's comment : Pity that the city government did not implement this plan.
Custom-made fixtures : Handrail Embedded Lighting, Luminous Obelisk
Main light source : HID, FL, Xenon
Brightness contrast level : 3
Design Period : 4 years

The Shiodome area redevelopment subdivided a very large site into several blocks. This still expanding belt-shaped redevelopment representing a new type of business center draws urban core revival high-rise housing and commercial facilities.

The Dentsu Head Office in Block A was designed by Jean Nouvel, Jon Jerde and Obayashi. Shiodome City Center and Panasonic (Former Matsushita Denkou) Head Office in Block B was designed by Nihon Sekkei and Kevin Roche. Block C, which includes a Shiodome tower and the Nippon Television Tower, was designed by KAJIMA DESIGN, Mitsubishi Jisho Sekkei and Richard Rogers Partnership. Assigned the lighting design for each of the three blocks, we formed three teams charged with creating distinctive designs for each.

Block A
DENTSU Head Office

2002 Tokyo, Japan
Design | Obayashi Tokyo Headquarters Office
of First-class registered architects,
Ateliers Jean Nouvel, The JERDE PARTNERSHIP
Client | DENTSU

In contrast to the office tower's stylish façade design, the commercial area makes ample use of low-positioned lighting to create a rhythm of light and shadow and also a warm yet lively atmosphere. The atrium, meanwhile, fuses these two lighting schemes with gleaming downlights and red lights on the bottom of elevators that endow the office tower with a lively nighttime appearance.

The project posed the challenge of how to integrate individually unique development blocks into the overall public light environment. When a development plan proceeds in blocks, coordinating the nighttime scene is much more difficult than for the daytime because the former is created entirely by artificial light and is therefore drastically affected by the lighting design scenario.

A poorly conceived overall illumination zoning plan seriously disrupts the site's sense of continuity, and, moreover, creating unity within an urban area cannot be accomplished without a clear overall color temperature plan. The abrupt presence of high-luminance walls, billboard light, and the like are irritating and disrupt a smooth line of view. The remarkable architecture and landscaping that appears at every turn in the Shiodome development required ingenuity that got to the core of the light environment of the public space linking the blocks together. We submitted and adjusted an overall plan to the town planning committee somewhat late, but it did not work well.

Block B
Shiodome City Center + Common-Use Area

2003 Tokyo, Japan
Supervisor | Kevin Roche John Dinkeloo and Associates
Design | Nihon Sekkei
Client | Alderney Investments, Panasonic (former Matsushita Denkou), Mitsui Fudosan

This block has contrasting light schemes guided by the concept "tangible light/information light": the historically significant restored trained station building has a tranquil light environment that takes advantage of the area's transplanted trees, while the sunken garden filled with people both passing through and pausing to relax has a lively light environment. Both areas have light features that convey "time" and presentations that visualize the passing of time.

Block C
Shiodome Tower + Exterior

2003 Tokyo, Japan
Design | KAJIMA DESIGN, Mitsubishi Jisho Sekkei,
Richard Rogers Partnership
Client | Nippon Television Network,
KAJIMA Shiodome development

In this public open space with its unique artificial ground we sought to create "the most tranquil environment in Shiodome" with uniform low color temperature light and light sources positioned as low as possible. Handrail lighting with specially developed optical controls clearly indicate the circulation route and create a pleasing ambience and unique nightscape that is easy on the eyes.

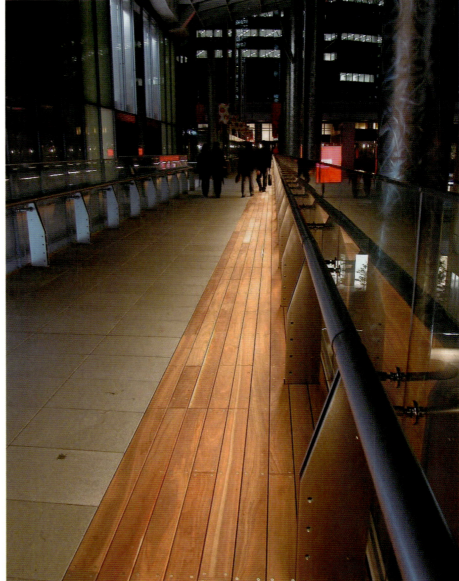

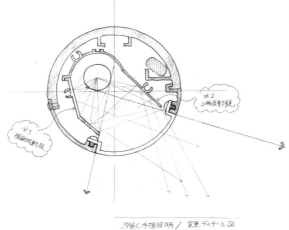

Block H
ACTY Shiodome

2004 Tokyo, Japan
Design | Urban Renaissance Agency,
TOHATA ARCHITECTS & ENGINEERS,
HEADS, PAC, Takenaka
Client | Urban Renaissance Agency

This is a landscape design highlighted by a stepped plaza called the "Step Garden."

The focal point is the large steps visible from Shimbashi and Shiodome Stations, where we installed an array of blue LED point lights in the step risers. Low-positioned lighting for the entire area gives the surface a bright appearance and creates a gentle light environment that takes into account the pedestrian's line of view.

Block D North-2
Shiodome Sumitomo Building

2004 Tokyo, Japan
Design | Nikken Sekkei
Client | Sumitomo Life Insurance,
Sumitomo Realty & Development

This multi-purpose office and hotel building is notable for a design that contrasts the building's dark colored stone exterior with its 40 meter-high glass covered atrium. The lighting plan as well focused on capturing this contrast in an elegant space.

Kagawa Prefectural Higashiyama Kaii Setouchi Art Museum

2004 Kagawa, Japan
Design | Taniguchi and Associates
Client | Kagawa Prefecture

Keyword : Blue Moment
Designer's comment : A space where time slows down
Custom-made fixtures : Fixed Point Spotlights
Main light source : IL, FL
Brightness contrast level : 4
Design Period : 2 years

This small art museum in Shamijima, Kagawa Prefecture was built to exhibit the work of Japanese artist Kaii Higashiyama. This serene building faces the Seto Inland Sea and has a view of the Great Seto Bridge. At the end of each day, the building's imposing slate gray wall extending like a marker between the park and sea shimmers amid magnificent nature as it absorbs the rays of the sun setting on the horizon of the Inland Sea. Before long, spotlights gently illuminate the contours of the wall as the sky is enveloped in a deep blue shroud.

    The lighting in the gallery, meanwhile, is designed to spontaneously draw the viewer towards the artwork, with special attention paid to a color temperature that compliments the artist's unique color palette.

At dusk the art museum's simple silhouette against the blue moment sky is an awe-inspiring site. Exterior lighting is designed to highlight how well the building harmonizes with nature. As the silhouette of the large wall takes form in the twilight, it is illuminated with the faintest of light, as if it were breathing on something soft and delicate. A concealed light source has the most impact, and with that in mind we applied a trial and effort process to selecting fixtures, illumination techniques, and other details, and worked out a design that casts the natural beauty and the beauty of the architecture in understated yet dramatic light.

The gallery spotlight system is deftly installed into the building while maintaining flexibility. To preserve the art, the system uses dimmer controlled halogen lamps, while color temperature conversion filters calibrate light color to bring out the beauty of the tranquil blue hues that can be described as a distinguishing feature of Kaii Higashiyama's art. We felt that light that properly captures the richness of the art and beautiful lighting designed to draw attention to architecture amid a natural setting were equally important.

The Tokyo Club

2005 Tokyo, Japan
Design | Taniguchi and Associates
Client | The Tokyo Club

Keyword : Harmony in the Townscape
Designer's comment : Members only! Entry inside no longer allowed.
Main light source : IL, FL
Brightness contrast level : 4
Design Period : 1 year

This members-only club sits in a quiet, tree-lined neighborhood. Given the neighborhood's character, the building needed an exterior that is not stand-offish and in harmony with the surroundings. With the comfort of guests inside the building in mind, the glass façade and face of the building that at first glance appears to be illuminated by light from inside is in fact lit-up from outside. For the benefit of passersby, considerable ingenuity went into details that hide fixtures and eliminate reflection in glass while also bathing the street in soft light.

The façade becomes increasingly transparent the higher up it goes thanks to well-balanced interior and exterior light, an effect that both provides a veil for the activity inside and creates an elegant exterior.

Chino Cultural Complex

2005 Nagano, Japan
Design | Studio Nasca
Client | Chino City

Keyword : Super Ambient Lighting
Designer's comment : Very happy to receive The Radiance Award!
Custom-made fixtures : Ventilation Embedded Up Light
Main light source : HID, IL
Brightness contrast level : 2
Design Period : 3 years

This facility next to JR Chino Station is a center for local cultural and creative activities. This complex including two auditoriums, an art museum, library, and an event space is noteworthy for being part of the station building itself.

The glass enclosed space next to the station is a library and studio. Sunny and open during the day, the character of the space dramatically reverses at night when the white ceiling is silhouetted in the night sky. The ceiling is completely free of lighting fixtures. Uniform uplighting that seems to come from nowhere transforms the building itself into a colossal lighting fixture.

Ambient lighting typically refers to illuminating an interior with soft light. This building, however, makes ample use of high-output ambient lighting, which we at LPA have named "super-ambient lighting." For the long and narrow library, we installed lighting fixtures on top of the 16 air-conditioning units that sit on the floor of the space. Lighting fixtures that go completely unnoticed use the white ceiling as a reflective panel and fill the room with light.

The top of each air-conditioning unit holds two 150W metal halide lamps with lighting angles adjusted to distribute illumination uniformly across the ceiling. The soft reflected light radiating from the ceiling produces only mild shadow and delivers floor illuminance of 100 lux. The library's "super-ambient lighting" is also deployed in the lobby, corridors, the auditoriums, and elsewhere. Without a doubt, "super-ambient lighting" is an essential tool of architectural lighting.

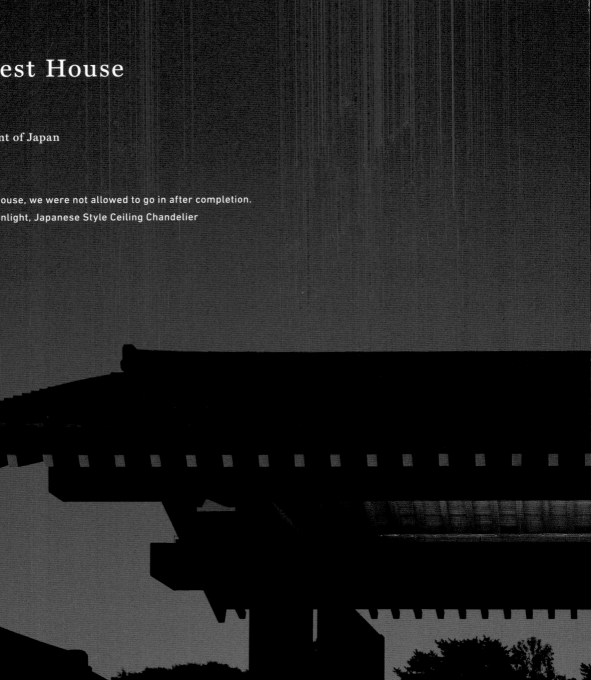

A Japanese-style guest house has been built in Japan's ancient capital of Kyoto. Welcoming foreign dignitaries to a state guest house built in the city symbolizing Japan's history and culture serves to deepen their understanding of and feelings of friendship toward Japan. The guest house is a one-story building enclosed by a Japanese garden on the grounds of Kyoto Gyoen National Garden. It includes a VIP room, conference room, dining room, reception hall, and tea house. The lighting design is especially fixated on gradations of light and shadow. Accomplishing the interior's seemingly infinite gradations of light and shadow required substantial time and effort.

The project's lighting design concept was "Japanese-style hospitality." The Western-style guest house in Tokyo's Akasaka district and the Japanese-style guest house in Kyoto have starkly contrasting light environments, so these two places also need significantly different light philosophies and lighting methods. We articulated our concept of Japanese-style light around a number of qualities: light without too much glitter and brightness, warm light, light and shadow rich in gradation, low-positioned light sources, and so on. The project's building committee included many leading authorities in the field of architecture.

The lighting design philosophy we presented to the committee proposed "Five Japanese Lighting Principles" that we felt were essential to the Japanese-style guest house:

1. Light and shadow rich in gradation
2. Light diffused by translucent and reflective surfaces
3. Light that changes with the occasion
4. Sequential light
5. The use of sunlight and fire

While the guest house is entirely traditional on the surface, it is extremely high-tech in substance. The lighting design and fixture manufacturing and installation likewise used sophisticated state-of-the-art technology. Kyoto is the home of traditional joinery craftsmanship, and this inspired the *washi* and wooden framework ceiling lighting system, which changes the shape of the intricate Japanese-style ceiling by means of computer control. The downlighting cast through small 30mm openings in the ceiling is an optical fiber lighting system throughout that enables subtle shifts in color temperature and brightness. Optical fiber downlights make it possible to definitively fine tune the light so that it complements the given occasion. In short, while Kyoto State Guest House aims for an ambience based on a genuine Japanese and traditional esthetic, the construction and design is technical and modern in the extreme. Indeed, the building might be best described as "low-tech in spirit, high-tech in execution."

The lighting design for this project moved forward in close collaboration with the building's architects, landscape architects, fixture manufacturers, and builders. Since almost all of the lighting fixtures and systems were specially designed for this project, we tested prototypes over and over and painstakingly performed onsite lighting adjustments.

Traditional Japanese architecture is fundamentally a handcrafted form, yet we all too easily forget the value of performing work on-site with a concrete approach. The spirit of Kyoto traditional craftsmanship is what made these extraordinarily high-quality lighting fixtures possible. The singular quality of this project is a tribute to the combined skill and ingenuity of its designers, fixture manufacturers, and builders and a true expression of the "made in Japan" spirit.

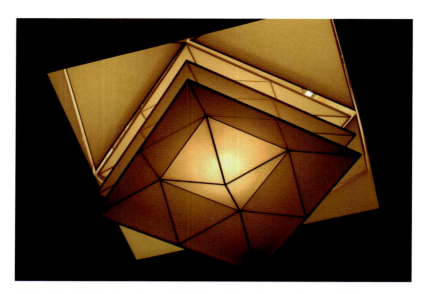

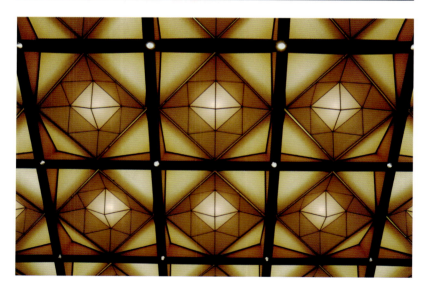

In the dining room, an ornamental ceiling of traditional design appears in place of Western chandeliers.

The ceiling lighting system features a retracting device that can change the ceiling into one of 15 different shapes. By the time it was completed, we had tried out numerous fixture designs and tested lighting onsite.

Lighting fixture details were built with traditional Kyoto joinery, while the system is controlled by state-of-the-art computer technology.

The 39th Tokyo Motor Show 2005 Nissan Booth

2005 Chiba, Japan
Design | Curiosity
Client | Nissan Motor

Keyword : Japanese Touch
Designer's comment : The festive mood during the construction was lots of fun!
Main light source : FL, HID
Brightness contrast level : 2
Design Period : 1 year

The concept for this project was "presentation with a Japanese touch." By fully exploiting the booth's emphasis on simplicity and texture we sought to avoid the bright and uniformly white lighting that is typical of most motor show exhibits. The entire surface of the *washi* wall enclosing the booth radiates warm color temperature light, bathing the whole space in soft light. Spotlights painstakingly positioned amid the pleasant glow of the *washi* wall's ambient light cast the contours of the cars in beautiful light. By bringing out a pleasant light and dark contrast, the lighting design adds to the booth's unique character.

Phase 4

Overseas to Asia

2005–2009

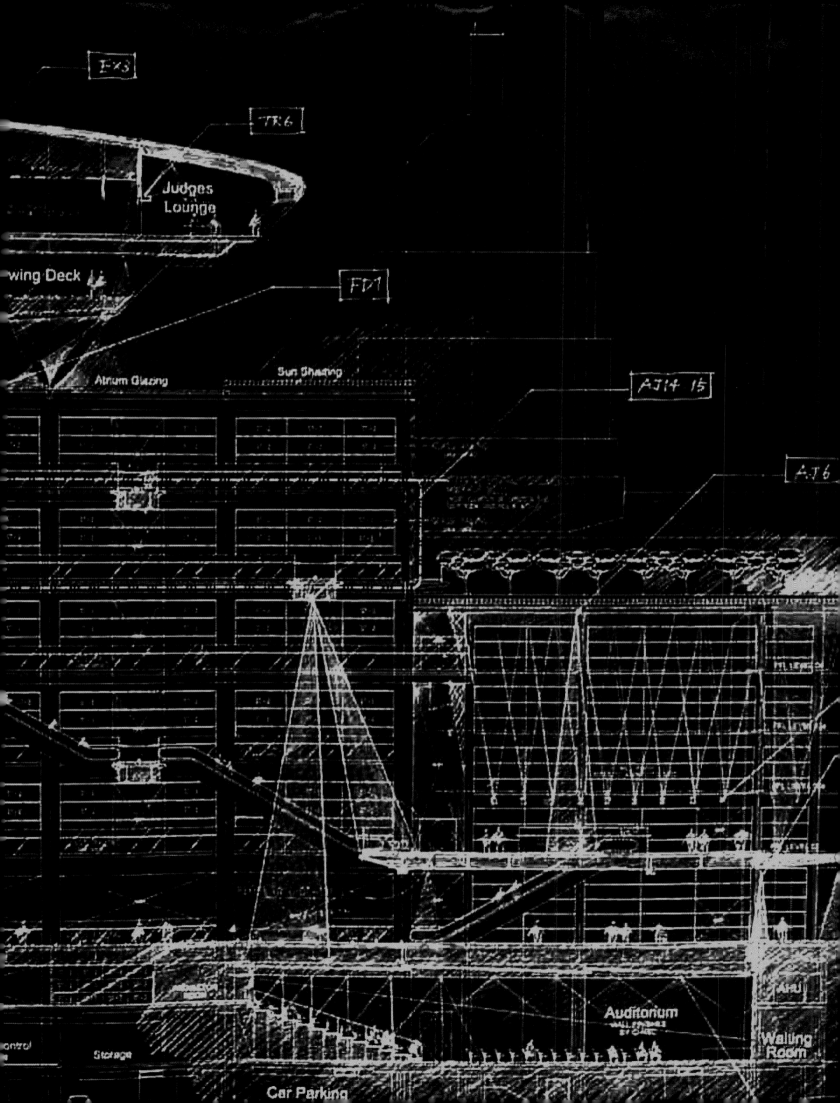

Overseas to Asia:

Learning from Singapore, China, and Hong Kong

Kaoru Mende

In 2000, ten years after LPA was established in Tokyo, we opened an affiliated company office in Singapore. The timing was ironic in that we had established LPA in Tokyo immediately after the collapse of Japan's bubble economy and here we had established a lighting design company in Singapore right after the Asian currency crisis of the late 1990s. What's more, around the time that we launched our Singapore venture many of the Japanese firms that had until then prospered there were in the process of leaving, and so I was often asked "why are you going to Singapore just now?"

In fact, we had a very good reason for opening up an affiliated office overseas: we wanted to absorb and experience the values and dynamism of the architectural lighting design profession in an internationally competitive environment. While there is no reason to question the judgment of clients, the quality of construction, and the like in Japan, we must not allow that to make us complacent. In short, we felt that we could further refine the technique and practice of architectural lighting by working with demanding clients from around the world in a globally competitive environment.

Our initial projects in Singapore were mostly luxury condominiums, and the various projects we became involved in after we first opened our office steadily came to completion starting around 2005. One George Street and the state sponsored projects Supreme Court of Singapore, National Library of Singapore, and National Museum of Singapore came to completion in rapid succession. Lighting Masterplan for Singapore's City Centre project was also completed in 2006 after three years of work. The Master Plan was commissioned by the Urban Redevelopment Authority (URA), the agency responsible for Singapore city planning. Our task was to work out guidelines for a unique and captivating urban nightscape unrivaled by any city in the world and lighting guidelines for the new construction that would achieve this thirty years in the future. The results of this project, which we might even characterize as "light urban planning," were presented to the public at a three-month long government sponsored lighting exhibition, and a steady renovation of Singapore's cityscape with unique and pleasant light according to government guidelines introduced at the exhibition is ongoing. This kind of urban planning with light is difficult to initiate in large Japanese cities such as Tokyo and Osaka, and therefore it truly personifies the significance and role of our crossing the ocean to work elsewhere in Asia.

The challenges we have undertaken in Singapore have led to collaborations with OMA, Zaha Hadid, Norman Foster, KPF, SOM, PCPA, and other internationally recognized architects and architectural firms and with clients initiating international projects in a variety of forms. These projects have also led to other overseas work outside of Singapore. Besides projects in Thailand, India, and Indonesia — countries near Singapore — our work in Singapore has also led to projects in the major Chinese cities of Beijing, Shanghai, Guangzhou, Hong Kong, Shenzhen, Chengdu, and Chongqing. In 2007, the National Centre for the Performing Arts in Beijing was completed, and Main Building of China Central Television (CCTV) was completed in 2008, also in Beijing. The lighting design for these two large-scale state sponsored projects did not include our being assigned the task of final installation and supervision, with the result that the lighting does not fully realize the intentions of our designs. Sophisticated lighting design does not come to fruition without filling in the details. The challenge of overseas projects is getting people to understand what is most important about the lighting design process. In a time when developing countries are focused on all kinds of construction projects, we again want to stress that the ultimate measure of lighting design value is not a conceptual image of the hoped for beautiful nightscape created by computer graphics but the quality of light crafted at the actual site. Lighting design in Asia is a hot, gale force wind that is sure to get stronger and stronger.

Expanding Terrain Light

Erwin J. S. Viray

No other continent has ever urbanized so fast and at such scale. The explosion in population in existing cities, the huge waves of migration from the countryside, and the dizzying pace of growth of new cities has no precedent in human history. But how sustainable can this be? This is the continent that will determine the future of the planet, if Asia is able to develop and bring its populations out of poverty in a sustainable manner, there is hope for us all.

LPA's Kaoru Mende realized the phenomena with prescience and foresight. LPA is one of the pioneers for bringing light consciousness an awareness of it, from illumination to luminance. Lighting Masterplan for Singapore's City Centre brought a new dimension on how we perceive the city. The seemingly generic city suddenly gains specificity. Even within the city, specific areas of the city attain a specific quality, a character, an atmosphere created by light. Lighting master plan highlights the aspects of globalization that makes cities the same and indistinguishable at some end. However, the vivacity and normality of everyday life in the city actually offer distinct and specific differences. That, I think, is the achievement of the opening of the horizon of the practice of LPA and Kaoru Mende beyond Japan: understanding the specific qualities of the places they work in, distinctive and specific places, brought to light with the techniques and technology available to make light bring along that consciousness. In LPA's design process, they assure that every city, every place is distinguished by certain characteristics which underpin the production and reproduction of its own specificity, and thus the uniqueness of the material and social existence. And despite the influence of globalization, urban areas develop different structures and dynamics; consequently they generate a great variety of urban forms and atmospheres. They offer a consciousness of the local city, the tourist city, the support city. Through a light plan we can offer distinct qualities to places that offer recognition and give orientation.

As a business plan on how a lighting design planner from Japan can provide services beyond its border, the exploration of LPA into South East Asia and Asia beyond also offers new avenues to innovations and inventions on how we operate our systems and business models. It offers new scenes for collaboration and distinction of minimal maximal differences, coupled with induced and produced similarities. The operation offers new ways of doing things beyond borders assimilating similarities while also recognizing differences.

In this phase, LPA and Kaoru Mende bring us beyond the borders of our personal space and territory to new borders of consciousness of light: operationally, emotionally, professionally.

One George Street

2005 Singapore
Design | Skidmore, Owings & Merrill, DCA Architects
Client | One George Street

Keyword : Layers
Designer's comment : We really emphasized architectural features.
Custom-made fixtures : Up Light Strip
Main light source : HID
Brightness contrast level : 4
Design Period : 3 years

One George Street is a 23 floor office building in Singapore's business district. Closely spaced rows of louvers to block the intense sunlight and four sky gardens give the façade a striking appearance. The piloti space contains the lobby and elevator core, which are enclosed in curved glass. The elevator core's opaque glass, the curved wall of transparent glass, and the lobby's wood ceiling creating a fascinating composition of contrasting materials.

With the emphasis on accentuating the wood ceiling with up-lighting from the floor, we analyzed the behavior of light on all the materials and worked out a balance of brightness between the vertical plane and floor. This dynamic architectural composition makes possible simple yet powerful architectural lighting details.

230

The wood ceiling up-lighting required strenuous analysis. It is easy to simply cast a ceiling in beautiful light, but here we also needed to find a comfortable balance between ceiling luminance, floor illuminance from light cast back from the up-lit ceiling, and wall luminance. The lobby needs illuminance of 50 lux, and to secure the minimum necessary brightness only with light reflected off the walls and ceiling, we used samples of the actual materials to calculate reflection ratios and work out the balance between floor illuminance and the combined ceiling and wall luminance. We repeated this process until we were sure that there would be no glare from reflected light and that the landscape outside would not be inundated by light from the lobby. Thus, the gradation dots printed on the curved glass walls keep ceiling luminance as seen from the exterior at a comfortable level and interior light reflected off the dots produces further brightness that together effectively modulate the quantity of light inside and outside the space.

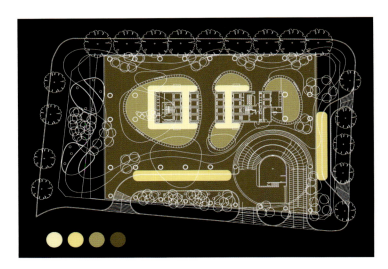

Supreme Court of Singapore

2005 Singapore
Design | Foster+Partners, CPG Consultants
Client | The Supreme Court, Singapore

Keyword : Precision Lighting Design
Designer's comment : Each judge had different preferences.
Main light source : HID, FL
Brightness contrast level : 4
Design Period : 4.5 years

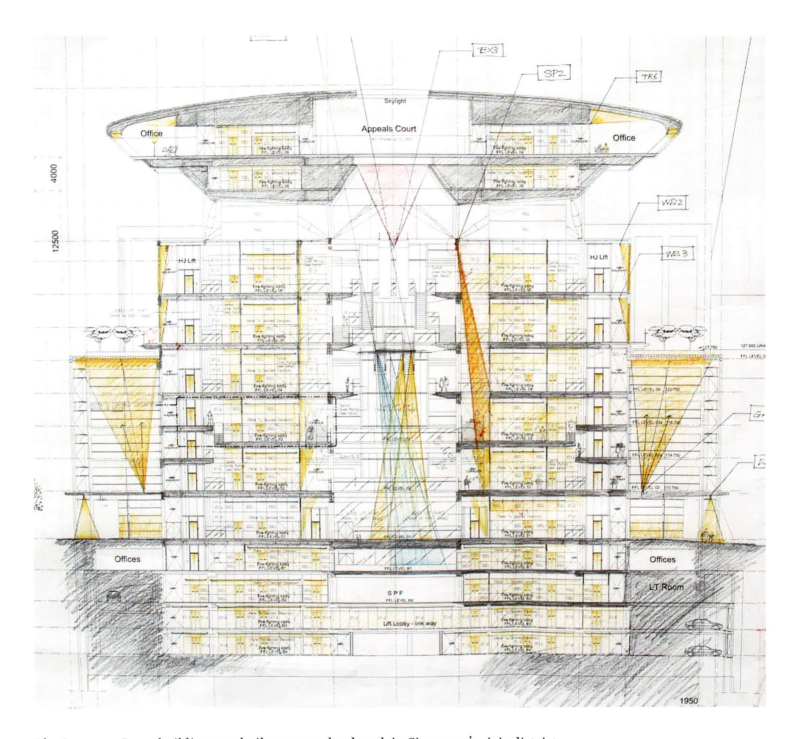

The Supreme Court building was built as a new landmark in Singapore's civic district, an area with preserved historical architecture. Our design theme for this multi-purpose facility partially open to the public focused on harmonizing the authority embodied by the court and the spirit of openness and transparency. In addition, we used the most advanced technology available at that time to produce a plan with the flexibility to accommodate future expansion. Just as a toplight brings in abundant natural light deep into the space during daytime we endeavored to create a comfortably bright spatial envelope at night that loses none of the sense of openness experienced in the day.

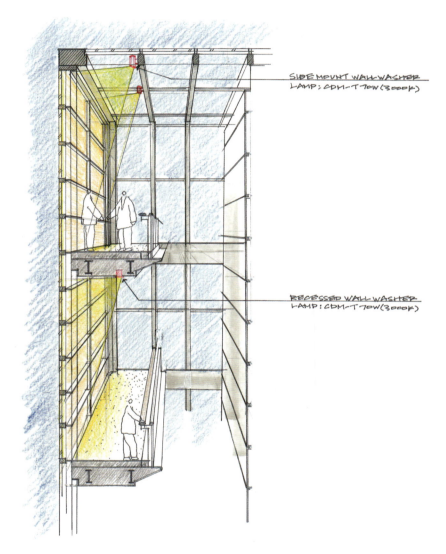

The exterior of this Supreme Court building standing in a district with preserved historical architecture uses a transparent marble inserted into a special glass. During the day, this gives the glass and aluminum panel building a stately air that harmonizes with the stone architecture around it. We carefully worked out the interior lighting so that at night light radiates through the stone and gives the building a warm glow. The base of the massive 66-meter wide circular disc that tops the building is lit with white light, an effect that makes it appear as if it might be a separate object suspended above the building.

 This novel design has become a new icon for the district both during the day and at night. The central atrium between the court room blocks on the left and right is the primary route to each floor and has a toplight that fills the space with ample daylight. Uniform lighting of the corridor walls facing the atrium softens the contrast of light and shadow produced by daylight during the day and envelops the entire space in warm light at night.

The Chedi Chiang Mai

2005 Chiang Mai, Thailand
Design | Kerry Hill Architects
Client | Suriyawong Holding

Keyword : Layers of Light
Designer's comment : Working with local contractor was tough, but we were happy with the results.
Custom-made fixtures : Low-position Pendant, Lantern
Main light source : IL, FL
Brightness contrast level : 5
Design Period : 3 years

This 84 room, four-story resort hotel sits on the shore of the Ping River in Chiang Mai, Thailand's second-largest city. Guest rooms face the river and enclose the courtyard, creating an ambience that takes hotel visitors away from the clamor of the bustling street.

In the corridors outside guest rooms, footlights spaced at regular intervals and floor stands in the corners create subtle shadow, while the neat rows of wooden vertical louvers of the building's façade add a sense of depth to the building when viewed from outside.

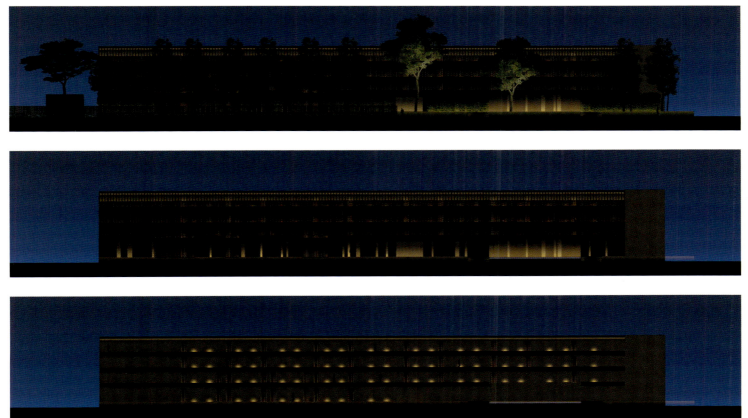

Guest room corridor light and the façade's wood louvers creates a layered lighting effect.

In daytime, sunlight pouring through the gaps in the wood louver façade cast beautiful shadow on the pure white surfaces of the long, straight corridors in front of the guest rooms. So as not to sully the elegant design of these corridors, ceilings are completely free of downlights.

Instead, lighting is furnished by 25W incandescent foot lamps placed inside small 200mm-square openings made in the wall at 3 meter intervals. At night, this orderly arrangement of foot lamps guides guests to their rooms. Lanterns at the ends of corridors provide pleasant faint light and ensure that guests do not lose their orientation. When looking at the façade from outside, the light from the foot lamps placed at fixed intervals behind the delicate wooden louvers create a striking rhythm of light and shadow.

National Museum of Singapore

2006 Singapore
Design | W Architects, CPG Consultants
Client | National Heritage Board,
National Museum of Singapore

Keyword : Glass and Stone Architecture
Designer's comment : Synchronizing color temperature was demanding work.
Custom-made fixtures : Track Lighting Wall Washers
Main light source : HID, FL
Brightness contrast level : 3
Design Period : 3.5 years

The restoration project for the old Singapore History Museum transformed the building into the new National Museum. The new museum combines the colonial-style Old Building and the glass architecture of the New Building, which also partially encloses a section of the Old Building. This experiment in preserving old architecture while adding something new to the cityscape embodies the character of a museum. We decided to highlight the contrast between the old and new façades with layered light. The lighting creates a striking scene by elegantly blending the classical solemnity of the stone structure with the modern lightness of the glass building.

The original Old Building was constructed in 1887 in the colonial-style. The façade and rotunda are given added solemnity with uplighting, while precisely positioned light accentuates the building's distinctive relief work. Warm light cast on the main façade and familiar face of the history museum creates a striking effect.

In contrast, the New Building has a glass-enclosed entrance. The Old Building façade is majestically lit-up at night with wall wash lighting from above and visible through the New Building's glass envelope. Interior lighting is limited to minimal spotlighting to suppress reflection off the glass and symbolically highlight just the Luminous Box (the museum's ticket counter) and rear façade.

Changi Airport Terminal 2 Upgrading

2006 Singapore
Design | Gensler and Associates International,
RSP Architects Planners & Engineers
Client | Civil Aviation Authority of Singapore

Keyword : 24-hour Lighting Operation
Designer's comment : Adjusting lighting after the final flight of the day
Main light source : HID, FL
Brightness contrast level : 3
Design Period : 4.5 years

Unfailingly admired by travelers from around the world, Changi Airport Terminal 2 underwent a major renovation 15 years after it first opened. The dynamic and open interior designed around a plant motif teeming with tropical plants and a newly built skylight transforms it into a modern, pleasant space filled with abundant sunlight. Light in the departure lobby changing hour-by-hour in-sync with the various functions of an airport that operates around — the clock dramatically reverses the day — and nighttime light environment and heightens the anticipation of travel.

Lighting Masterplan
for Singapore's City Centre

2006 Singapore
Client | Urban Redevelopment Authority

Keyword : Tropical Light
Designer's comment : We hope we are contributing to
beautifying Singapore's nightscape.
Main light source : HID, LED
Brightness contrast level : 2
Design Period : 3 years

We were commissioned by the Singapore government's Urban Redevelopment Authority (URA) to develop a 30 year lighting master plan and lighting guidelines for Singapore City Centre. The City Centre consists of five major districts: Orchard, Bugis, Singapore River, the Central Business District (CBD), and Downtown at Marina Bay.

Urban lighting in Asia at the time of the project was invariably conceived along Western lines, but our emphasis was on distinctive urban lighting for this unique city. We felt that Singapore's nightscape and urban lighting should be heavily tinged with the climate, history, ethnicity, culture, and other qualities that make it an exceptional city.

A wide-ranging discussion about what makes Singapore unique gave us the following five features, which we then worked to dynamically reflect in the city's nightscape.
1. Hot humid climate: a cool, refreshing nightscape
2. Intense sunlight: rhythmical light and shadow
3. Tropical greenery: beautiful and lush greenery, even at night
4. Ethnic diversity: the intermingling of diverse lighting effects
5. Water-rich landscape: the reflection of light off the city's waterfront

We also meticulously surveyed the city and analyzed its light environment. This greatly clarified the characteristics as well as the weaknesses of the city's light environment and what needed to be improved. The latter included poor vertical luminance, inappropriate color temperature, glare from light sources, low color rendering, a lack of shadow, and an inadequate operation plan. To work out how to implement these improvements and to make sure that the new project would satisfy the general principles for high-quality light, our proposal required advance consultation with the relevant Singaporean government bodies.

The five main districts all have their own characteristics and concerns, so we developed different lighting concepts for each one: an elegant and composed nightscape for Orchard, frenetic excitement and artistic ambience for Bugis, the interplay of light and water for Singapore River, façade and building top lighting that complements building-type for CBD, and a three-dimensional nightscape of mutually reflected light for Downtown at Marina Bay.

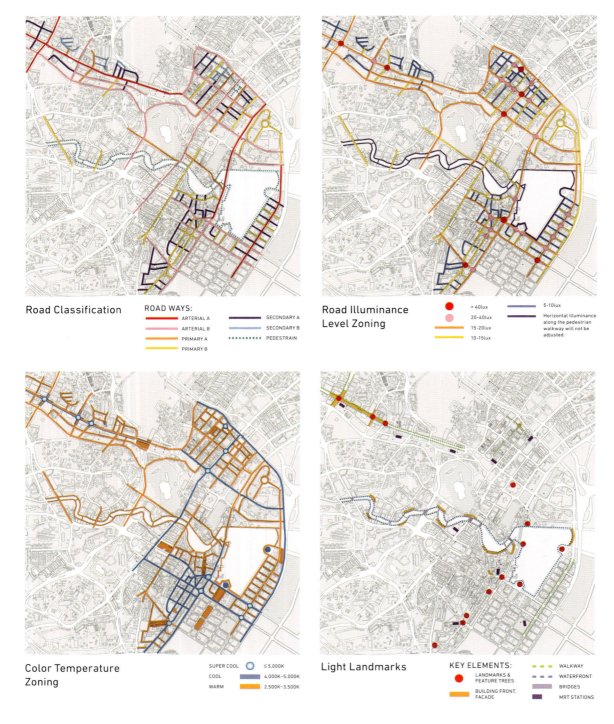

Road Classification

ROAD WAYS:
ARTERIAL A
ARTERIAL B
PRIMARY A
PRIMARY B
SECONDARY A
SECONDARY B
PEDESTRAIN

Road Illuminance Level Zoning

> 40lux
20-40lux
15-20lux
10-15lux
5-10lux
Horizontal illuminance along the pedestrian walkway will not be adjusted.

Color Temperature Zoning

SUPER COOL ≦5,000K
COOL 4,000K–5,000K
WARM 2,500K–3,500K

Light Landmarks

KEY ELEMENTS:
LANDMARKS & FEATURE TREES
BUILDING FRONT, FACADE
WALKWAY
WATERFRONT
BRIDGES
MRT STATIONS

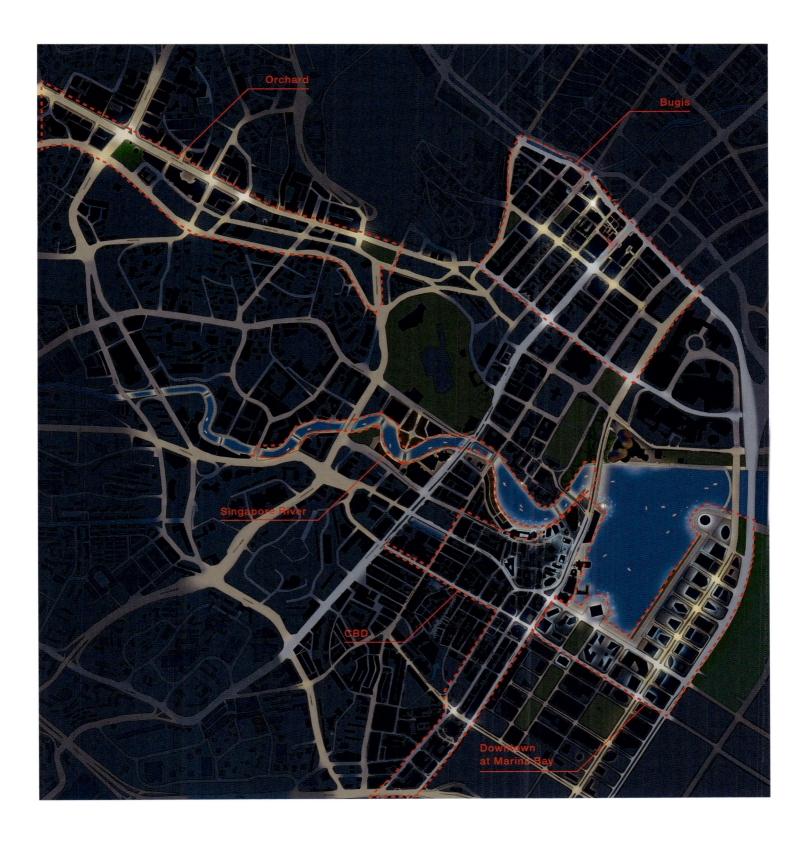

Night image of the complex of unique districts that makes up Singapore's City Centre (above). The master plan aims to create an attractive nightscape by designing distinctive light environment for each district based upon general guidelines. We began with an analysis of the light environment, traffic conditions, and other factors for the main thoroughfares that are the backbone of the city plan (P250 above left). We then used this information to work out light zoning (P250 above right), color temperature zoning (P250 bottom left), and light landmarks (P250 bottom right) and illuminance distribution, which became the foundation of master plan.

Orchard

The two kilometer long boulevard called Orchard Road runs straight through the City Centre and is lined with trees more than 20-meters high, luxury hotels, and shopping malls. In order to create an entertaining and pleasant light environment worthy of one of the world's most famous shopping areas and one that casts the people coming to the district in beautiful light even after sundown, we deployed seven strategies:
1. Three types of tree lighting, 2. High color-rendering light sources, 3. Rhythmical light placement to enhance contrast, 4. Consistent and stimulating shop fronts, 5. A light urban axis that forms a tangible path, 6. Light that changes dynamically, and 7. Lighting that create continuity for the three intersections.

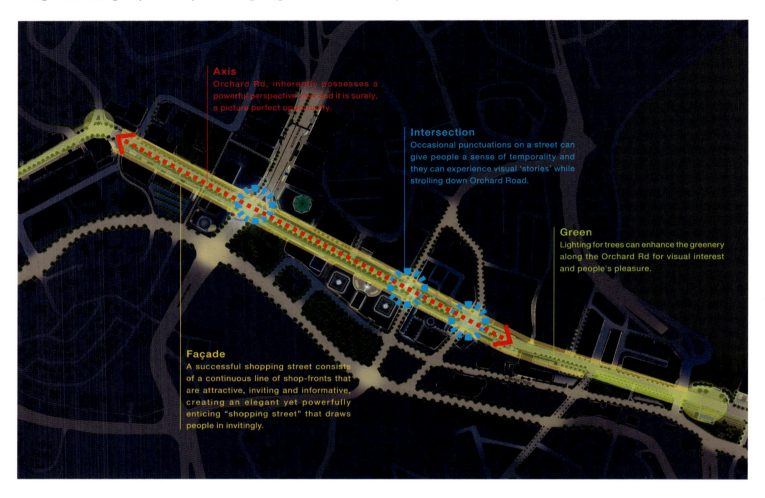

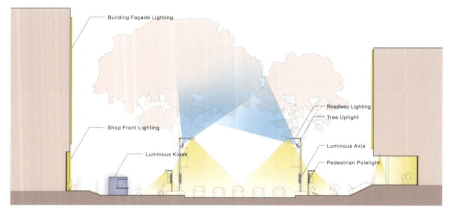

Functional road lighting that minimizes glare and illuminated trees create a beautiful street alive with greenery. Pedestrian paths illuminated with light sources with excellent color rendering give the pedestrian mall a sense of continuity. Moreover, lights installed in the orderly arranged kiosks and street furniture gives the street a lively appearance.

Original Photo

Proposed Rendering (CG)

Bugis

Bustling Bugis with its schools, libraries, and other public facilities, and shops and food stalls sitting right next to a large shopping mall has an atmosphere that embodies the chaotic energy of Asia. This culture, art, and entertainment district is sure to become even livelier in the years ahead. The lighting aims to maintain Bugis' daytime energy after dark. Lighting public, religious, and other prominent buildings scattered throughout the district creates street corner light landmarks. In addition, the plan adds to the lively and boisterous street atmosphere by making media walls, signboards, art installations, and the like a dynamic part of the nightscape.

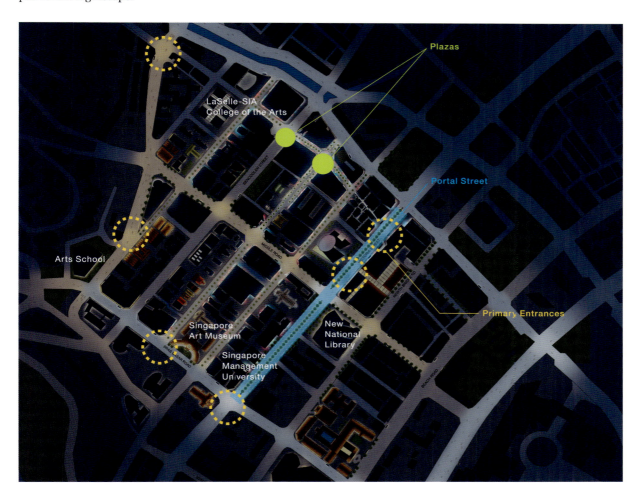

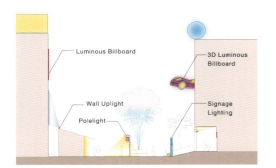

The Façades of the booths lining the street are a luminous canvas and even the illuminated signage and huge 3D designs make a contribution. Victoria Street needs a symbolic presence, so light columns line the median and give the street a dynamic look.

Original Photo

Proposed Rendering (CG)

Singapore River

The pedestrians who come to enjoy the roughly 3-kilometer riverfront district need a pleasant walking area. The strikingly picturesque nightscape and its reflection in the sweeping water is one of Singapore's most valuable scenic resources. Located next to CBD, the district includes Boat Quay, filled afterhours with workers who come to relax at its restaurants and bars along the water, Clarke Quay, popular with families and groups who come to enjoy the diverse entertainment on offer there, and Robertson Quay, a stretch of hotels and condominiums dotted with bars and other establishments. We worked out lighting method proposals that complement the character of each of these three areas.

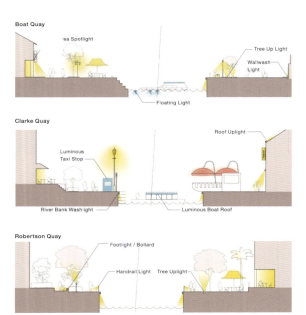

At night the waterfront is full of people dining and taking walks. Lights installed in walls and trees, railing, and other elements ensure a glare-free environment. Lighting installed in the river taxis going up and down the river serves to entertain viewers with the sight of the boats moving on the surface of the darkened water. In addition, jellyfish motif lighting fixtures are installed beneath the water's surface.

Original Photo

Proposed Rendering (CG)

CBD and Downtown at Marina Bay (DTMB)

The first thing that impresses a visitor entering Singapore City Centre from Changi International Airport is the cluster of skyscrapers. A number of skyscraper projects are in progress in the newly developed DTMB district. Assigned to build lighting for the skyline they will form, we want to create a novel nightscape around a "bundles of light" concept. An energetic nightscape symbolizes Singapore's identity as a business hub. In addition, the street lighting that is the foundation of urban lighting needs to meet the functional requirements of traffic safety and be elegant at the same time. Moreover, important traffic junctures forming light focal points will ease the tension resulting from a field of vision constricted by high-rise buildings.

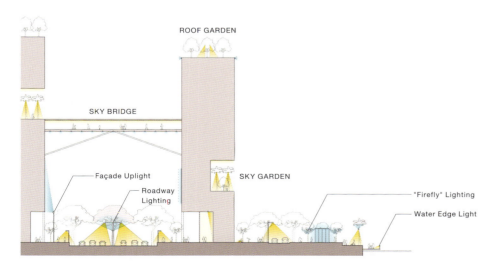

The still growing cluster of skyscrapers is a symbolic area that needs a distinctive nightscape. We recommended the color temperature, color rendering, illuminance, lighting method, light pollution measures, fixture attachment, operation, and other lighting design details appropriate for the use and position of each skyscraper.

Midland Square

2006 Aichi, Japan
Design | Nikken Sekkei
Client | Toyota Motor, The Mainichi Newspapers,
Towa Real Estate

Keyword : Transformation of Light
Designer's comment : Numerous and meticulous adjustments made together with the architects.
Custom-made fixtures : Transformable Balloon Light, LED Panel
Main light source : HID, FL, LED
Brightness contrast level : 3
Design Period : 4 years

Midland Square is a multi-purpose facility of offices and shops in front of Nagoya Station. The design concept makes extensive use of the most advanced LED lighting available at the time to create an interior space that is both ethereal and kinetic. "Light Balloons" spontaneously descending and ascending in the immense atrium give performances of light and sound that greatly heighten the shopping experience and enhance the facility's unique atmosphere.

The mist and light motif of the spacious Sky Promenade on the top floor transforms it into a sea of clouds where visitors can enjoy an indoor walk and appreciate the surrounding nightscape.

The design for the central atrium of the low-rise commercial building features 27 slowly ascending and descending "Light Balloons." These molded contrivances contain LED lighting fixtures in the three primary colors and digital controls that subtly change their hue. The elevators and bridges that span the atrium for getting around the facility have illuminated walls and floors that serve as large radiant surfaces that both enhance visibility and provide the necessary functional illumination. Soft, diffused light becomes a stage enveloping facility visitors.

The spacious 220-meter wide Sky Promenade on top of the high-rise office tower is designed as a walk in the sky that follows a north-south-east-west circuit.

We installed LED dots behind the punch metal wall at the building core. This LED source follows the eye movement of the visitors walking through the course and flashes spontaneously. The light reflects off the glass that encloses the Sky Promenade and becomes part of the beautiful Nagoya nightscape, creating a fantastic light experience like no other place.

OMOTESANDO akarium

2006 Tokyo, Japan
Client | Meiji Jingu, Harajuku Omotesando
Keyaki Organization

Keyword : Japanese Light realized by High-tech
Designer's comment : Very expensive installation!
Custom-made fixtures : Giant LED Lantern
Main light source : LED
Brightness contrast level : 4
Design Period : 0.5 years

akarium was a one month illumination event held during the Christmas and New Year season. The street was lit up for the first time in 8 years around the theme of "a people- and eco-friendly town" that protected the neighborhood's *keyaki* (Japanese elm) from damage. Street lamps symbolizing the traditional Japanese paper lanterns that are a unique part of Japanese culture lined the street leading to the famous Meiji Shrine. The large street lamps were existing street lights covered in a two-layer semi-transparent fabric with computer controlled LED fixtures that delivered both high-tech illumination and bathed the whole street in a gentle and colorful glow like flickering candlelight.

Nicolas G. Hayek Center

2007 Tokyo, Japan
Design | Shigeru Ban Architects, Studio on Site
Client | The Swatch Group (Japan)

Keyword : Function and Ambiance
Designer's comment : We hope the plants are happy, too.
Custom-made fixtures : Spot Light System for Potted Plants
Main light source : HID
Brightness contrast level : 3
Design Period : 2 years

The Nicolas G. Hayek Center serves as a showroom and corporate office for the Swatch Group. The building faces Ginza Chuo-Dori Street and has a broad, open plan that creates a sense of continuity between the street and the interior space. The piloti-supported ground floor is dotted with elevated showcases for each brand and has a wall completely covered with plants. The primary design theme was a light environment that makes use of the green wall but without interfering with the room's function as a captivating showroom. The lighting casts an illumination of 2,000 lux on the green wall during the day and from the evening onwards gradually changes light intensity and color. The brightly lit green wall and minimal light elsewhere combine to create a space rich in contrast.

Projects that advocate green walls are common, but we had yet to see one successfully make it to the actual competition phase with the original vision of verdant greenery intact. After all, plants intended to grow from the nourishment of sunlight must be nurtured with artificial light. We conducted our research and understood the requirements, but this project was not a plant growing facility. The building is broadly open to Ginza Chuo Dori Street and the green wall contributes substantial greenery to the urban surroundings. The lighting fixtures and equipment needed to be aesthetically pleasing and, of course, could not be allowed to detract from the architectural design and purpose of the showroom. Based on several months of theoretical analysis and technical research we decided on morning to evening illumination of 2,000 lux using 4,200K metal halide lamps.

General ambient lighting is provided by spotlights embedded in the inter-floor layer opposite the green wall. Meticulous planning and on-site adjustments led us to employ wall wash downlights for the upper part, adjustable downlights for the lower part of the green wall, and indirect supplemental lighting for areas in shadow. The contrast between the vividly illuminated greenwall and the composed showroom creates a pleasant environment.

National Centre for the Performing Arts

2007 Beijing, China
Design | Paul Andreu Architect
Client | Owners Committee of National Centre for the Performing Arts

Keyword : Aesthetically Pleasing during Daytime
Designer's comment : Unfortunately, we were not given site supervision.
Main light source : HID, IL
Brightness contrast level : 3
Design Period : 3 years

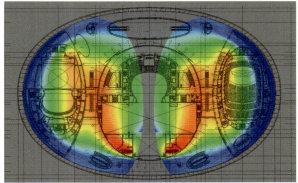

This national theatre covered by an immense dome holds a 2,416 seat opera house, 2,017 seat concert hall, 1,040 seat concert hall, and other performance venues. We were commissioned to design the lighting for the dome's public area after construction had already begun and was entering its final stage. The light environment inside the dome makes use of natural light and therefore demanded the most meticulous attention to detail. We analyzed how perspective shifted inside the space and worked out the lighting design with simulations that ranked in order of priority 12 types of background luminance.

Regrettably, we were not commissioned to supervise the work and the lighting does not achieve the environment our design intended. This is a common issue for state projects in China, and it reminded us just how important it is to entrust the entire project process — from design through construction and supervision — to the same organization.

Banyan Tree Phuket, Doublepool Villas

2007 Phuket, Thailand
Design | Laguna Resorts & Hotels Public
Client | Laguna Banyan Tree

Keyword : Reflected Landscape
Designer's comment : Discovering the refractive properties of water
Custom-made fixtures : Underwater Sea-firefly Lighting
Main light source : IL
Brightness contrast level : 5
Design Period : 3 years

This luxury resort in Phuket, Thailand features a lagoon surrounded by Thai-style villas. The illuminated edges of the villa's tall roofs reflect off the placid surface of the lagoon to create a tranquil nightscape on the opposite shore. Every villa private pool has indicators installed on the bottom that flicker like fireflies, endowing them with an enchanting glow that complements the surface of the lagoon.

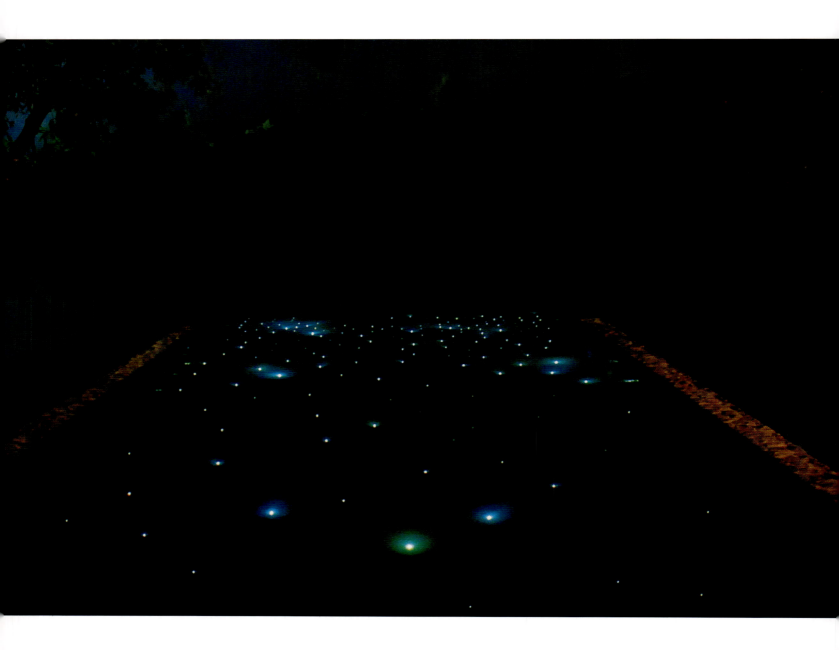

The pools of each villa and the enchanting light floating within them stand out against the clear, blue sky. Our design focused on how to present the pools that make this resort so distinctive.

The lighting for the private pools adjoining the lagoon can be adjusted with a scene and dimmer switch inside the room. When a pool's bright lighting is extinguished the points of light from 150 or so light particles randomly arranged on the bottom of the pool appear. The particles of light originate from optical fibers embedded in the seams of the tile on the bottom of the pool. The fibers have a gradated arrangement that makes their number appear greater the farther one is from the villa. In addition, their placement was painstakingly worked out to make sure that the light particles do not appear to be aligned with the tile seams. Finally, while a single optical fiber is 0.75mm in diameter, we randomized the size of every light particle by varying the number of optical fibers at each point.

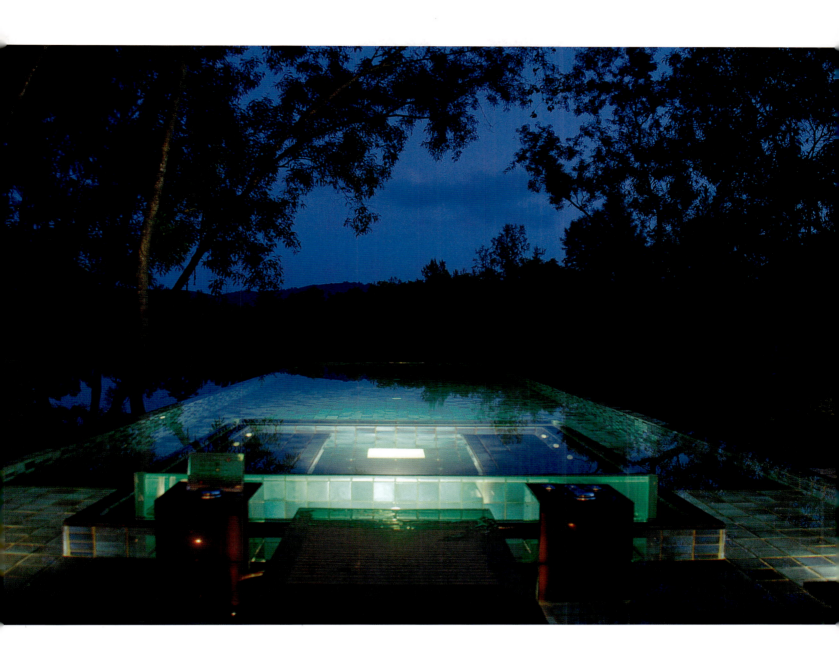

Akita International University, Nakajima Library

2008 Akita, Japan
Design | Mitsuru Man Senda and
Environment Design Institute
Client | Akita International University

Keyword : Ambient Lighting
Designer's comment : A comfortable darkness makes it easy to concentrate.
Custom-made fixtures : Bookshelf Lighting
Main light source : FL
Brightness contrast level : 3
Design Period : 1 year

This library open 24 hours a day was built on the university campus. The library's semi-circular Great Hall has an Akita cedar ceiling and ambient light radiating from the bookstacks along its walls that endow the space with a warm ambience. The ceiling cast in uplighting from the maintenance deck using a simple method highlights the room's distinctive features. Fluorescent lighting fixtures installed on top of the book stacks illuminate the spines of the books on the shelves below and bring into relief the vast number of books that are the room's main attraction. In addition, reading desks have task lighting for every chair with settings that library visitors can use to adjust the light to their liking. Given that the library is open around-the-clock, and also from the viewpoint of location and operation, we strove for a convenient, economical, and practical design that is easy-to-operate and only uses the most common fixtures.

Hilton Niseko Village

2008 Hokkaido, Japan
Design | Hashimoto Yukio Design Studio, Tanseisha
Client | Citigroup Principal Investments (Japan)

Keyword : Lightscape with a Fireplace
Designer's comment : The difficulties of renovation work
Custom-made fixtures : Decorative Lighting
Main light source : IL, FL, LED
Brightness contrast level : 4
Design Period : 1 year

Niseko is famous as a resort destination blessed with some of the finest powder snow in the world. This 499 room hotel named after the region reopened after a major renovation. Our lighting concept for this hotel surrounded by the great outdoors uses warm-textured materials and balanced light and shadow to express the rhythm of nature.

In the lobby, we made use of existing columns and fire from the suspended fireplace in the center of the room to create a space symbolizing the spirit of the resort hotel. The rhythmical arrangement of light and shadow steers attention to the center and creates a circular layer of light.

International Commerce Centre

2008 Hong Kong
Design | Kohn Pedersen Fox Associates, Wong & Ouyang
Client | Sun Hung Kai Properties

Keyword : Dynamic Lighting Environment
Designer's comment : Does everyone sense the dragon?
Custom-made fixtures : Buried Adjustable Up Light System
Main light source : HID, LED
Brightness contrast level : 3
Design Period : 2 years

This 484-meter tower built in West Kowloon is presently Hong Kong's tallest skyscraper. Along with IFC Tower across the bay on Hong Kong Island, the building is a defining landmark amid the nightscape of Victoria Harbor.

The dragon-motif tower façade has LED linear lighting installed in gaps between the exterior's overlapping curtain walls programmed to create a variety of scenes. This dynamic and elegant lighting design endows the Hong Kong nightscape with a new and more refined appearance. In addition, the lighting design of the office lobby highlights its dynamic spatial composition by merging the function and beauty that characterize the space.

Swarovski Ginza

2008 Tokyo, Japan
Design | Tokujin Yoshioka Design
Client | Swarovski Japan

Keyword : Space of Sparkling Light
Designer's comment : Repeated lighting experiments with a very special purpose
Custom-made fixtures : Luminous Crystal Steps
Main light source : HID, LED
Brightness contrast level : 3
Design Period : 1.5 years

When it opened on Ginza Chuo Dori Street, Swarovski Ginza became Japan's first Swarovski Crystal flagship store. Based on the "Crystal Forest" design concept created by designer Tokujin Yoshioka, Swarovski Ginza is the first store of a phased worldwide expansion to 1,300 stores planned by the Swarovski Crystal brand of crystal jewelry and other crystal goods. Our lighting design is themed around the sparkle of crystal, the delicate light and shadow and pure transparency of the shop's newly designed wall materials, and the rhythm of reflected light inside this 256㎡, two-level store.

Stairway steps are filled with cut and polished crystals. The appearance of the crystals changes depending on their distance from the light source.
To determine the distance that achieves the best effect, we did several experiments using actual crystals and the five-layered combinations of materials; non-slip reinforced glass, crystal, prism acrylic panel, LED and specular reflector panel, were conducted to decide on the best distance to achieve maximum effect from the crystals (P280). There are no fixtures mounted to illuminate the stainless steel façade. Instead, surrounding street lights reflecting off the material create a façade appearance unique for the Ginza district (P281).

Alexandra Arch, Singapore

2008 Singapore
Design | Look Architects
Client | Urban Redevelopment Authority

Keyword : Shifting Landmark
Designer's comment : Walking on the bridge is a simple and elegant experience.
Main light source : LED, FL

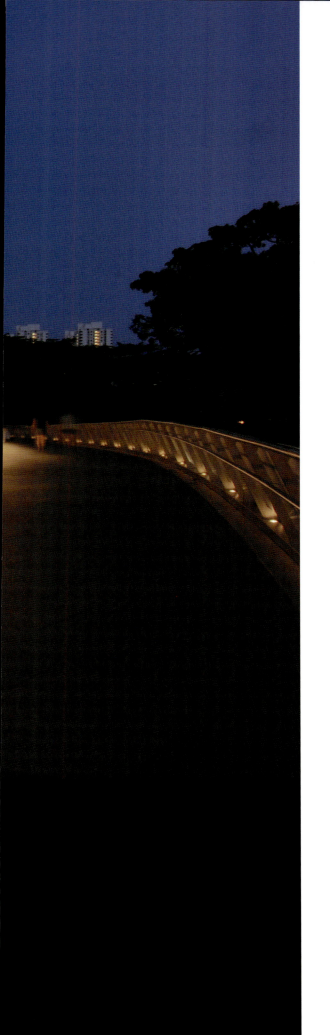

This iconic pedestrian bridge is a vital connector that overlooks a busy expressway and an adjacent forest. It connects to a tree top canopy walk in one of the greenest parts of Singapore. Its folded leaf shape is echoed by the lighting scheme, by using indirect washes of light and color.

  As day turns to night, the lighting operation is a series of carefully calibrated and smooth color transitions that gradually blend colored light over 20 minute intervals. The colors are very selective, that move from a warm white to sunset orange and therafter to a deep midnight blue.

W Hong Kong

2008 Hong Kong
Design | Wong & Ouyang, GLAMOROUS
Client | Sun Hung Kai Properties

Keyword : Fireflies Wafting in the Woods
Designer's comment : Piles of sample branches were all over my desk.
Custom-made fixtures : Branch Shaped LED fixture
Main light source : IL, LED
Brightness contrast level : 4
Design Period : 3.5 years

W Hotel built in the tower of Hong Kong's Kowloon Station complex has the stylish design characteristic of the hotel brand. We aimed for sophisticated, high-quality light that would be a clear departure from the vaunted gaudiness of Hong Kong's million dollar nightscape.

The building's podium includes an atrium that appears amid the urban landscape as a colossal glass box. To complement the interior design concept of "forest," our lighting design motif for the space was "fireflies alight among the trees." Novel light filters produced by LED lights appear as little sparkles of light from inside the room while from outside they form an immense façade of glittering light that dazzles passersby.

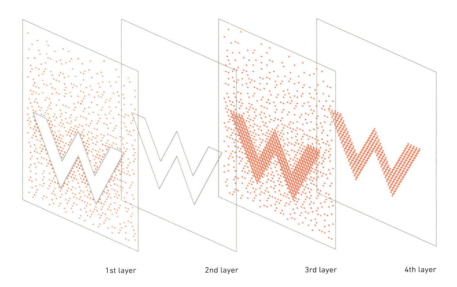

1st layer　　2nd layer　　3rd layer　　4th layer

Inside the 38-meter high glass box hangs a two-layer screen within which the small branches of the "forest" are assembled. Acrylic chips attached to the surface of the branches emit LED light programmed to make the "W" logo periodically emerge from the sparkle of the gigantic box.

By gradually reducing the density of the LED array inside one layer, the "W" naturally emerges from amid the thousands of light particles. In addition, a different LED pattern for each of the overlapping screens gives the overall display a sense of depth. Likewise, the façade is given further depth by up-lighting the whole branch screen assembly and subtly changing the light.

We evaluated LED intensity and the cut of acrylic chips by testing countless samples to ensure that the sparkle has presence not only nearby but as far as Hong Kong Island two kilometers away.

ION Orchard

2009 Singapore
Design | Benoy Architects,
RSP Architects Planners & Engineers
Client | Orchard Turn Developments
Co-Lighting Consultant | Parsons Brinckerhoff

Keyword : Dynamic Organically Shaped Façade
Designer's comment : At any rate, we were hard at work.
Custom-made fixtures : LED Media Louvre
Main light source : LED, HID
Brightness contrast level : 1
Design Period : 2.5 years

This is a multipurpose commercial facility built at a prime location on Singapore's famous Orchard shopping street. The building's podium and most distinctive feature is a striking organically curved glass façade that at night projects the media art of local artists. To both preserve the view inside and outside the facility and beautifully present the media art, we painstakingly worked out the positioning and details for the glass façade louvers and the LEDs installed in them. In sharp contrast to the imposing presence of the large canvas, we proposed a design that conveys slow and gentle natural phenomena and crafts an artistic and refined look for the Orchard district.

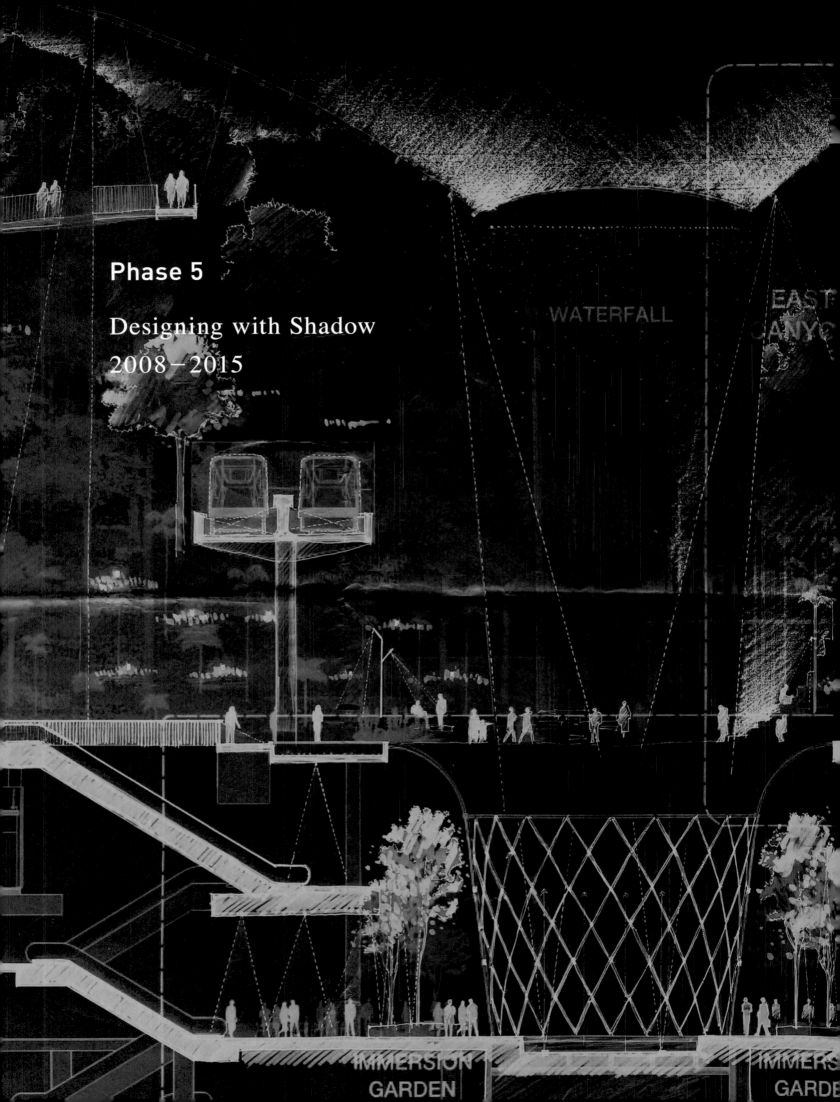

Phase 5

Designing with Shadow
2008–2015

Designing with Shadow:

New Lighting Values Taught in 2011

Kaoru Mende

In 2010, we released a book entitled *Designing with Shadow*. It was inspired by the idea that light design is actually the careful and meticulous arrangement of shadow. Light in enormous volume is a social phenomenon in Japan, so we wanted to assert that lighting design is not concerned with the amount of light but with the quality of light.

In fact, we had wanted to use that title for the first book that we released in English in 2000, ten years before *Designing with Shadow*. The Australian publisher handling the book's publication flatly refused our proposed title, however, insisting a book entitled *Designing with Shadow* would not sell. I was not fully satisfied with their reasoning, and when I look back on that time I also recall a similar expression that was likewise rejected by an overseas audience. The phrase was "the beauty of darkness," which was the title for a lecture I had been invited to do in Frankfurt, Germany. The Germans packed into the hall insisted that there is no beauty in darkness, that in darkness lurk repulsive things, the evil spirits that dwell in mountains and rivers. Like the aforementioned "designing with shadow," for them, it seemed, "the beauty of darkness," was merely the wordplay of a stoic Japanese brandishing high-minded *wabisabi* idealism. Their hearts were set on exciting light design and, alas, the titles "the beauty of darkness" and "designing with shadow" both received a poor reception.

Ten years passed, bringing us to the year before the release of the long-awaited *Designing with Shadow*. Then, on March 11, 2011, the Tohoku Earthquake and Tsunami struck, causing extensive natural destruction as well as the worst kind of manmade calamity with the nuclear accident at Fukushima. 20,000 people lost their lives, people were forced from their communities and homes, ruined infrastructure led to blackouts. People had the frightening experience of cities shrouded in darkness after losing electricity.

Of course, cities gradually recovered electric power, but urgent calls to curtail power consumption led by public facilities brought about light environments conserving energy at levels never before experienced. Confronted by this terrible tragedy, we Japanese contemplated for the first time the excessive brightness that until then had been a part of our daily lives. Now, what is meant by "excessive brightness"? 3.11 made Japanese take note on a national level of the extravagant energy waste and unnecessary light that characterized twentieth-century light environments. Nonetheless, support once again grew for restarting nuclear power plants and there was also the extraordinary development of more illumination than ever before justified by the low power consumption made possible with the arrival of LED. Coming from a perspective that condemns this kind of grotesque binge lighting, we are convinced that the phased elimination of nuclear power and the development of natural energy are urgent priorities. We need to embrace low levels of light and aim for a society with modest and stable growth on a global level.

Our lighting design work from 2010 to the present includes a number of projects coming to completion embodying the "designing with shadow" philosophy. The lighting for Commemorating the 50th Anniversary of the Reconstruction of MEIJI JINGU [akarium] conveyed the significance of the deep shadow that dwells within traditional Japanese architecture by making the all-important darkness enshrouding Meiji Jingu the main attraction. The lighting design for Sengukan Museum built at the Ise Shrine outer shrine stresses sequential shadow. In a different context, the resort hotel projects in Bali, Phuket, and India aim for a harmonious balance between natural light and artificial light guided by ecological lighting design themes. Preservation and Restoration of the Tokyo Station Marunouchi Building completed in 2012 features state-of-the-art LED and control technology that accentuates the building's delicate balance of shadow. At Gardens by the Bay, Bay South, one of the largest scale ambitious public garden recently completed in Singapore, choreographed organic light creates enchanting encounters with shadow.

There is no question that "designing with shadow" will play a vital role in achieving the sustainability and comfort sought by urban life in the generation ahead.

Shadow's Light

Erwin J. S. Viray

One of the immediate thoughts when we hear the word shadow will be *In Praise of Shadows* by Junichiro Tanizaki. Tanizaki writes, "...the beauty of a Japanese room depends on a variation of shadows, heavy shadow against light shadow — it has nothing else." LPA and Kaoru Mende astutely capture the idea of creating light with shadows. On second thought how could such seeming contradiction be possible?

In trying to understand the concept in the operation of LPA and Kaoru Mende in interrogating the intrinsic nature of science and art of light, luminance, and illumination, I dwell on the works of LPA I have experienced like Tokyo Station Marunouchi Building. On closer look, it is actually very subtle gradations of light and shadow playing in the space. It seems that shadow's light is not necessarily the contrast between darkness and light. I realized that shadow's light played by LPA lay bare the perpetual rhythm of light in space that we often are not conscious of. There is a delicate shadow balance. In LPA's shadow's light, we observe how light is not just one streak but many gradations, we observe how the walls and materials reflect and absorb light, we can see a vibration in space that often is invisible. These words, and the works of LPA further awaken association with sfumato by Leonardo da Vinci, where chiaroscuro was used to bring to light presence by using techniques "to tone down," "to evaporate like smoke," to produce fine shading that evoke soft imperceptible transitions between color and tones, and create a space of beauty and atmospheric effects, which is the pursuit of light in shadow's light. I recall an experience in Minami Dera in Naoshima. In a Dark Black Building crafted by Tadao Ando, James Turrell makes us aware of the light that constantly exists, yet the sudden darkness withholds from us, and thus, it takes time for our eyes to slowly adjust and eventually see the light.

In this phase, LPA and Kaoru Mende help us see in the darkness — light, slowly opens our eyes to the light in the shadow, a revelation, to make us conscious of Shadow's light!

Commemorating the 50th Anniversary of the Reconstruction of MEIJI JINGU [akarium]

2008 Tokyo, Japan
Client | Commemorating the 50th Anniversary of the Restoration of Meiji Jingu Committee

Keyword : Illuminating Shadows
Designer's comment : We were stunned by the darkness and scale of the shrine.
Custom-made fixtures : Aurora Lantern
Main light source : LED, IL, FL
Brightness contrast level : 5
Design Period : 1.5 years

To celebrate the 50th anniversary of the reconstruction of the main sanctuary of Meiji Jingu and on the occasion of the shrine visits to take place at night, an imaginative light design was put in place along the path approaching the shrine and for the shrine itself. At night, the shrine's vast 700,000㎡ grounds retain a darkness that makes one forget that it is located right in the center of Tokyo. We felt that this darkness is a vital part of the shrine experience, so we put in place a design that minimally yet effectively illuminates shrine approaches and gates and the main sanctuary around the concept of light in harmony with forest darkness. Visitors walking on the approach were beckoned deeper and deeper into the grounds until they were welcomed by the main sanctuary appearing out of the darkness. The large crowds of people making their first nighttime visit were enchanted by a world of light and darkness that conveyed the history of Meiji Shrine.

The lighting design used the space's unique features to highlight the nighttime route toward Meiji Jingu within the forest grounds. A great deal of analysis went into a design that successfully captured "Japanese beauty" against a moonlit background with minimal yet effective illumination.

The neatly ordered rafters and bracket complexes at the South Deity Gate (*minami-shinmon*) and the Outer Shrine (*gaihaiden*) that lead to the Inner Shrine (*honden*) are softly illuminated, creating balanced light and shadow that accentuates the beautiful forms of traditional Japanese architecture. The same technique was adopted for the Inner Shrine, where spotlights illuminated the undulating curves of the shrine's *karahafu*-style roof.

At the Great Gate (*ootorii*), illuminating the gate as well as the trees lining the approach sharpened the contrast between the gate's powerful presence and the lush, green vegetation around it and also added perspective to the approach as it nears the Inner Shrine.

The South Shrine Approach (*minami-sando*) was covered with gravel that illuminated the path with a blanket of blue light. At the Sacred Bridge (*shinkyo*), the silhouettes of passersby create a beautiful scene against a background given added depth by individually illuminated trees.

Alila Villas Uluwatu

2009 Bali, Indonesia
Design | WOHA, CICADA
Client | Bukit Uluwatu Villa

Keyword : Ecological Resort
Designer's comment : Very thankful for the sunset and darkness of Bali
Custom-made fixtures : Villa Lantern Light
Main light source : IL, LED, FL
Brightness contrast level : 4
Design Period : 4 years

This villa-style resort located in Uluwatu on the southern tip of Bali sits atop a cliff overlooking the sea, giving guests a direct view of the sea. The design achieves a fitting and pleasant resort light environment with minimal illumination guided by a "minimum light" concept that makes the most of surroundings much darker than in an urban setting. Rather than rely solely on the natural warmth of incandescent lamps, we also used other ecological light sources such as fluorescent lamps and LED and made ample use of techniques such as ambient lighting based on a thorough analysis of their compatibility with the architecture's exterior color and materials. Our goal was to create a new kind of resort light environment that merges candlelight and LED.

Resort lighting design has tended to rely solely on the natural warmth of low-cost incandescent lamps, but for this project we made ample use of fluorescent lamps and incandescent color LED to achieve an ecologically sound facility.

For the entrance reflection pool, we went so far as to do away with underwater lighting in favor of arcade light around the pool reflected off the water's surface. The arcade's extremities are up-lit with halogen lamps, while transom and corridor lighting employ LED ambient lighting. LED was not yet a reliable light source at the time of the design and quality varied widely, however, so we worked out the most suitable light by comparing the color temperature of numerous samples. Overall area brightness is kept in balance with a programmed dimming system that gently changes intensity in concert with the change in external light. The cabana protruding over the steep cliff has minimal lighting to enhance the view of the spectacular sunrises and sunsets so that it stands out as a place where the light environment adds immediacy to the surrounding nature.

303

Aman New Delhi

2009 New Delhi, India
Design | Kerry Hill Architects
Client | Lodhi Property

Keyword : Light and Shadow of India
Designer's comment : Tough site work, but the *jaali* silhouettes were a delight.
Custom-made fixtures : Ceiling Up Light in Guest Rooms
Main light source : IL
Brightness contrast level : 5
Design Period : 5 years

Aman New Delhi was the first city hotel of the Aman Resorts luxury hotel chain. The interior of this ten-floor, one-underground floor tower-style building is memorable for a design that adapts the traditional sunshade screens called *jaali* to a contemporary setting.

During the day the intense sunlight casts beautiful *jaali* shadow upon the walls while at night the warm glow of incandescent light radiating from the rooms highlight their silhouettes so that they completely reverse form as the day passes. Covering open sections with *jaali* from the bottom floor to the top creates modern architecture around a traditional motif.

Crafted with a variety of materials and techniques, *jaali* screens are a traditional element of Indian architecture. The *jaali* screens at Aman New Delhi are arranged in both traditional and contemporary settings, and we therefore deployed lighting appropriate for each.

Most striking of all is the rigid, glass-fiber reinforced concrete *jaali* of the building's façade. The guest rooms and residential units are arranged in an L-shape around the beautiful courtyard's unpretentious greenery and have an open side facing the courtyard covered by *jaali* screens that stands as a powerful symbol of the hotel.

The spa, library, bar and lounge, and other amenities located below ground level are covered by an atrium ceiling. The lighting plan takes advantage of the natural light coming in through the atrium and is designed to gradually transform the scene in harmony with the changing light from outside.

In addition, the edge of the outdoor pool in the spa area is softly illuminated with underwater lighting while the corridor has rhythmically arranged wall lighting and column shadow that come together to create a light environment befitting an urban resort.

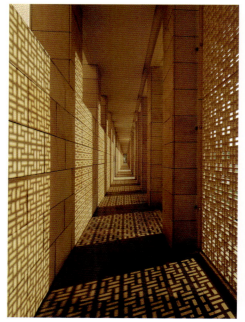

Tang Plaza
Façade Enhancement

2009 Singapore
Client | Tang Holdings

Keyword : Timeless Beauty
Designer's comment : Focusing for over 100 spotlights!
Custom-made fixtures : Super Narrow Spotlight
Main light source : HID, LED
Brightness contrast level : 3
Design Period : 2 years

This was a lighting enhancement project for Orchard Road's most iconic building located at a prime junction. The design casts in elegant light the stately and composed architecture, the red eave undersides, and elaborate Chinese-style motif of this distinguished landmark standing at a choice location. The use of super-narrow angle high-efficiency spotlights and LED fixtures reduces energy consumption by 70%.

A series of on-site lighting tests and a meticulous decision-making process that included the client's participation was an especially significant aspect of this enhancement project. The fact that a design themed around beautiful shadow and light and a lighting scheme free of all excess can contribute to significantly reduced power consumption serves as a valuable lesson for future landmark lighting design.

OSAKA "City of Light"

2010 Osaka, Japan
Client | OSAKA "City of Light" Planning & Promotion Committee

Keyword : A Necklace of Light
Designer's comment : Urban lighting always requires patience.
Custom-made fixtures : Turner Light, Underwater LED Luminary for Seawater
Main light source : LED
Brightness contrast level : 3
Design Period : 10 years

"OSAKA City of Light" Planning & Promotion Committee was launched in 2004 to reinvigorate the Osaka cityscape with light and make it recognized around the world as a city of light. In the ensuing 12 years, we have participated in and supported the project as a committee member and general supervisor.

In 2010, the deliberations and planning led by the Committee were compiled in the Plan for "OSAKA City of Light in 2020." Guided by the theme of "using light to bring out the qualities that make Osaka what it is", the Masterplan's lighting design principles fully exploit the city's untapped appeal. The Masterplan also includes a variety of proposals that make use of Osaka's topography, history, culture, and more, such as "Axis on the Network of Lights," "Calendar of Illumination Event," and "A Hundred Scenes of Osaka Night."

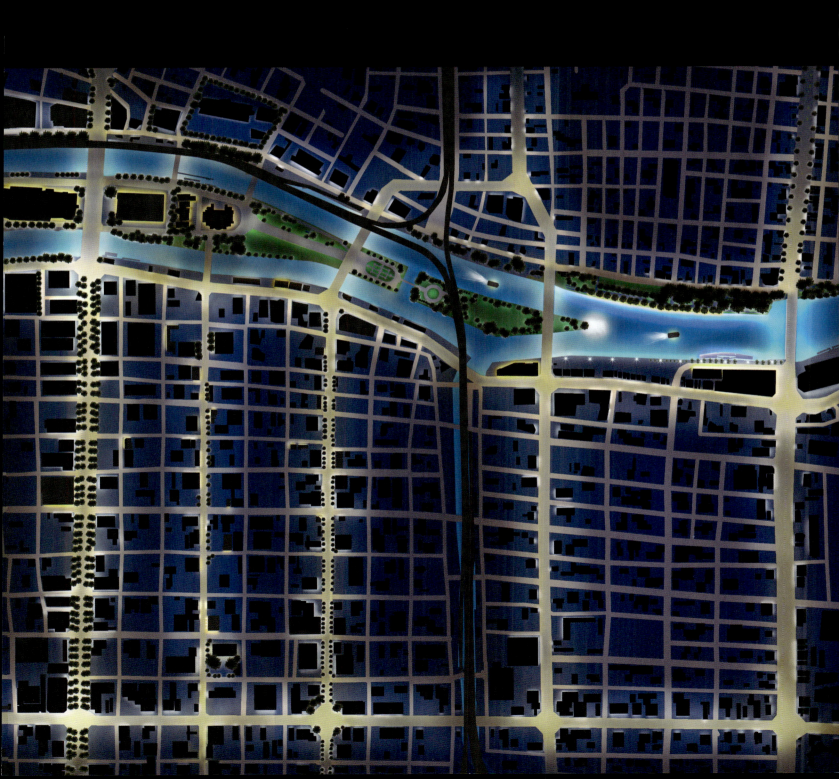

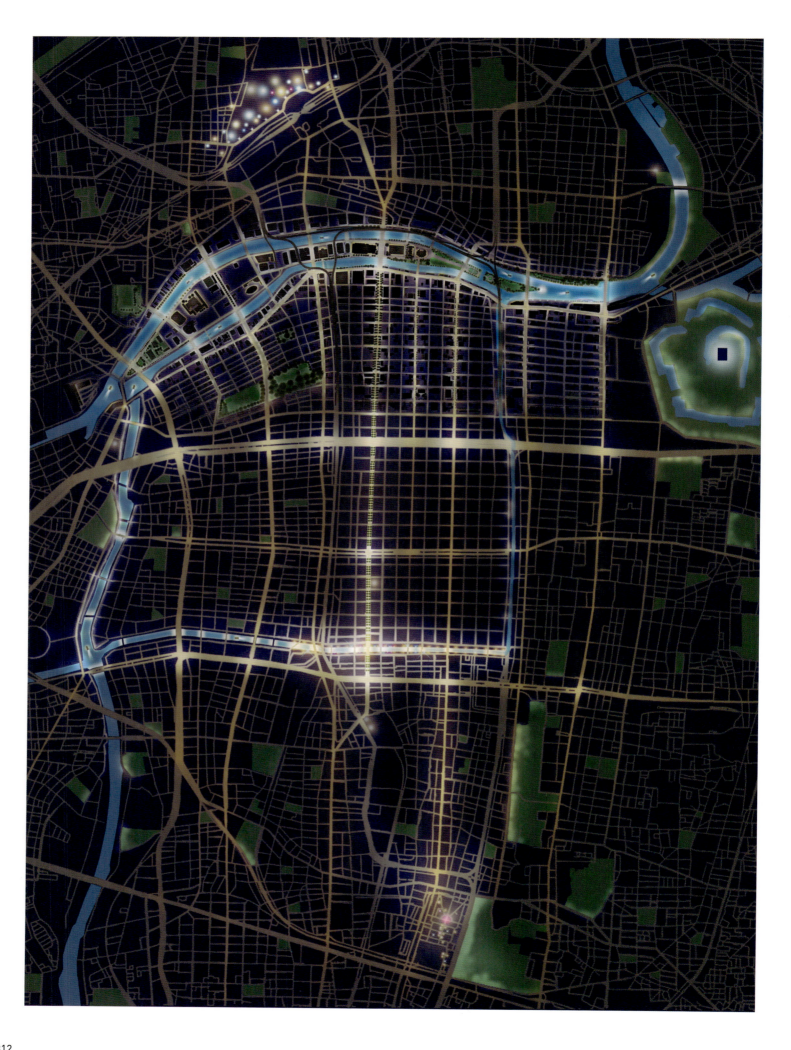

The plan for "OSAKA City of Light in 2020" consists of a three parts. The first part is titled "Illumination Grand Design" and establishes the direction of the light environment as based on such concepts as "Axis on the Network of Lights," "Calendar of Illumination Event," and "A Hundred Scenes of Osaka Night."

The second part summarizes the technical means by which the Master plan is to be achieved. Finally, the third part details the specific action plan for the project as it moves forward. This section is divided into three year phases through the year 2020 for achieving the "City of Light Osaka" vision.

The second part is especially important because it establishes three viewpoints around which urban lighting will realize its role in the city of Osaka: comfortable urban lighting, urban lighting that expresses city identity, and environmentally-friendly urban lighting, which the Master plan refers to as "Comfort," "Identity," and "Ecology" for short. The Master plan greatest accomplishments have been as a forum for different groups representing government, citizens, and business to engage in a dialogue on how to achieve the "City of Light Osaka" concept and as the framework under which its participants directly experience and analyze light in the cityscape.

A revision of the second part issued later on in order to expedite the process of appraising the cityscape titled "Osaka 'City of Light' Technical Guidelines" includes a comparison of the latest LED light sources with existing light sources, important points concerning lighting techniques, and technical guidelines for adding and subtracting light in a manner that brings out the unique characteristics of each area in the heart of Osaka. These guidelines are the basis for creating a dramatically beautiful nightscape for Osaka by 2020.

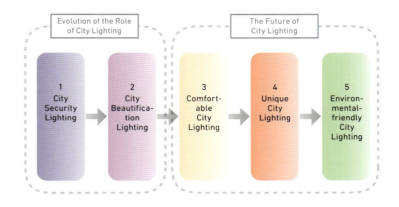

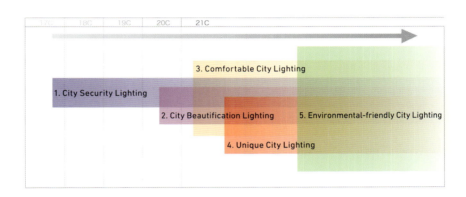

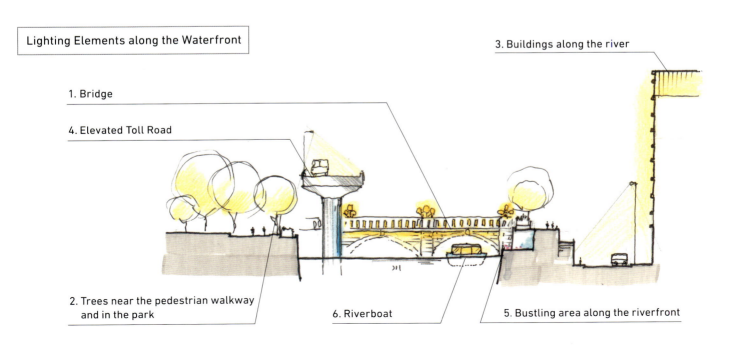

Lighting Elements along the Waterfront

1. Bridge
2. Trees near the pedestrian walkway and in the park
3. Buildings along the river
4. Elevated Toll Road
5. Bustling area along the riverfront
6. Riverboat

Original street view of mockup area

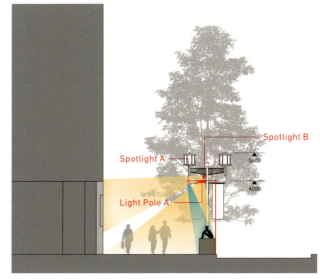

Lighting Methods added to mockup area

■ Light Pole A (sidewalk lighting) : compact metal halide CDM-T35W (3,000K)
→ Downward facing fixtures to increase lux levels and use of lamps with good quality color rendering and low color temperature (warm tones) leads to improved lighting effects.
■ Spotlight A (sculpture lighting) : compact metal halide CDM-T70W (4,200K), 10° light distribution
→ Originally, the lighting is insufficient resulting in under-represented sculptures. Increase volume of light and use a white color tone, different from the sidewalk lighting, for dramatic effects.
■ Spotlight B (wall planar lighting) : compact metal halide lighting CDM-T70W (3,000K), 30° light distribution
→ Highlight the building wall with a wash to create a sense of brightness. Color filters can also be used for special lighting features.

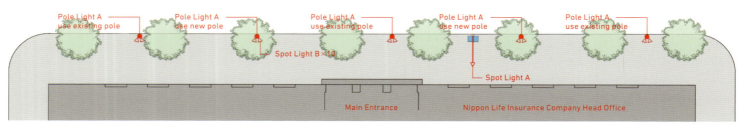

Fixture layout of mockup

Images during mockup

A Social Experiment

Central Osaka includes Midosuji Boulevard (National Route 25), a 4 kilometer, 44 meter wide main street running north to south lined by 949 gingko trees. Despite being a highway of a scale found nowhere else in the world, a number of problems — insufficient lighting, streetlight glare, high-pressure sodium lamps with low color rendering, and so on — made it evident that it desperately needed better lighting. In order to revitalize the light along Midosuji Boulevard, the Ministry of Land, Infrastructure, Transportation and Tourism (MLIT) decided to conduct a two-month "light pilot study" aimed at the public. The study, which was made available to the public via the Internet, included a questionnaire survey on the effect of light in urban environments.

For the study, we did a detailed survey of Midosuji Boulevard and prepared content that was easy for the public to understand and learn. The study included how light sources with different color rendering properties act on human skin and vegetation, how light cast off buildings walls effects street brightness, the effect of stage lighting cast on sculptures placed on sidewalks, and so on.
Through these diverse studies, the public learned about lighting methods and how lighting works and also became aware of how important it is that Osaka's own citizens create the city's light environment.

Sample Questionnaire

Results of Questionnaire

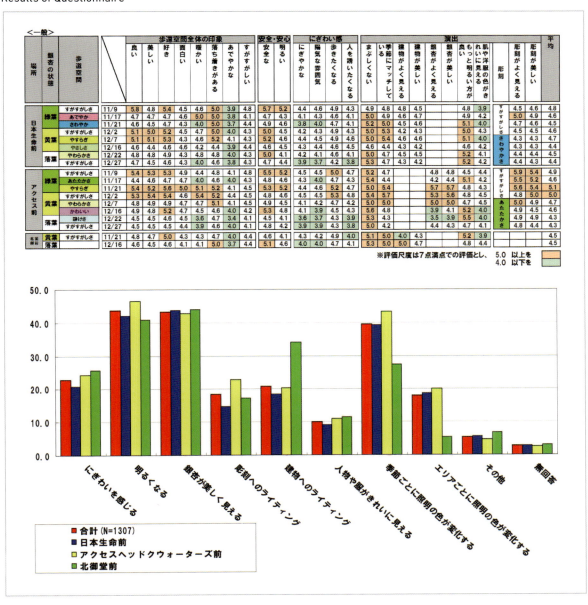

Working out the lighting for Yodoyabashi and Oebashi bridges

Yodoyabashi and Oebashi bridges stand at the north end of Midosuji Boulevard, Osaka's main street. While the two bridges are of different lengths, they share the same shape and stately elegant stone design. Installing new lighting fixtures along the side of either of these bridges was unthinkable, so we illuminated them with lighting originating from the service roads.

Projector spotlights casting pinpoint light free of all excess highlight only the graceful form of the bridges, while the reflection of the scene on the river's surface deepens the sense of passing time for the people walking through the area. A plan to light up the bridge with LED is moving forward and a street lighting upgrade to achieve glare-free lighting is also planned.

Supervising the scenic lighting for Minami-Tenma Park

Minami-Tenma Park situated on the north bank of the Okawa River on the east side of Nakanoshima in central Osaka is a place well-known among the city's residents for its cherry blossoms. The indirect LED lighting along the river was designed with the view from the shopping facility on the opposite shore in mind. This ambient lighting extending a distance of 400 meters is the product of exhaustive analysis to ensure that the light source is not visible from the opposite shore and is designed so that the ripple of waves from the sightseeing boats sailing up and down the river creates a multi-color change in the color on the surface. We like to call this lighting techinque "Turner lighting" because it adopts a color motif reminiscent of the watercolor paintings of the English painter William Turner.

Kanagawa Art Theatre and NHK Yokohama Broadcasting Station

2010 Kanagawa, Japan
Design | Hisao Kohyama Atelier, Architecture Planning and Landscape Associates,
Hidetoshi Ohno + Architecture Planning and Landscape Design Workshop
Client | Urban Renaissance Agency

Keyword : Cultivating a Sense of Anticipation
Designer's comment : Check and recheck for the perfect lighting.
Custom-made fixtures : Façade Screen
Main light source : FL, HID, LED
Brightness contrast level : 4
Design Period : 1.5 years

This 1,200 seat urban-style theatre is located in Yamashita-cho, Yokohama. To optimize its operation facility is operated together with the adjacent civic hall. The illumination of the glass screen that is the exterior's most notable feature serves as a "welcome light" for the hall's visitors. Since this is a public facility, the design both creates a theatrical light ambience using long-life discharge lamps, fluorescent lamps, and LED to reduce running cost and maintenance frequency.

The design also avoids exposing nearby homes to light pollution. We also did the lighting design for the permanent outdoor the Remains of Yamashita Foreign Settlement exhibit discovered during construction and for the Former Yokohama Settlement No. 48 Building, which still stands at site.

The exterior of this ten-floor, one-underground floor building has a glass screen affixed with a unique pattern. Fluorescent lamps installed between the glass and roll screen inside illuminate the entire building, welcoming visitors to performances with an effect that is like a cocoon of light. During periods of normal operation, when the building is not conducting performances, the lighting operation plan synchronizes with the passage of time by gradually and randomly turning off lamps. The interior includes an expansive 30 meter-high atrium ceiling. Theatrical-like shadow created by indirect lighting from high-sidelights and spotlights located on the 8th floor accentuate the brick wall and floor.

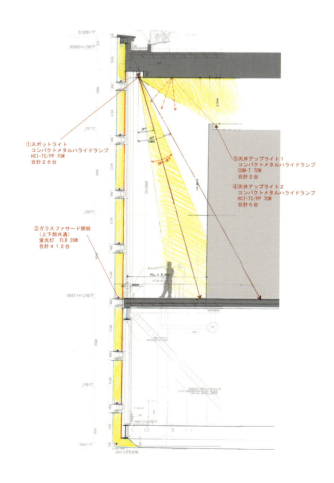

St. Regis OSAKA

2010 Osaka, Japan
Design | Nikken Sekkei, Taisei, GLAMOROUS, GA Design International
Client | Sekisui House

Keyword : Osaka Modern
Designer's comment : Sensitive and detailed hotel lighting
Main light source : IL, FL
Brightness contrast level : 4
Design Period : 3 years

This hotel designed around the concept of the "beauty of Azuchi-Momoyama culture" that flourished in Osaka in the latter half of the 16th-century is the first hotel in Japan for the St. Regis luxury hotel brand of Starwood Hotels & Resorts. Light and shadow are tinged with the magnificence and splendor of Azuchi-Momoyama beauty. Interiors filled with the soft glow of understated light are the result of careful study of decorative lighting designs and techniques for incorporating light into interior elements. Everything needed to achieve comfort — the ideal brightness balance, light source selection, verifying lighting details, dimming level, etc. — were carefully considered to ensure that the effect is like "an invitation to a mansion" that defines the St. Regis brand.

The lighting for the driveway apron overhang models the St. Regis New York design (above left). Inside, an exclusive elevator takes guests to the 12F reception lobby, a large room with vaulted ceilings. In the lobby, interior and roof garden lighting are balanced, so even at night the field of vision naturally moves from the interior to the garden and to the view beyond (P325 above). In the roof garden, ripples in the white sand are distinguishable through blue light and large rocks shaped like a dragon lurking in the sand are also illuminated, simulating a Japanese moonlit night (P325 bottom right). Beyond the reception area is a bar. The softly illuminated gilded ceiling and contrasting dark green walls combine to exude a certain dignified bar atmosphere (P325 bottom left).

The 12F Italian restaurant designed by GLAMOROUS, with dramatic floor-to-ceiling windows, uses warm light to softly enhance relief work and symbolical chandeliers. Lighting operations for the restaurant are controlled and adjusted to change based on a time schedule (above right). Soft light illuminates wall-mounted ceramic relief work to greet guests in the 1F French restaurant, also decorated with several unique, large Bordequx lamp shades (left).

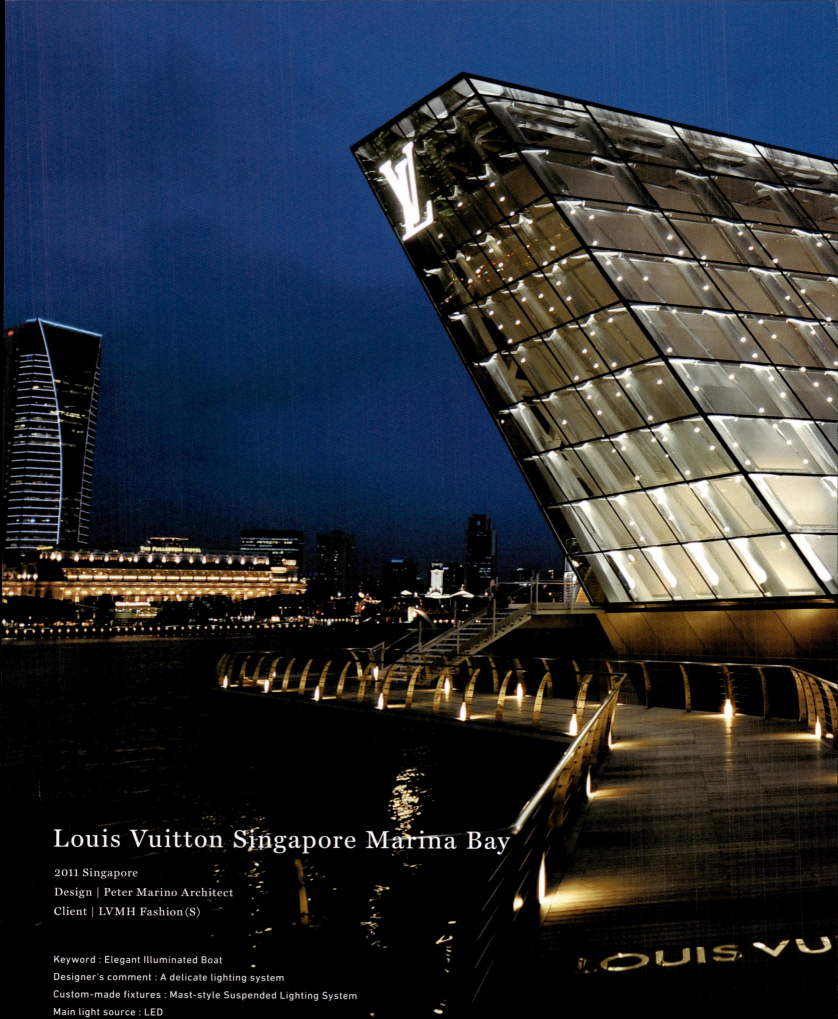

Louis Vuitton Singapore Marina Bay

2011 Singapore
Design | Peter Marino Architect
Client | LVMH Fashion (S)

Keyword : Elegant Illuminated Boat
Designer's comment : A delicate lighting system
Custom-made fixtures : Mast-style Suspended Lighting System
Main light source : LED

Surpassing even the excitement of recent years brought by the ongoing development of the Marina Bay Sands district, Louis Vuitton has opened a strikingly original, large-scale island-style shop right on top of the water. Guided by the concept "Elegant Illuminated Boat," we sought to create for this novel building a sophisticated light scene that also harmonizes with its surroundings. For the extremely porous sunshade specified by the architect to both regulate daytime light and reveal the shop interior at night, we tested numerous large-scale mock-ups that led us to a lighting scheme that conveys the energy within the shop when seen close-up but at a distance appears as a solid object.

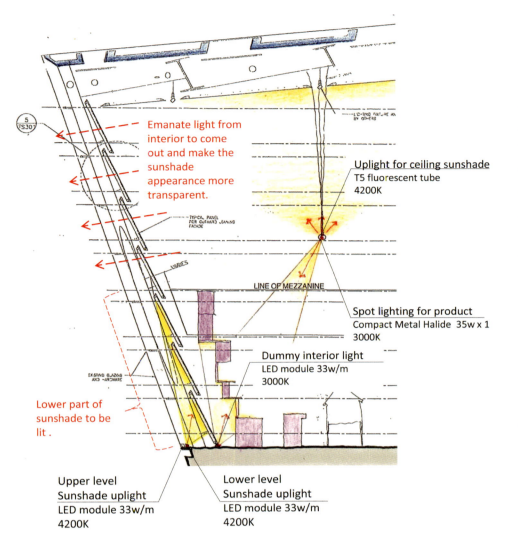

We paid particular attention to seamlessly integrating the lighting into the unique sunshade-covered interior of this spacious, glass pavilion-enclosed two-level atrium.

Lighting ducts for base lighting are unobtrusively placed between ceiling sunshade panels. Lighting fixture units designed to look like boat masts hang over display shelves and counters are installed with spotlights to highlight the merchandise below. Fluorescent lamps attached to the top of the mast-style fixtures provide uplighting for the ceiling shade and artwork and also greatly contribute to the space's overall brightness. For the two-level space, lighting fixtures integrated into the design complement the characteristics of each sales area and effectively showcase the products on display. For the low-ceiling space, every effort was made to keep lighting fixtures in the background by both minimizing glare and highlighting the merchandise with discreetly directed light.

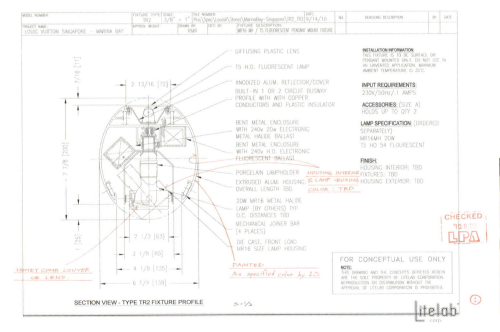

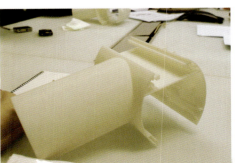

Reflections at Keppel Bay

2011 Singapore
Design | Studio Daniel Libeskind, DCA Architects
Client | Keppel Land

Keyword : Iconic Lighting
Designer's comment : At night, the "Sharpness" of the building is a delight to see.
Custom-made fixtures : Façade edge light
Main light source : LED, HID
Brightness contrast level : 4
Design Period : 5 years

A landmark development on the waterfront of Singapore, the lighting brief was to be iconic and true to its architectural form, yet suitable for a residential atmosphere. Façade lighting emphasizes the tapering edges of the towers and celebrates the profile of the buildings' crowns. The public areas have integrated LED lighting strips that accentuate the strong graphic geometries. Linear lighting both direct and indirect is predominant, and custom details that integrate the lighting with other building services were especially developed for the project.

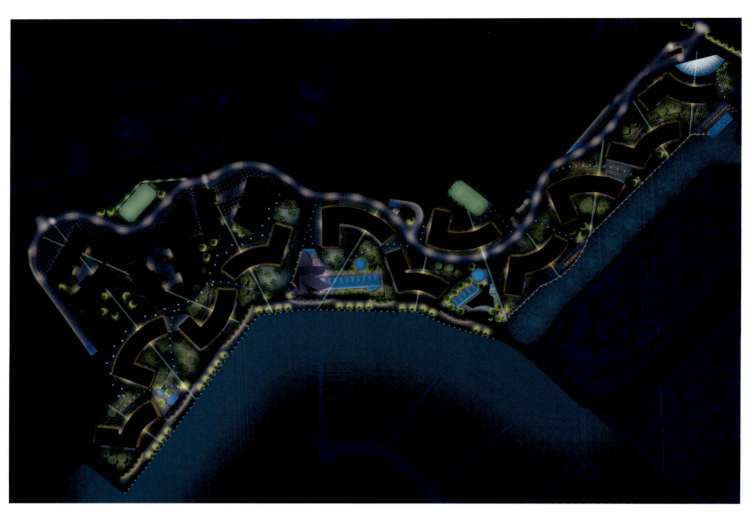

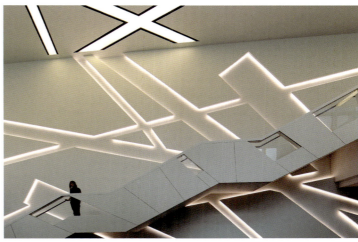

At the entrance to the basement car park, crystal glass is uniquely illuminated for a dramatic presentation (top left). In the main lobby, indirect lighting emphasizes the geometric patterns extending over the walls and ceiling and also highlights the architectural uniqueness of the structure (top right). View of the landscape from the sky garden which connects the six towers (above left). Soft light emits from windows and glass façade of the gym and clubhouse, creating a comfortable contrast with the bronze trim (above right, bottom).

We tried to enhance the visibility of the iconic crown and building profile of this project so that it could be visible from afar using a combination of slim LED profiles with diffuse emission for the façade edges, and very focused metal halide spotlights for the building crown. To show a natural character, we sought to create a gradation of light that peaked at the apex of the crown and gently faded away. The landscape lights are intentionally devoid of pole lights that would be out of place with the strong vertical character of the towers. The shallow reflection pools within the common areas have a grid of twinkling fiber optic light points that create a random sparkling effect depending on the water movement. This is a beautiful sight especially from the skyterraces and the interiors of the residences, when one is looking down.

on the Bund

2011 Shanghai, China
Design | HBA, John Portman & Associates
Client | New Union

Keyword : Lighting to Exude Historical Dignity
Designer's comment : The most beautiful nightscape on the riverfront
Main light source : HID, LED
Brightness contrast level : 4
Design Period : 3 years

This hotel in Shanghai's Bund district is the first hotel in Asia for the Waldorf Astoria luxury brand. It consists of a restored and refurbished heritage building built in 1910 and a new tower rising up behind it. Façade lighting painstakingly positioned to complement its ornamental features and a vivid and captivating presentation of architectural elements gives the building a conspicuous, eye-catching presence in an area in which buildings of the same architectural style are common. The interior lighting consciously contrasts and harmonizes ornate decorative lighting fixtures dating from a time close to that of the hotel's construction and modern architectural lighting.

NUS Education Resource Centre

2011 Singapore
Design | W Architects
Client | National University of Singapore (NUS)

Keyword : Soft Campus Lighting
Designer's comment : Very satisfied to see students enjoying the space
Custom-made fixtures : All Cold Cathode Tube
Main light source : Neon
Brightness contrast level : 3
Design Period : 3 years

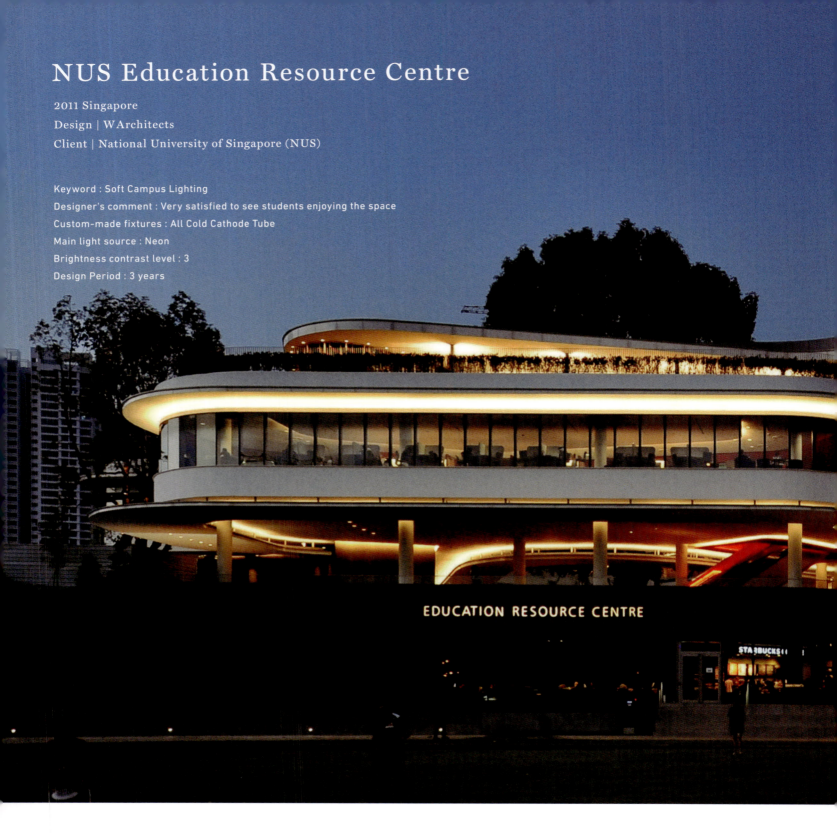

This project sits in the heart of the new campus of the National University of Singapore. Following the architectural profile, the exterior lighting for this round-the-clock center for students living in the adjacent residential blocks is mostly indirect. The reflected light from the contoured surfaces creates both visual interest as well as a gentle glow.

Inside, both daylight and artificial lighting are controlled to provide the students a glare-free environment. Completely silent automated shear blinds are synchronized with the lighting levels. Lighting closely matches the interior finishes and colour schemes, so that each zone has a distinct identity.

Sengukan Museum

2012 Mie, Japan
Design | Akira Kuryu Architect & Associates, Tansei Institute (Display)
Client | Jingu Shikinen Zoueicho

Keyword : Sequential Light
Designer's comment : Intricate lighting adjustments made on sacred ground
Custom-made fixtures : Luminous Ceiling, Ceiling Washer
Main light source : IL, FL, HID, LED
Brightness contrast level : 4
Design Period : 3 years

The Shikinen Sengu Ceremony performed every 20 years at Ise Shrine is an event of great significance for Japanese. For the 62nd Shikinen Sengu Ceremony, a new archive has been built next to Magatama-ike Pond of the Outer Shrine dedicated to the history, meaning, art, and traditions of Shikinen Sengu. Inside this archive building covered by a beautiful 45° *kirizuma*-style roof in emulation of the main shrine is a life-size model of a portion of the outer shrine's main sanctuary that visitors can view close up. The lighting is designed to give continuity to the building's entire spatial sequence, from the entrance to the sacred encounter. Another design theme was how to present with indoor light a shrine that under normal circumstances would be outdoors.

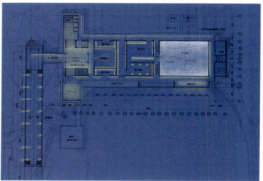

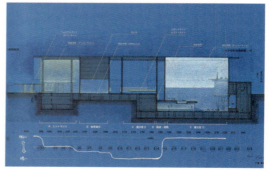

In the beginning, we drew several sketches of light and studied sequences of light according to the circulation route of the museum (above).

Linear floor lighting guides the eye from the main approach deeper into the building (top, middle left). In the entrance hall, the gabled ceiling is softly lit for a dynamic display of light (bottom left). The north corridor is a prelude to the galleries, with faint daylight reflecting off sand in a miniature, low-level, window garden and slit lighting illuminates several works of art (P341 top). This gallery displays models depicting an ancient midnight ceremony. To portray this dim, outdoor, ceremonial setting, the lux level of the entire gallery is reduced to only showcase and accent lighting for models (P341 bottom left). Past the stairwell, where lighting is reduced further, is the main shrine gallery with a luminous ceiling simulating a natural skylight (P338-339).

A combination of basic corridor lighting and gallery lighting creates a comfortable gallery setting in the south corridor. From dusk, corridor light also doubles as soft façade lighting (below right). The rest area is designed to also accommodate after-hour events. Glare control is carefully assessed from guest seating for an unhindered view of the stage and pond (bottom right). After dusk, interior lighting glows softly over the garden. The beautiful nightscape, complete with surrounding greenery, is quietly reflected in the pond (P342).

Our quest to create light worthy of this beautiful architecture on the shore of
Magatama-ike Pond of the Outer Shrine was guided by the following three lighting concepts.

1. Sequential light

We strived to create continuity from the entrance to the main sanctuary with gradual and seamless shadow transitions between corridors and exhibit rooms. Since this facility has more visitors during daytime than at night, we focused on creating a memorable spatial experience by balancing daylight and artificial light and contrasting brightness between adjoining spaces. The light sequence assumed to follow the circulation route of visitors starts from the entrance and links spaces together in a sequence that becomes gradually darker and culminates in the space with the luminous ceiling.

2. Light integrated into the architecture

We worked out lighting methods and details that erase the presence of lighting fixtures and conform with the conditions of the architectural space. Most important in this regard is that instead of fixtures attached to the *kirizuma* ceiling, highly intricate, custom-made lighting fixtures are concealed within the luminous ceiling that transform the ceiling itself into a lighting fixture.

3. Nightscape reflected on water

Creating an exterior with "warm light radiating from the inside" is a feature of Japanese architecture, and our design reflects the serene form of the architecture in Magatama-ike Pond, itself surrounded by luxurious greenery.

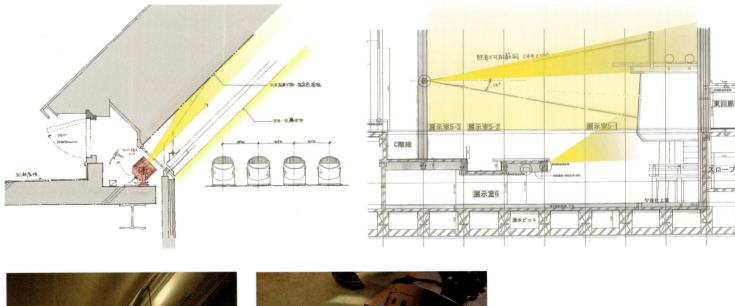

84 custom-made spotlights installed inside a limited space comprising a 400mm wide pocket illuminate the 10m long membrane ceiling in the gallery that displays a life-size replica of main sanctuary of the outer shrine. In addition, spotlights shine down on the gilded detail of the elaborately designed roof, giving the display an awe inspiring presence, as if glittering under the morning sun.

China Central Television (CCTV)

2012 Beijing, China
Design | OMA
Client | China Central Television

Keyword : Changing Nightscape
Designer's comment : The OMA communication model was stimulating.
Main light source : FL, HID
Brightness contrast level : 3
Design Period : 3 years

CCTV, the state-run television station upon which China has placed its reputation, is an extraordinary company, a growing and dominant media force not only in China but around the world. Construction of a new headquarters building with an intended completion date before the 2008 Beijing Olympics has been delayed due to fires and other setbacks.

This huge 600 million Euro project combines the 52 floor CCTV facility and 30 floor TVCC facility on the same site in a strikingly shaped volume with a 553,000m² total floor area. Our assignment was to design lighting for every space in and around the building, with the exception of special lighting in the CCTV studios.

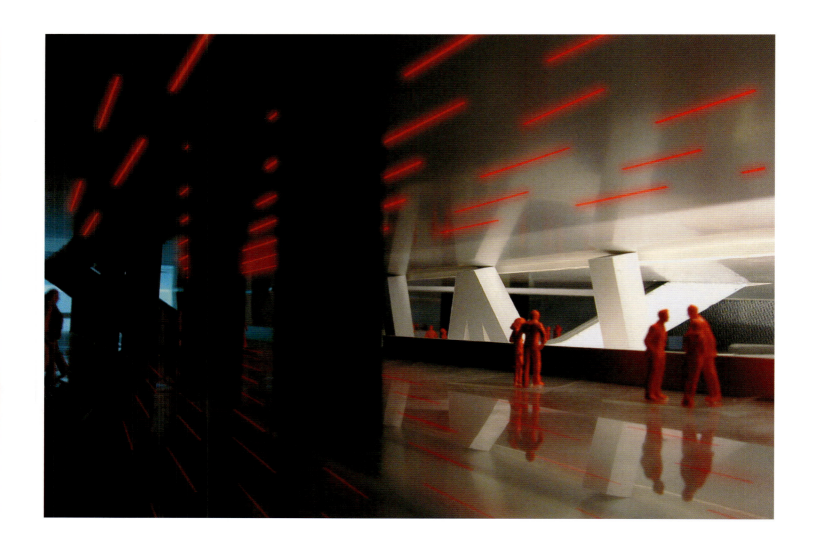
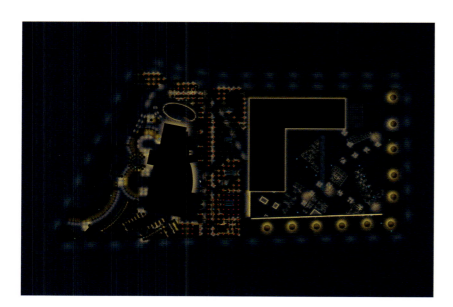

Adapting our lighting design to the accomplishments amassed by the designer OMA, was a grueling effort for which we only had six months to complete. We organized 15 LPA staff members into three teams, one each dedicated to CCTV and TVCC and a third dedicated to the exterior. Every month, 4 or 5 staff members traveled to Rotterdam to attend OMA workshops.

Our work began at OMA, where a place was secured for us to analyze the design details and ideas of the project's mocks-ups, which were updated every day, and massive number of blueprints. While in Rotterdam, we followed a detailed agenda and interacted with the other participants in the project from morning to night. Once we felt we grasped the content and aims of the architectural design, we turned to working out sketches of the lighting design scheme. We brought fiber optic equipment to insert into building models and fill out images. We hung our sketches on the wall and debated their merits. And, along with these exhaustive discussions, we positioned lighting fixtures in countless reflected ceiling plans and worked out detailed fixture specifications.

Finishing reflected ceiling plans for 52 floors was an impossible task. Proposing avant-garde lighting schemes still meant consuming all our time grinding through details. In the end, we were unable to renew the contract for the construction supervision phase and the lighting was not installed as we had intended in numerous places. The experience was a painful reminder of how vital it is to have an agreement that covers the entire project process, from initial design to final supervision.

Ocean Financial Centre

2012 Singapore
Design | Pelli Clarke Pelli Architects, Architect 61
Client | Keppel Land

Keyword : Architecture Cutting into the Wind
Designer's comment : The simple lighting design is actually very eye catching.
Custom-made fixtures : Lobby Pendant Light
Main light source : LED
Brightness contrast level : 2
Design Period : 6 years

This 43 floor office building is curved softly like a ship. A dense RGB-W LED dot matrix installed in the curtain wall dims in phases, creating a scene like a ship riding the wind off Marina Bay. In the lobby, we illuminated the 12-meter high core wall to bring out both a sense of brightness and the architectural solemnity of the space. The steel and glass canopy at the plaza features lights installed in the truss structure that both showcase its unique structure and provide ambient lighting. The slow flickering of the green wall, which comprises maps of the World, Southeast Asia and Singapore further adds dynamism to the plaza.

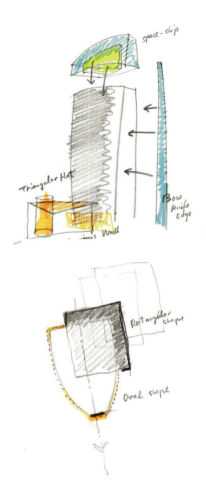

The truss-construction plaza canopy and green wall add a festive atmosphere to the plaza (P350). Wall washers brushing the inner core wall and custom-made pendants create ambience in the office entrance (below). Using partial models of the tower-tip lantern with optical fiber helps to share design image with clients (above). A concept sketch of architectural design vocabulary transformed into lighting elements (right).

Preservation and Restoration of the Tokyo Station Marunouchi Building

2012 Tokyo, Japan
Design | Design consortium consisting of the East Japan Railway Tokyo Construction Office,
JR East Tokyo Electrical Construction and System Integration Office,
JR East Design and JR East Consultants
Client | East Japan Railway

Keyword : Sustainable Nightscape
Designer's comment : Continuous days of late-night work
Custom-made fixtures : Custom-made LED Flood Light, Retractable Multiple Spot Light System
Main light source : LED, HID
Brightness contrast level : 4
Design Period : 3 years

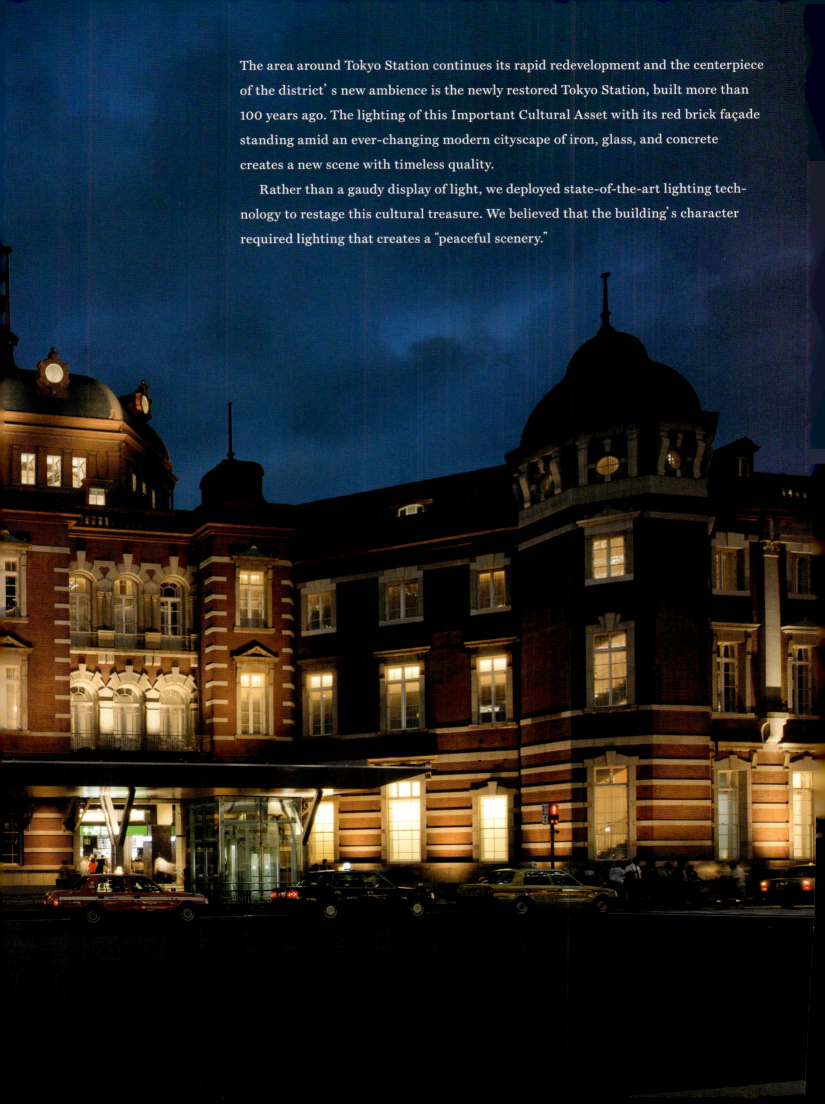

The area around Tokyo Station continues its rapid redevelopment and the centerpiece of the district's new ambience is the newly restored Tokyo Station, built more than 100 years ago. The lighting of this Important Cultural Asset with its red brick façade standing amid an ever-changing modern cityscape of iron, glass, and concrete creates a new scene with timeless quality.

Rather than a gaudy display of light, we deployed state-of-the-art lighting technology to restage this cultural treasure. We believed that the building's character required lighting that creates a "peaceful scenery."

On-site lighting mockups

Studies using a scale model of the station

The three year process from design to final light-up ceremony started with studying models of the building and numerous on-site mock-up lighting experiments. The lighting of each particular element—red brick façade, columns, balconies, slate roof, dome roofs, and so on—was meticulously checked and worked out. The final result is subtle and beautiful illumination.

Five Lighting Design Strategies and Six Fundamental Lighting Elements

1. Creating contrast among building elements

The building façade extends 400 meters north to south and consists of four architectural elements: the central section (A), the north and south domes (B), the north and south edges of the façade (C), and the overall building façade (D). Uniformly illuminating the entire exterior would not only consume vast amounts of energy it would decrease the value of the light by half. Carefully balanced light and shadow is essential to the design. Our study to find the perfect and most picturesque balance for a poised and beautiful presentation arrived at a luminance ratio of A:B:C:D = 7:10:5:3.

2. Dramatic gradation

Rather than sharp contrasts of light and shadow, creating a composed overall presentation is best achieved with gently and naturally diminishing gradation. When illuminating the exterior, highlighting the roundness of the domes, and so on, we made every effort to cast beautiful gradations of light from the ground up.

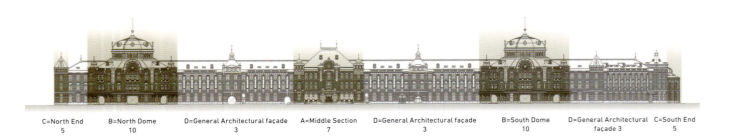

| C=North End | B=North Dome | D=General Architectural façade | A=Middle Section | D=General Architectural façade | B=South Dome | D=General Architectural façade | C=South End |
| 5 | 10 | 3 | 7 | 3 | 10 | 3 | 5 |

3. Light suitable for each type of material

The exterior deploys four types of materials: brick, stone, slate, and copper sheeting. We assumed that each of these materials has different light requirements and cast different kinds of light on them to find the most suitable color temperature for each. The color temperature of light casts on the natural slate roof is 4,200K and on the copper sheeting 3,500K. To recreate the best light environment for the station's stately red brick façade, we accent the finely crafted granite columns with 3,000K to contrast with the 2,300K cast on the brick. As light radiates from the ground upward the color temperature gradually changes from warm to cool hues. Inside the building, 2,200K light cast on the drapery achieves a warm ambience. Stable color temperatures within the 2,200K to 4,200K range are achieved with the latest LED technology.

4. Sustainable lighting system

Lighting design can no longer rely on inexhaustible energy sources. Most important is easy maintenance and low running cost. Besides the use of long-lasting LED, sustainable lighting requires sustainable, waste-free, and durable mounting detail. Sustainable design also rests on timeless lighting design uninfluenced by the latest fads that also creates environmentally-friendly light.

Reduced environmental burden

The lighting design uses LED only and also minimizes the brightness for nighttime scene transitions. This achieves significant energy conservation by reducing energy consumption by 56% compared to consumption before the station's preservation and restoration.

< Energy Reduction (daily average) >

	Power consumption	CO₂ emissions
Before renewal	134[kWh]	56[kg]
After renewal	59[kWh]	24[kg]
Energy Reduction	75[kWh]	32[kg]

Keys to a Low Carbon and Low-Impact Environmental Design

1. Adopt the use of highly efficient, long life LEDs
2. Apply the use of high quality luminaries
3. Vertical Planar Brightness
4. Targeted Light Distribution
5. Integrate dimming controls and scene operations

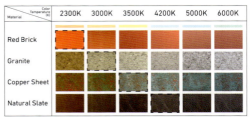

The most suitable color temperature for each material

5. Well-presented and energy-efficient operation

Lighting brightness and on-off transitions are time controlled. The lighting scheme both creates an almost imperceptibly changing nightscape and conserves energy.

Over the course of the day, from dusk to lights out, the lighting plan deftly transforms the scene. Moreover, operation takes into account seasonal power demand, including programs synchronized with holidays throughout the year.

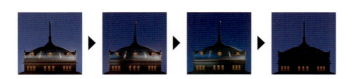

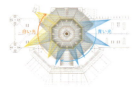

Lights are turned on at dusk, when there is still some natural light in the sky, and then gradually fade as the evening progresses until finally dissolving entirely in the night sky around 9PM. The tops of domes are carefully illuminated at 8 locations. Gradually changing light color continually transforms the scene like the waxing and waning of the moon.

Six Fundamental Lighting Elements

1. Illuminated red brick façade
A bottom section softly illuminated in warm light accentuates the red brick.

2. Illuminated columns
The white granite columns spaced amid the red brick are illuminated to accent the overall design.

3. Illuminated main arches
Fastidious illumination of the arches located in the building's south, north, and center create subtle shadow.

4. Illuminated dome roofs
The beautifully shaped domes are illuminated as the building's signature feature. Light operation continually transforms the illumination as time passes.

5. Linear illumination of the slate roof
A linear band of light accentuates the building's south-to-north horizontal axis.

6. Window lighting
Warm light from the windows is a key element of the exterior at night.

Completion and Opening Ceremony

Focusing and dimming control configuration

Operation	Daytime to Sunset	Sunset to 21:00	21:00 ~

Dome concourse lighting

The relief work on the third and fourth floor walls and dome ceilings is carefully illuminated with 4,000K to 5,000K light during the day and 3,000K at night. People on their way through the station pausing for a moment to look above them are a common sight. The third floor area opposite the hotel room windows, especially, has fixtures that eliminate as much glare as possible so that the lighting inside the domes can also be appreciated from inside guest rooms.

Overall illuminance of the concourse floor restrained to around 50 lux and highlighted ticket machines and gates define the concourse space and clarify circulation routes within it. Illuminated dome ceilings and indirect lighting of the walls that enclose the periphery contribute brightness. Strikingly strong light cast into the center of the circle serves to highlight the dome's circular form.

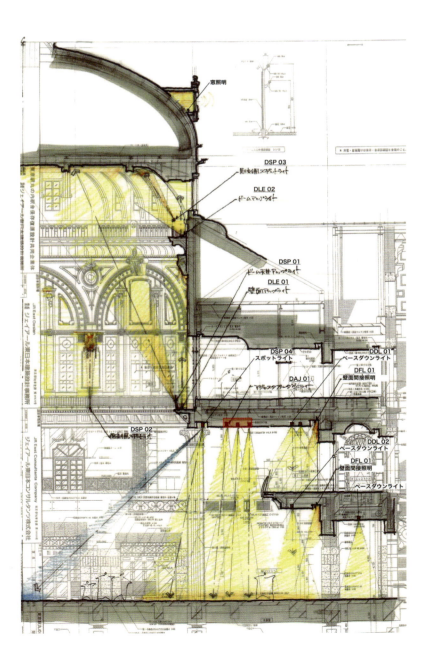

The Star

2012 Singapore
Design | Andrew Bromberg of Aedas, ICN Design International
Client | Rock Productions (Cultural Complex) /CapitaLand (Retail Complex)

Keyword : Unique in Appearance
Designer's comment : A bold façade design
Main light source : HID, LED
Brightness contrast level : 3
Design Period : 4 years

This building is part of the large-scale development that has begun in the Buona Vista district over the last several years. The lower section is a semi-outdoor, naturally ventilated atrium containing a galleria shopping mall. The upper section is a multi-purpose facility enclosed in a novel polyhedral mass holding a large, 5,000 seat hall. At night, sharply defined lines of light showcase the building's striking form while the front façade lends an ethereal quality to the theatre volume within.

A new landmark has been built next to Buona Vista Station.

Our main theme was how to showcase at night the striking presence of this polyhedral volume that seems to have been carved from solid form. Spiral shaped gaps encircling the polyhedron's periphery serve as ramps and openings. Like light radiating from fissures, the gaps become simple bands of light that accentuate the building's complex formal design. The 5,000K light bands are intended to contrast with the warm light of the interior.

The "Bowl Skin," as the theatre volume is called, is visible through the curved, glazed glass of the front face, which encloses it like a shell composed of linear acute-angles. Light radiating from folds forming a skin drape of soft curves and the Bowl cast in blue light create a striking exterior. During events, the blue light organically and imperceptibly changes, as if the activity inside were the act of breathing itself.

Warm toned lighting and blue light illuminate the ceiling to create contrast against the rows of burgundy seating in the large auditorium (above). In the foyer, blue light illuminating the main wall and white light radiating through the folds create a striking contrast (right). By illuminating the bottom lip of the auditorium block, softly reflected light also adds ambiance to the shopping area below (P364 above right). Downlights equipped with spread lenses create a carpet of light along the outdoor deck connecting the theatre and the station (P364 above left). The semi-outdoor shopping mall's minimal lighting is so energy efficient that it has been awarded a gold green mark (P364 bottom).

Kaga Katayamazu City Spa

2012 Ishikawa, Japan
Design | Taniguchi and Associates
Client | Kaga City

Keyword : Public Bathhouse Connected to Nature
Designer's comment : What do you think about this level of darkness?
Main light source : FL, LED
Brightness contrast level : 5
Design Period : 2.5 years

The former Katayamazu public bath was reopened as a city spa. This modern glass building cast in sharp light on the shore of greenery-fringed Shibayamagata Lagoon keeps alive hot spring culture and serves as a new place where citizens of the community and tourists can mix together. By keeping light to a minimum and highlighting the view of the lagoon and greenery, the hot spring's two unique baths — one facing the lagoon, the other facing the forest — preserve a view of the scenery while also maintaining privacy. This is a new kind of spa in which the seasons and nature extend their presence into the space through spacious openings, even at night.

Gardens by the Bay, Bay South

2012 Singapore
Design | Grant Associates, Wilkinson Eyre Architects, CPG Consultants
Client | National Parks Board

Keyword : Organic Lighting
Designer's comment : On-site adjustments for this expansive project required an all-out effort.
Custom-made fixtures : Variety of Organic Bollards
Main light source : LED, HID
Brightness contrast level : 4
Design Period : 4 years

With the construction of the Singapore Flyer and Integrated Resorts, Singapore's Marina Bay district has experienced frenetic development over the last few years. This development includes Gardens by the Bay, a waterfront garden composed of three areas totaling 101 hectares, among which the largest is Bay South. For this project, we proposed "Entertainment with Organic Lighting" as our concept for adapting outdoor entertainment to a new age.

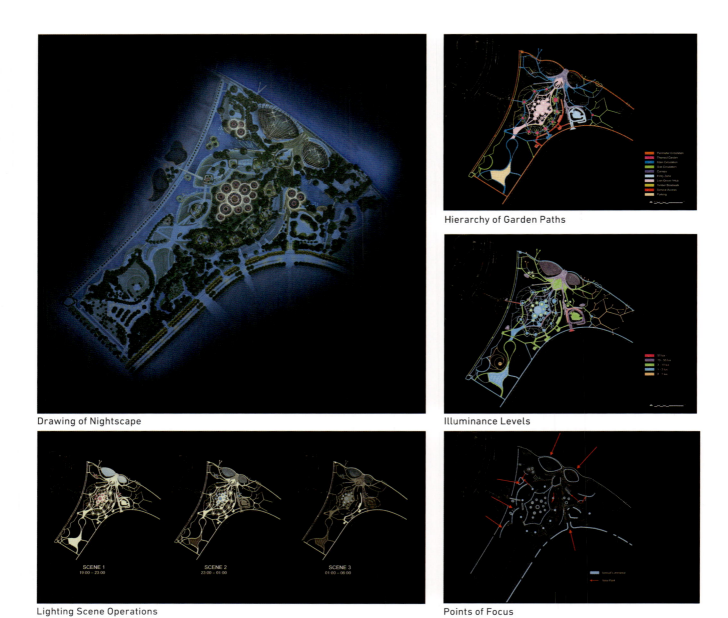

Drawing of Nightscape

Hierarchy of Garden Paths

Illuminance Levels

Lighting Scene Operations

Points of Focus

Two huge, waterfront glass domes called cooled conservatories and 18 "Supertrees" create a fantastic never-before-seen landscape on this expansive 54 hectare site. The Gardens also features many other unique facilities and areas, and integrating them all into a single, sophisticated and exciting nightscape needed an underlying core of common rules. We began by creating a lighting master plan and creating individual plans for the garden path hierarchy, illuminance levels, color temperature, main lighting method, focal point, and operation. At the same time, based on these various plans, we created conceptual drawings of the nightscape and performed studies.

Outdoor Garden

We incorporated the lighting into the landscape and interpretation design of each of the ten theme gardens that dot Bay South so that lighting fixtures are unobtrusive during the day and effectively showcase the features of each place at night. Garden paths feature a variety of fixtures custom-made in line with the parameters of the master plan, such as light poles whose light is reminiscent of sunlight streaming through trees, paper lanterns that cast plant motif shadows on the ground, and organic, winding and twisting bollards. The fabrication and supervision of high-quality custom lighting fixtures at overseas facilities became a key factor as the project moved forward.

We also designed lighting environments for other areas of the Gardens and created plans intended to guide visitors strolling through the Gardens with low-key light to unexpected encounters with beautiful scenery.

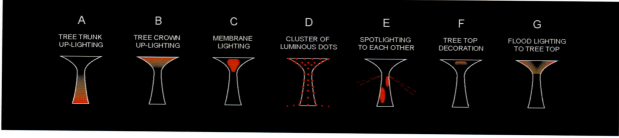

Supertrees

The Bay South Garden includes 18 novel 25 to 50-meter high vertical gardens called "Supertrees." Solar panels are installed on top of several Supertrees. During the day, their huge canopies cast shadow, while at night programmed lighting makes them appear to breathe, creating a space where visitors feel the vitality of the forest and sense the extraordinary.

The 6 lighting items installed on the Supertrees are programmed like a musical performance, organically transforming their appearance with a process as natural as breathing.

Clustered in three locations, all 18 Supertrees have synchronized lighting programs. In addition, visitors can take night walks on the aerial walkway between the two 42-meter high Supertrees.

Conservatories

"Cloud Forest" and "Flower Dome" are the Gardens' two climate-controlled cooled conservatories. Highlighted by the sturdy rib structure supporting their glass façades, their appearance creates a captivating nightscape, even from the opposite shore.

Cloud Forest

This 0.8 hectare, 58-meter high cool and moist dome recreates a tropical highland environment. Upon entering the Conservatory one is met by a breathtaking waterfall cast in dramatic light tumbling from a mountain covered in plants native to habitats nearly between 1,000 to 3,500 meters above sea level. From time to time a thick mist is released, enveloping the mountain in a thick fog and sending down bands of shimmering, mystical light from the aerial walkways.

Flower Dome

Visitors entering this 1.2 hectare, 38-meter high cool and dry dome are greeted by a large flower field populated by Mediterranean plants that at night is choreographed with light. The Flower Dome also has numerous baobab trees, palms, and other plants that are lit up to showcase their distinctive shapes.

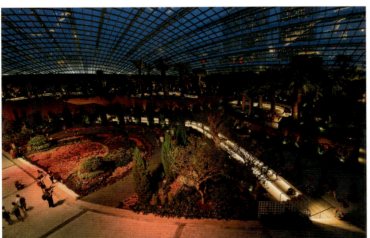

PARKROYAL on Pickering

2013 Singapore
Design | WOHA, Tierra Design
Client | UOL Group

Keyword : A Sense of an Outdoor Environment Inside
Designer's comment : The lighting from several luminous panels has a striking effect.
Custom-made fixtures : Variety of Lanterns
Main light source : HID, LED, IL
Brightness contrast level : 4
Design Period : 5 years

This hotel and office multi-purpose facility planned as a new landmark for this section of Chinatown leading into the Central Business District is designed around a "Hotel in the Garden" concept. A view of the street is visible through the pool from the deck on the 5th floor. The podium section and defining exterior feature has a "valley" motif showcased with lighting at night. The garden concept also extends to the interior, which is integrated with outdoor space by well-choreographed lighting.

City hotel exteriors this striking are few and far between. The plant-covered exterior exemplifies a new hotel concept unique to this city-state of everlasting summer. Following the architectural concept, the first concern of the lighting design was drawing attention to the vegetation, exploring not only how to enhance the guest's spatial experience but how to use the nighttime lighting of tropical architecture to contribute to the nightscape of a tropical city.

After consulting with the architect, we arrived at a two-pronged "light emitting surface/double-function" strategy for reducing environmental burden while maximizing effect. A "light-emitting surface" affects perception so that the space seems brighter in a psychological sense. In other words, instead of illuminance levels, the technique focuses on the perception of the person in the space. "Double-function" refers to our use of a single lighting method for both exterior corridor lighting for guests and urban scenic lighting. From the very start, we treated guest room lighting as an element of the exterior, working out design with one lighting method that fulfills two functions.

Landscape lighting provided entirely by solar storage equipment installed on the roof is another noteworthy endeavor of this remarkable hotel.

The Interlace

2013 Singapore
Design | OMA / Ole Scheeren,
RSP Architects Planners & Engineers
Client | CapitaLand Singapore, Hotel Properties and a third shareholder

Keyword : Framed Scenery
Designer's comment : The floating building blocks look very 'playful' at night.
Custom-made fixtures : Pole lights for the pedestrian zones.
Main light source : HID
Brightness contrast level : 3
Design Period : 3 years

This unique residential development is located in one of Singapore's greener areas in the south. The development consists of 31 six-story high superblocks. The blocks are stacked so as to form a hexagonal grid containing courtyards. This arrangement frames the view, which is further defined by the lighting of the soffits in each block.

We employed different lighting strategies that complement the thematic character of each zone within the development's large 8 hectare area. We also created custom lighting fixtures for outdoor areas.

InterContinental Osaka

2013 Osaka, Japan
Design | NTT Facilities + Ilya, BILKEY LLINAS DESIGN,
Hashimoto Yukio Design Studio, Ilya
Client | NTT Urban Development, Mitsubishi Estate, and others

Keyword : The New Osaka Nightscape
Designer's comment : Focusing LEDs was a unique experience.
Main light source : LED, FL, IL
Brightness contrast level : 4
Design Period : 3.5 years

"Contemporary Luxury" is the defining concept of this tower-style hotel north of Osaka Station that includes luxury residences. From the entrance to the guest rooms, diverse light creates an ambience of hospitality. For the 20th floor lobby, which boasts a panoramic view, and the restaurant floor, the lighting design reduces glare and minimizes the reflection of lighting in glass, creating a light environment ideal for appreciating the Osaka nightscape. Ambient lighting of the shell-shaped two-level atrium ceiling of the 2nd floor wedding chapel creates an atmosphere fitting for starting a new chapter in life.

Basic Studies on Lighting Plan for Railroad Station

2013 Tokyo, Japan
Collaborative Research |
East Japan Railway
Tokyo Electrical Consultation and
System Integration Office,
Nihon Tetsudou Denki Sekkei

Keyword :
Better Lighting Environment by Reducing light
Designer's comment :
A no-go for "survey" fieldwork
Main light source : FL, LED, HID
Brightness contrast level : 1
Design Period : 1.5 years

The shortage of electricity after the Tohoku Earthquake and Tsunami prompted a re-evaluation of light environment volume and quality, including facilities whose functions are mainly public in nature, train stations foremost among them. We began by documenting current conditions and conducting base studies with the cooperation of East Japan Railway and others in order to establish how much light is actually necessary and sufficient inside train stations. We then derived from the study results basic principles for achieving suitable light environments and formulated a foundation for analyzing train station lighting environments. Currently, the study results are being applied to drawing up renovation plans for several train stations aimed as part of a schedule for creating outstanding lighting environments in the years ahead.

Train Station Lighting: Three Issues

Issues that became apparent as the survey progressed can be broadly categorized into the following three:

Plan consists only of uniform floor illumination

While all kinds of specifications have been established for station lighting design, for light there are only guidelines for intensity — specifically, floor illumination — and no guidelines for evaluating light in terms of the space or light quality. Uniform illumination is important, but when it is made the only criteria light intensity easily becomes excessive. Moreover, these plans select glary fixtures with poor light volume color conversion and color rendering and direct the lighting only to the floor, resulting in dim walls and ceilings.

No operation plan

Most large-scale buildings have a timer and sensor system that turns lights on and off and controls light intensity so that the light environment is only as bright as necessary for the given time and situation. The few train stations that now have light operation systems provide suitable light environments and achieve energy efficiency by providing only the light needed for each time segment — morning, noon, night, after station shops have closed, and so on.

No correspondence with the building plan

Stations are administered by different bodies due to complex area divisions, resulting in individual lighting plans for each division and department. When there is no uniform approach, the boundaries between these division and departments may have too much lighting installed or a light environment that abruptly changes. Moreover, the lighting at these stations is not well-coordinated with the building plan or with other building infrastructure so that the light becomes a visual impediment and illuminates places that do not need to be lit up.

Train station survey schedule

The study was conducted from September 2011 through January 2013 at 17 locations in 5 train stations. The stations selected are expected to directly apply the results in upcoming lighting plans, have a large volume of users, and lighting equipment that is in relatively good condition. Study areas were concourses with significant foot traffic, ticket gates, platform stairs, and passages around shopping areas inside the station (ecute).

Location	Study date	Locations	Passengers
Tokyo Station	2011.09.08	Keiyo Street / Gin no suzu (plan only)	380,000
Shinagawa Station	2012.03.23	Concourse / ecute South	320,000
Akabane Station	2012.09.12	ecute corridor / Concourse central / Ticket gate / Platform stairs	90,000
Osaki Station	2012.11.09	Concourse / Overpass / Ticket gate / Platform stairs	130,000
Yotsuya Station	2013.01.15	Concourse / Ticket gate / Corridor inside gate corridor / Corridor outside gate / Platform stairs	90,000

Number of passengers as of 2010

Study flow

The general flow of the studies is as follows.

1. Produce in advance plans for several different lighting schemes by switching circuits on and off, covering lighting fixtures, attaching and detaching spotlights, and so on.

2. Perform grid floor illumination measurements and take fixed-point photographs and document and verify the light environment for each scene.

3. Recommend as the light environment the best low-light scene and then document and investigate issues concerning current lighting conditions.

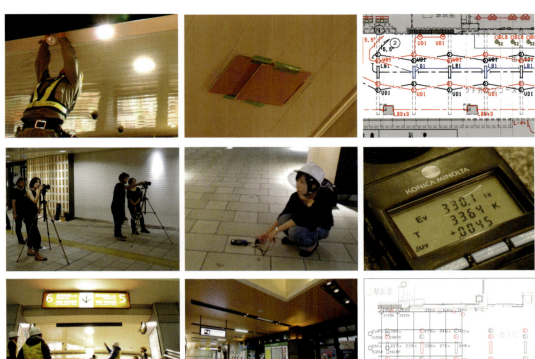

Study example: Akabane Station Concourse

Late at night on September 12, 2012, we performed and documented a lighting operation test at JR Akabane Station. This is one of the scenes that we documented and recommended from among the seven we measured at the station's concourse.

Full lighting

Recommended scene (during shop business hours)

Lighting fixture installation layout and fixture usage for recommended scene

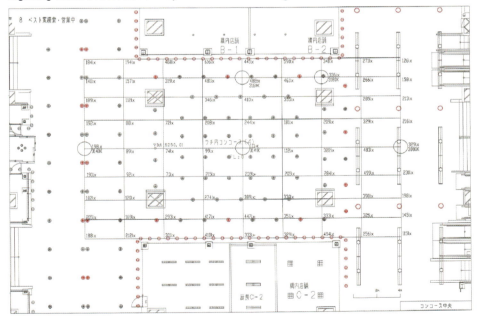

*Fixtures marked in red are illuminated during the recommended scene

Power consumption under full lighting and under the recommended scene

Scene		All Lights On	Proposed Scene / Business Hours	Proposed Scene / Closing Hours	Construction Costs (Percentage of necessary fixture installation)
	General Downlight FHT 42W × 2	100% 84 × 76 =5,880W (18.6W/m²)	61% 84 × 46 =3,864W (12.2W/m²)	61% 84 × 46 =3,864W (12.2W/m²)	61%
	Downlight LED 15W	100% 15 × 50 =750W (2.4W/m²)	100% 15 × 50 =750W (2.4W/m²)	100% 15 × 50 =750W (2.4W/m²)	100%
TOTAL		21.0 W/m²	14.6 W/m²	14.6 W/m²	
Percentage of fixtures used			69.5%	69.5%	71.0%

*width of corridor × width of storefront + 5m area=316.8m²

Switching on the entire array of uniform and compact fluorescent base downlights uniformly fills the space with bright light. We therefore studied how best to distribute the light. The space has a high ceiling and a planar surface with a mostly uninterrupted line of view, so it has comfortable forward and left-right views. Our study shows that in a location like this extinguishing the central downlight array draws attention to the shops on the side and vertical luminance on the walls and secures a sense of brightness.

Study example: concourse inside the Shinagawa Station ticket gate

Late at night on March 23, 2012, we performed and documented a lighting operation test at JR Shinagawa Station. These are four of the scenes that we documented and recommended from among the eight that we measured at the station's concourse.

1. Conditions at the time of the study
(power saving mode)

Only one-fourth of downlights were illuminated. As a result, while the area in front of stores was well-lit by interior store lighting and ceiling uplights it also made the stairs on the opposite side seem poorly lit.

2. Full lighting

An extremely bright effect. Besides floor illumination with downlights, pillar highlights and ceiling ambient lighting were among lighting elements intended to complement the space. Illuminating all of these at the same time, however, made the space so bright that each element lost its impact. In addition, the ceiling ambient fluorescent lights were directly visible, causing glare in places.

3. Fluorescent downlights only

The space with only the base lighting high-light distribution fluorescent downlights illuminated. Overall, since illumination is almost entirely uniform and the vertical plane lacks brightness, the result is a dim effect despite average illuminance.

4. Pillar highlights, etc. switched on

Scene with the fluorescent downlights dimmed and the pillar highlights and shop front ceiling uplights illuminated. Since much of this lighting is in the field of view and the vertical surfaces of the pillars and ceiling are illuminated, the scene creates a bright effect.

5. Highlighting added in front of stairs
(recommended scene)

Spotlights deployed before the stairs highlight the stairway. As a key station area traversed by a huge number of people, a concourse needs to provide a suitable sense of brightness and pedestrian safety while also making it easy to get around the station. Distributing the appropriate amount of light only where it is needed reduces power consumption while also providing functionality and a sense of design.

Luminary layout and fixtures to be used during proposed lighting scene
*The red notations are fixtures to be used during the proposed scene.

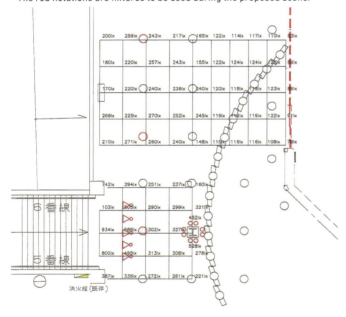

Original Scenes and Proposed Scene Power Consumption

Scene	Surveyed Scenes				Proposed Scenes	
	1. Original Scene at Time of Survey (Energy-Saving Application)	2. All Lights On	3. Fluorescent Downlights Only	4. Highlights to Columns Added	Until 22:00 (Business Hours)	After 22:00 (Closing Hours)
Shutter	Open	Open	Open	Open	Open	Close
General Downlight CFL(FHT) 42W × 3 (Incandescent)	29% 126 × 5 =630W (3.8W/m²)	100% 126 × 17 =2142W (12.9W/m²)	100% 126 × 17 =2142W (12.9W/m²)	18% 126 × 3 =378W (2.3W/m²)	18% 126 × 3 =378W (2.3W/m²)	OFF
Ceiling Cove Lighting FL(Seamless1m) 31W (Incandescent)	OFF	100% 31 × 11 =341W (2.0W/m²)	OFF	24.3 × 3 =72.9W (1.6W/m²)	100% 31 × 11 =341W (2.0W/m²)	100% 31 × 11 =341W (2.0W/m²)
Ceiling Cove Lighting FL(FHF) 32W (Natural White)	100% 32 × 12 =384W (2.3W/m²)	100% 32 × 12 =384W (2.3W/m²)	OFF	OFF	OFF	OFF
Column Highlights LED 6.9W (Incandescent)	OFF	100% 6.9 × 8 =55.2W (0.3W/m²)	OFF	100% 6.9 × 8 =55.2W (0.3W/m²)	100% 6.9 × 8 =55.2W (0.3W/m²)	100% 6.9 × 8 =55.2W (0.3W/m²)
Storefront Downlights HID 70W (Incandescent)	OFF	100% 70 × 4 =280W (1.7W/m²)	OFF	OFF	OFF	OFF
Spotlights (track lighting) HID 35W (White)	OFF	100% (Even Layout) 35 × 6 =210W (1.3W/m²)	OFF	OFF	83% (Before Stairs) 35 × 5 =175W (1.1W/m²)	83% (Before Stairs) 35 × 5 =175W (1.1W/m²)
TOTAL 1 Span (Width 10.4m × Length 16m = 166.4m²)	6.1 W/m²	20.5 W/m²	12.9 W/m²	4.2 W/m²	5.7 W/m²	3.4 W/m²

Examples of scenes recommended by the studies

We performed tests in spaces under all kinds of conditions, but the one thing common to every station was uniform and excessive floor illumination. Minimizing base light brings out pillar, wall, and ceiling light and heightens the visibility of illuminated signs. In particular, eliminating glary objects, floor-only illumination, and objects with poor color tone can improve the quality of the light environment. It is also important to consider the brightness contrast with adjacent space and diffusing light in a way that takes into account the depth of the space.

Yotsuya Station corridor outside ticket gate

Yotsuya Station ticket gate

Akabane Station ecute corridor

Tokyo Station Keiyo Street

Shinagawa Station ecute corridor

Osaki Station ticket gate

*Left: full illumination. Right: recommended scene

Summary

To improve station lighting quality for future, new construction and renovation plans it is especially vital that we break away from existing standards and processes. We formulated seven principles required for accomplishing an outstanding station light environment. Besides thoroughly understanding the organization and functions of a space, a lighting plan that follows these principles will achieve not only safety and functionality but a comfortable and environmentally-friendly light environment. These studies compiled large amounts of measurement data, but were evaluated only from a designer's perspective. Looking ahead, we hope that station lighting design will be based on objective evaluations using various criteria for evaluating space and carry out statistical studies using test subjects.

Seven station lighting principles

1. Appropriate illumination : Break the habit of illuminating floors only and avoid excess illuminaton
2. Vertical luminance : Plan wall, pillar, ceiling and other surface luminance and create a well-lit space without relying on floors
3. Pleasant shadow : Hightlight important areas, such as ticket gates and before stairs
4. Light operation : Program lighting to fit each time frame: daytime, nighttime, late at night, etc.
5. Glare-free : Enhance user comfort and worker safety by eliminating glare
6. Pleasant color temperature : Create an inviting ambience with low-color temperatures
7. Energy sustainability : Design a lighting system with long-term sustainability by eliminating waste and excess

Proposal for A New Nightscape for Sumidagawa River

2013 Tokyo, Japan
Client | Tokyo Metropolitan Government

Keyword : Versatile Riverside
Designer's comment : Looking forward to the implementation
Main light source : LED, HID
Brightness contrast level : 4
Design Period : 0.5 years

Original photos

A vision for a beautiful nightscape ten years from now has been planned that will create a "hustle and bustle area," "historic area," and "gate area" for three areas encompassing a total distance of 23.5 kilometers along the Sumidagawa River. We worked out measures for harmonizing glare with the surrounding darkness for all three areas and developed a practical plan that secures both choreographed lighting and the functional lighting needed for public safety. These landscapes also take the view from the opposite shore into account and field experiments were performed for some sections.

Proposed lighting scenes

Victoria Theatre & Victoria Concert Hall

2014 Singapore
Design | W Architects
Client | Ministry of Culture, Community and Youth,
National Art Council Singapore, Singapore Symphony Orchestra

Keyword : Old Meets New
Designer's comment : Unifying LED color temperature was painstaking work.
Custom-made fixtures : Modern/Classical Pendant Light
Main light source : LED, FL, HID, IL
Brightness contrast level : 4
Design Period : 4 years

This was a preservation and restoration project for a 100-year old historical building. Facing the front, the building consists of a clock tower in the center, a concert hall on the right, and theatre on the left. Guided by the concept of communicating "Old meets New" with light, the lighting design employs methods suitable for both the historical appearance and new design and that draw attention to their presence in the same place. The elaborate motifs and traditional look of the chalk façade is fastidiously illuminated in warm light, while the newly added spiral staircase for the concert hall and theatre timber seat box interior façade appear in bright relief through the glass enclosure. In this way, the latest lighting technology announces a new beginning for a historical building well-known to the public.

The Otemachi Tower

2014 Tokyo, Japan

Design | Taisei Design Planners Architects & Engineers,
Kohn Pedersen Fox Associates, Michel Desvigne Paysagiste, SIMPLICITY
Enterprising Body | Tokyo Tatemono

Keyword : Nature in the Urban Forest
Designer's comment : Enjoyable exterior lighting, even from inside
Custom-made fixtures : Moving Moonlight
Main light source : FL, LED, HID
Brightness contrast level : 3
Design Period : 5.5 years

This is a multi-purpose facility newly built at the intersection of Eitai Dori and Daimyo Koji in Tokyo's Otemachi district. The black clad exterior of the Otemachi Tower is given extra gravity with a distinctive slit light and ambient lighting at the summit. Lighting highlights the abundant natural greenery of "Otemachi Forest," the natural woodland recreated at the foot of the tower, and functions as a device for making the greenery's presence felt among the people going back and forth inside "Otemori" atrium. Every night at 8pm the forest is illuminated for 30 minutes by a xenon searchlight mounted on top of the tower, about 200-meters above ground.

Populated by pre-forest trees cultivated in Chiba Prefecture and then transplanted at the site, "Otemachi Forest" has the untamed atmosphere of an ancient and untrammeled woodland. Full-color LED spotlights light up spots in the forest, while a year-round light operation program that changes light color in harmony with the color of the leaves emphasizes the transitions of the four seasons. In addition, for 30 minutes starting at 8pm, light from the top of the tower shines down like moonlight on the forest, casting the shadows of leaves as it moves in a slow figure-eight pattern. The lighting uses a xenon searchlight and an automatic controller employing a system that extends a tip reflector panel at the appointed time. The system successfully casts light from a position about 200-meters above ground without pedestrians being aware of its source.

The illuminated forest visible through the glass curtain wall installed east to west along the four-level atrium "Plaza" uniting the space from the second underground floor to the ground floor gives the expansive exterior a presence in the interior.

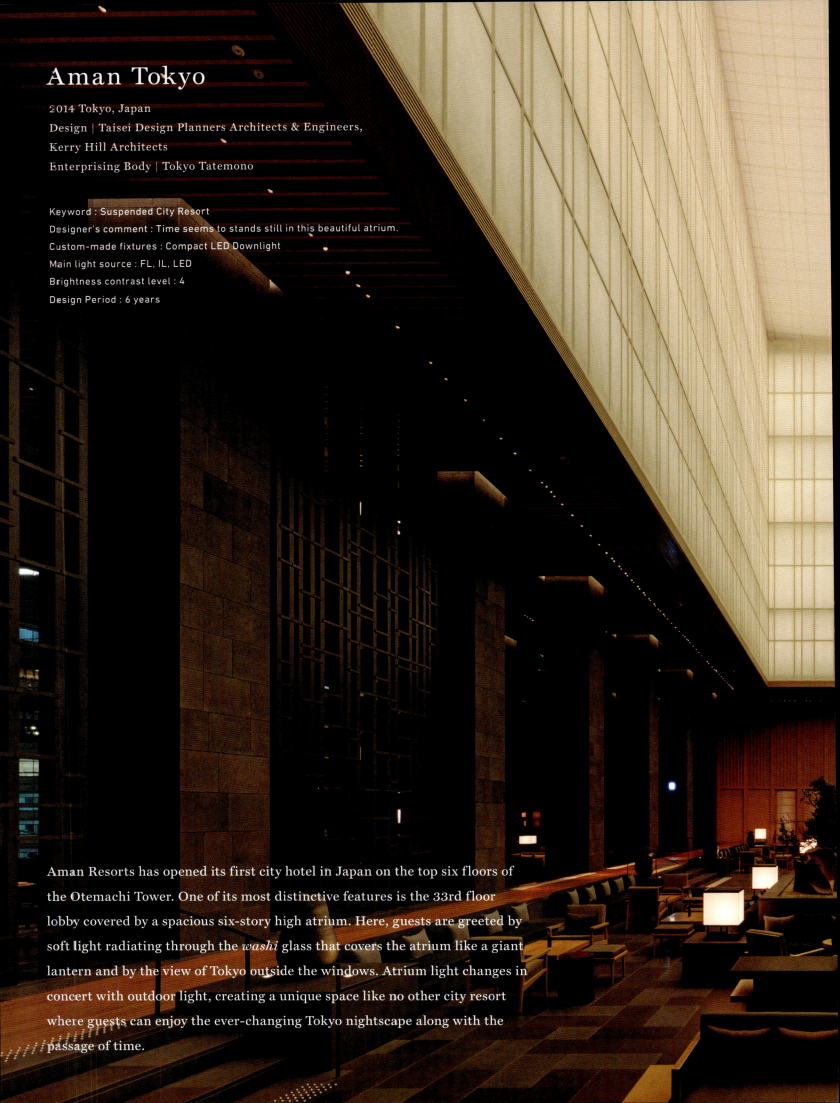

Aman Tokyo

2014 Tokyo, Japan
Design | Taisei Design Planners Architects & Engineers,
Kerry Hill Architects
Enterprising Body | Tokyo Tatemono

Keyword : Suspended City Resort
Designer's comment : Time seems to stands still in this beautiful atrium.
Custom-made fixtures : Compact LED Downlight
Main light source : FL, IL, LED
Brightness contrast level : 4
Design Period : 6 years

Aman Resorts has opened its first city hotel in Japan on the top six floors of the Otemachi Tower. One of its most distinctive features is the 33rd floor lobby covered by a spacious six-story high atrium. Here, guests are greeted by soft light radiating through the *washi* glass that covers the atrium like a giant lantern and by the view of Tokyo outside the windows. Atrium light changes in concert with outdoor light, creating a unique space like no other city resort where guests can enjoy the ever-changing Tokyo nightscape along with the passage of time.

Upon arriving at the first-floor entranceway and taking the elevator direct to the 33rd-floor, guests are met by a huge space enclosed by a six-story atrium ceiling. The *washi* glass wall that encloses this space has a 600mm deep maintenance space inside installed with fluorescent lamps that turn it into an immense lantern-like lighting fixture radiating light through the entire wall. So that the light emitting surface does not cast unneeded shadow, the position of lighting fixtures and the dimensions and shape of the internal structure were painstakingly worked out with on-site experiments.

The Tokyo nightscape visible through the lobby windows is one of the great pleasures that make high-rise city hotels so special, and in order to ensure a pleasant nighttime view, we paid special attention to minimizing the reflection of lighting in glass. At every turn, and including guest rooms, lighting is devised so as to reduce reflection. For example, areas facing windows use only glareless downlights.

In the guest room, the sitting area near the window, or *engawa*, lux levels are reduced so room lighting does not obstruct the view or atmosphere (right). In the 33F pool area, to reduce reflection in the glass and allow full enjoyment of the Tokyo nightscape, cove lighting around the pillars and floors stand lamps are the only lighting elements (below).

d'Leedon

2014 Singapore
Design | Zaha Hadid Architects, RSP Architects Planners & Engineers
Client | CapitaLand Residential Singapore,
Morganite (A consortium led by CapitaLand Singapore,
together with Hotel Properties and two other shareholders)

Keyword : Linear Continuity
Designer's comment : Residents can enjoy the strong graphical linear light.
Custom-made fixtures : Most fixtures
Main light source : LED
Brightness contrast level : 4
Design Period : 5 years

A large scale residential development in the heart of Singapore, the lighting scheme for d'Leedon is closely aligned to the unique architectural language of the project. This challenging scheme relies on continuous linear lighting profiles to achieve a seamless architectural expression — right from the entry to the development to all the public areas. A minimum number of bollards and pole lights were used. The continuous lighting profiles helped in creating a low contrast illumination which varied from space to space depending on the architectural expression. Almost all the lighting for the public areas were designed with LEDs.

In Facilities Pool 1, unbroken linear light traces the pool boundary and provides safety light when the underwater pool lights are switched off after 11pm (top). In Facilities Pool 2, a combination of underwater LED lights and spotlights on poles hidden between the palm trees on the pool deck ensures completely uniform pool lighting that also complies with the latest Singapore code requirements (above left). Linear light that expresses the architectural character of the complex is present everywhere, such as the softly glowing fabric covered pavilions (P403 above left), the solid surface walls of the lobby entrance (P403 above right), and the embedded uplights in the sculptural hanging gardens (P403 bottom). The low contrast illumination cast by the unbroken linear profiles is visually relaxing.

Oita Prefectural Art Museum

2015 Oita, Japan
Design | Shigeru Ban Architects, Studio on Site
Client | Oita Prefecture

Keyword : Lighting Contributes to the Town
Designer's comment : Also anticipating use at night
Custom-made fixtures : Luminous Louvre Ceiling
Main light source : LED, HID
Brightness contrast level : 3
Design Period : 3 years

This art museum designed for flexibility is equipped to accommodate all kinds of events, including exhibitions, collection exhibits, and galleries featuring the work of prefectural residents. Most importantly, since the first-floor exhibition room has movable walls that can be adapted to any layout — from precisely partitioned, enclosed exhibits to open-plan exhibits integrating the atrium into the layout — the lighting has the same degree of flexibility.

The 10-meter high atrium faces the boulevard and features an open plan enclosed in an 80-meter long, six-meter high glass horizontal folding door, creating a space where citizens can feel the presence of art as they unwind, even at night. The exterior is a wood latticework structure in the image of traditional bamboo art covered with glass. At night, the exterior is illuminated in gentle light that also provides light for the street.

CapitaGreen

2015 Singapore
Design | Toyo Ito & Associates, Architects
Client | CapitaLand, CapitaCommercial
Trust and Mitsubishi Estate Asia

Keyword : Urban Forest
Designer's comment : Acquiring energy saving certification was an arduous journey.
Custom-made fixtures : Glare-free Exterior Downlight
Main light source : LED, HID
Brightness contrast level : 1
Design Period : 3.5 years

CapitaGreen is the newest office tower in Singapore's Central Business District. As high-rise buildings become more and more common in the city, CapitaGreen stands out among them for an exterior more than half covered with plants that contributes more greenery to the skyline. The lighting was guided by the concept of showcasing this greenery in elegant light. The color temperature of lighting for the vegetation covering the façade changes in gradation from incandescent colors to white color from ground floor to the top.

The summit of the building features a red and white petalled structure which is part of a "cool void" that harvests the cooler and fresher air from the top of the building and around the sky forest and circulates it via air handling units to every office level. Uplighting the void etches its shape as a symbol in the night sky.

A lighting control system slowly and continuously varies the intensity of the façade lighting as if to suggest that the building itself is a living, breathing plant.

Minna no Mori Gifu Media Cosmos

2015 Gifu, Japan
Design | Toyo Ito & Associates, Architects
Client | Gifu City

Keyword : Architecture as a Luminaire
Designer's comment : How unique!
Custom-made fixtures : Sphere Pendant, Ring Pendant
Main light source : LED, FL, HID
Brightness contrast level : 3
Design Period : 4 years

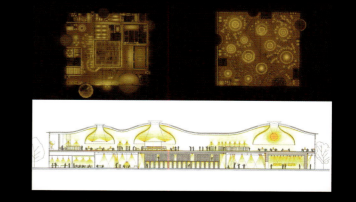

This multi-purpose public facility located in the center of Gifu City is scheduled to open in July 2015. Conceived as a center for community "knowledge, culture, and ties," the facility includes a central library, community activities exchange center, and exhibition gallery. The library enclosed by a soft, undulating wood roof and latticework walls utilizes to the fullest solar, wind, and other natural energy sources and is designed to harmonize with the lush forest planned around it. Low color temperatures and pleasant shadow create a tranquil and composed space reminiscent of deep forest living. Facility visitors are warmly greeted by a light environment amid a peaceful ambience imbued with nature's presence.

Keyword : Connecting People and Art through Light
Designer's comment : Historical architecture needs to be handled with the greatest care.
Custom-made fixtures : Luminary Mounting Box
Main light source : LED
Brightness contrast level : 4

National Gallery Singapore is a new visual arts institution that oversees the largest public collection of modern art in Singapore and Southeast Asia.

Situated in the heart of the Civic District, the Gallery is housed in the City Hall and adjacent former Supreme Court building — two important heritage buildings symbolic of Singapore's nationhood. A distinctive metal and glass canopy screen known as " the veil" integrates the two buildings at roof level, creating a civic plaza in the sky. Exterior lighting will be entirely LED with dimmer controls and lighting inside the windows will become more prominent as the night deepens. Along with showcasing the buildings' historical architecture, we have made every effort to create a welcoming ambience with the use of warm lighting as well as create beautiful artwork lighting using a highly efficient LED system. The official opening is scheduled for November 2015.

Ping An Financial Centre

Shenzgen, China
Design | Kohn Pedersen Fox Associates, AECOM
Client | Ping An Insurance (Group)

Keyword : Sleek Landmark
Designer's comment : Reminiscent of Gothic architecture
Main light source : LED, HID
Brightness contrast level : 3

Scene1 18:00-21:00

Scene2 21:00-23:00

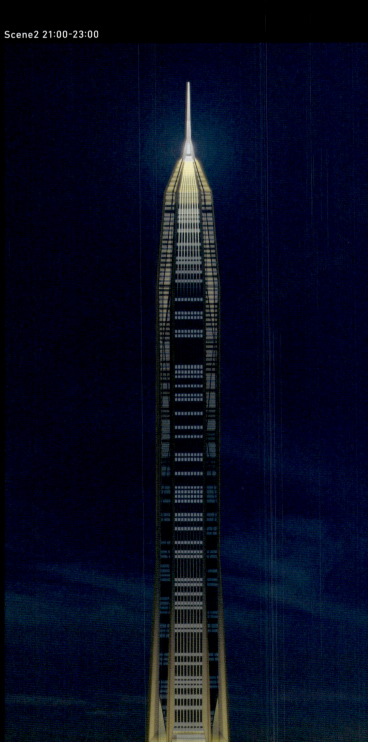

This is a 115 floor, 660 meter high tower in the planning stage for central Shenzhen. Scheduled for completion in 2016, construction is moving ahead at a feverish pace. Once completed, it will be the tallest tower in China.

The elegant, needle-topped tower's geometrical structure has been made a visible part of the building's design. The lighting design relies mainly on individually controlled LED light sources that will bathe the façade in beautiful, gradated light as if the light were streaming down from the firmament.

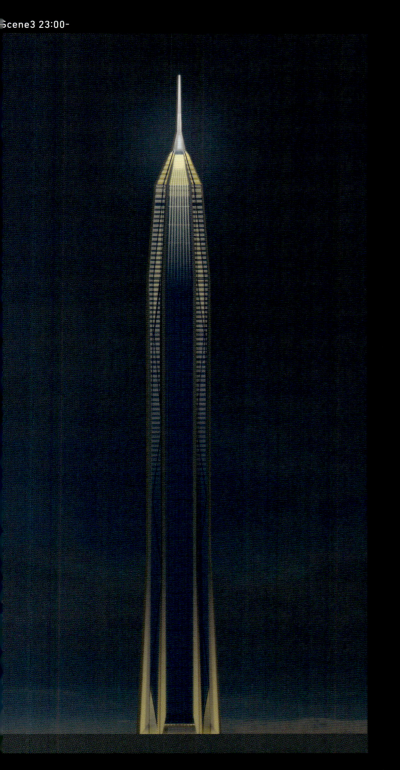

Scene3 23:00-

Scene4 Festive Time

Jewel Changi Airport

Singapore
Design | Safdie Architects, Benoy Architects,
RSP Architects Planners & Engineers
Client | Jewel Changi Airport Trustee

Keyword : 24-hour Amphitheater
Designer's comment : Waiting to experience Singapore's latest landmark
Custom-made fixtures : Tunable White LED Downlights; fixing, suspension Lights
Main light source : LED
Brightness contrast level : 2

Jewel Changi Airport is a new mixed use complex featuring attractions, retail offerings, a hotel, and facilities for airport operations strategically located in the heart of Singapore Changi Airport. With the concept theme of creating a 24 hour amphitheater, a dynamic lighting scheme will be adapted in Jewel where the interior lighting will be changed gradually according to the time of the day. Using state-of-the-art-adaptive LED technology, users in Jewel will also enjoy white lighting in an environment where tunable white technology and advanced lighting controls are used. Jewel is currently under construction and is scheduled for completion by end 2018.

Index / Photography Credits / Profiles

Index

The number after a project name indicates the page number.

Art Gallery and Museum

Shimosuwa Municipal Museum — 030
1993 Nagano, Japan
Design=Toyo Ito & Associates, Architects
Client=Shimosuwa Town

Chihiro Art Museum Azumino — 086
1997 Nagano, Japan
Design=Naito Architect & Associates
Client=Chihiro Iwasaki Memorial Foundation

Fukushima Lagoon Museum — 092
1997 Niigata, Japan
Design=Jun Aoki & Associates
Client=Niigata City (former Toyosaka City)

Fukui Children's Science Center — 106
1998 Fukui, Japan
Design=Mitsuru Man Senda and
Environment Design Institute
Client=Fukui Prefecture

Iwate Museum of Art — 122
2000 Iwate, Japan
Design=Nihon Sekkei
Client=Iwate Prefecture

Osaka Maritime Museum — 124
2000 Osaka, Japan
Design=Paul Andreu Architect,
Port & Harbor Bureau, City of Osaka
Client=Port & Harbor Bureau, City of Osaka

National Museum of Emerging Science and
Innovation (Miraikan) — 152
2001 Tokyo, Japan
Design=Nikken Sekkei and Kume Sekkei
Design Joint Venture
Client=Japan Science and Technology

Chihiro Art Museum Tokyo — 164
2002 Tokyo, Japan
Design=Naito Architect & Associates
Client=Chihiro Iwasaki Memorial Foundation

Nagasaki National Peace Memorial Hall
for the Atomic Bomb Victims — 170
2003 Nagasaki, Japan
Design=Kyushu Regional Development Bureau,
Akira Kuryu Architect & Associates
Client=Ministry of Health, Labour and Welfare

Kagawa Prefectural Higashiyama Kaii
Setouchi Art Museum — 202
2004 Kagawa, Japan
Design=Taniguchi and Associates
Client=Kagawa Prefecture

National Museum of Singapore — 240
2006 Singapore
Design=W Architects, CPG Consultants
Client=National Heritage Board,
National Museum of Singapore

Sengukan Museum — 338
2012 Mie, Japan
Design=Akira Kuryu Architect & Associates,
Tansei Institute (Display)
Client=Jingu Shikinen Zoueicho

Oita Prefectural Art Museum — 404
2015 Oita, Japan
Design=Shigeru Ban Architects,
Studio on Site (Landscape)
Client=Oita Prefecture

National Gallery Singapore — 410
Ongoing Singapore
Design=Studio Milou Singapore
Client=National Gallery Singapore

Commercial Facility

Tokyo Design Center — 016
1991 Tokyo, Japan
Design=Mario Bellini, Obayashi
Client=Sowa Estates

Pachinko Parlor II — 032
1993 Ibaraki, Japan
Design=Kazuyo Sejima & Associates
Client=Kinbasha

Shibuya PARCO Façade Lighting — 046
1995 Tokyo, Japan
Client=PARCO Promotion

Shinjuku I - LAND PATIO — 058
1995 Tokyo, Japan
Design=Housing & Urban Development,
Nihon Sekkei
Client=Housing & Urban Development

Queen's Square Yokohama — 100
1997 Kanagawa, Japan
Design=Nikken Sekkei ,
Mitsubishi Estate Architectural & Engineering
Client=T·R·Y 90 Associates, Mitsubishi Estate,
Urban Renaissance Agency, JGC

Nicolas G. Hayek Center — 262
2007 Tokyo, Japan
Design=Shigeru Ban Architects,
Studio on Site (Landscape)
Client=The Swatch Group (Japan)

Swarovski Ginza — 278
2008 Tokyo, Japan
Design=Tokujin Yoshioka Design
Client=Swarovski Japan

ION Orchard — 288
2009 Singapore
Design=Benoy Architects,
RSP Architects Planners & Engineers
Client=Orchard Turn Developments
Co-Lighting Consultant=Parsons Brinckerhoff

Tang Plaza Façade Enhancement — 308
2009 Singapore
Client=Tang Holdings

Louis Vuitton Singapore Marina Bay — 326
2011 Singapore
Design=Peter Marino Architect
Client=LVMH Fashion (S)

Theatre and Hall

Opera House in Frankfurt Auditorium Ceiling — 018
1991 Frankfurt, Germany
Design=Toyo Ito & Associates, Architects
Design Collaboration = TL YAMAGIWA Laboratory
Client=Frankfurt City

Kyoto Concert Hall — 048
1995 Kyoto, Japan
Design=Arata Isozaki & Associates
Client=Kyoto City

Toyama International Conference Center — 110
1999 Toyama, Japan
Design=Maki and Associates
Client=Urban Renewal of Otemachi District, Toyama

Nara Centennial Hall — 114
1999 Nara, Japan
Design=Arata Isozaki & Associates
Client=Nara City

National Centre for the Performing Arts — 266
2007 Beijing, China
Design=Paul Andreu Architect
Client=Owners Committee of National Centre
for the Performing Arts

Kanagawa Art Theatre and
NHK Yokohama Broadcasting Station — 318
2010 Kanagawa, Japan
Design=Hisao Kohyama Atelier,
Architecture Planning and Landscape Associates,
Hidetoshi Ohno + Architecture Planning and
Landscape Design Workshop
Client=Urban Renaissance Agency

Victoria Theatre & Victoria Concert Hall — 390
2014 Singapore
Design=W Architects
Client=Ministry of Culture, Community and Youth,
National Art Council Singapore,
Singapore Symphony Orchestra

Office Building

Panasonic Data & Communication Center — 024
Current: BANDAI NAMCO Mirai-Kenkyusho
1992 Tokyo, Japan
Design=Nikken Sekkei
Client=Panasonic
(former Matsushita Electric Industrial)

DENTSU Head Office — 198
2002 Tokyo, Japan
Design=Obayashi Tokyo Headquarters Office of
First-class registered architects, Ateliers Jean Nouvel,
The JERDE PARTNERSHIP
Client=DENTSU

Shiodome City Center + Common-Use Area — 199
2003 Tokyo, Japan
Supervisor=Kevin Roche John Dinkeloo
and Associates
Design=Nihon Sekkei
Client=Alderney Investments, Panasonic
(former Matsushita Denkou), Mitsui Fudosan

Shiodome Tower + Exterior — 200
2003 Tokyo, Japan
Design=KAJIMA DESIGN, Mitsubishi Jisho Sekkei,
Richard Rogers Partnership
Client=Nippon Television Network,
KAJIMA Shiodome development

Shiodome Sumitomo Building — 201
2004 Tokyo, Japan
Design=Nikken Sekkei
Client=Sumitomo Life Insurance,
Sumitomo Realty & Development

One George Street — 228
2005 Singapore
Design=Skidmore, Owings & Merrill, DCA Architects
Client=One George Street

Midland Square —— 256
2006 Aichi, Japan
Design=Nikken Sekkei
Client=Toyota Motor, The Mainichi Newspapers,
Towa Real Estate

China Central Television (CCTV) —— 344
2012 Beijing, China
Design=OMA
Client=China Central Television

Ocean Financial Centre —— 348
2012 Singapore
Design=Pelli Clarke Pelli Architects, Architect 61
Client=Keppel Land

The Otemachi Tower —— 392
2014 Tokyo, Japan
Architect=Taisei Design Planners Architects
& Engineers
Façade Design=Kohn Pedersen Fox Associates
Landscape Basic Design=Michel Desvigne Paysagiste
Commercial Environment Design=SIMPLICITY
Enterprising Body=Tokyo Tatemono

CapitaGreen —— 406
2015 Singapore
Design=Toyo Ito & Associates, Architects
Joint Engineering Design=Takenaka,
RSP Architects Planners & Engineers
Client=CapitaLand,
Capita Commercial Trust and Mitsubishi Estate Asia

Public Facility

Toyonokuni Libraries for Culture Resources —— 052
1995 Oita, Japan
Design=Arata Isozaki & Associates
Client=Oita Prefecture

Sendai Mediatheque —— 142
2000 Miyagi, Japan
Design=Toyo Ito & Associates, Architects
Client=Sendai City

Kani Public Arts Center —— 154
2002 Gifu, Japan
Design=Hisao Kohyama Atelier
Client=Kani City

Hiroshima City Naka Incineration Plant —— 188
2004 Hiroshima, Japan
Design=Taniguchi and Associates
Client=Hiroshima City

Chino Cultural Complex —— 208
2005 Nagano, Japan
Design=Studio Nasca
Client=Chino City

Supreme Court of Singapore —— 232
2005 Singapore
Design=Foster + Partners, CPG Consultants
Client=The Supreme Court, Singapore

Kaga Katayamazu City Spa —— 366
2012 Ishikawa, Japan
Design=Taniguchi and Associates
Client=Kaga City

Minna no Mori Gifu Media Cosmos —— 408
2015 Gifu, Japan
Design=Toyo Ito & Associates, Architects
Client=Gifu City

Educational and Medical Welfare Facility

Center for Advanced Science and
Technology, Hyogo —— 034
1993 Hyogo, Japan
Design=Arata Isozaki & Associates, ADH Architects,
Peter Walker William Johnson and Partners (Landscape)
Client=Hyogo Prefecture

Katta General Public Hospital —— 166
2002 Miyagi, Japan
Design=Architects Collaborative (Taro Ashihara
Architects, Koh Kitayama + architecture
WORKSHOP, Hideto Horiike + URTOPIA)
Client=Shiroishi Hoka Nicho Association

Akita International University,
Nakajima Library —— 272
2008 Akita, Japan
Design=Mitsuru Man Senda and
Environment Design Institute
Client=Akita International University

NUS Education Resource Centre —— 336
2011 Singapore
Design=W Architects
Client=National University of Singapore (NUS)

Transportation Facility

Kyoto Station Building —— 094
1997 Kyoto, Japan
Design=Hiroshi Hara + Atelier ϕ
Client=West Japan Railway,
Kyoto Station Building Development

Changi Airport Terminal 2 Upgrading —— 244
2006 Singapore
Design=Gensler and Associates International,
RSP Architects Planners & Engineers
Client=Civil Aviation Authority of Singapore

Preservation and Restoration of the Tokyo Station
Marunouchi Building —— 352
2012 Tokyo, Japan
Design=Design consortium consisting of the East
Japan Railway Tokyo Construction Office, JR East
Tokyo Electrical Construction and System Integration
Office, JR East Design and JR East Consultants
Client=East Japan Railway

Basic Studies on Lighting Plan
for Railroad Station —— 384
2013 Tokyo, Japan
Collaborative Research=East Japan Railway Tokyo
Electrical Consultation and System Integration Office,
Nihon Tetsudou Denki Sekkei

Jewel Changi Airport —— 414
Ongoing Singapore
Design=Safdie Architects, Benoy Architects,
RSP Architects Planners & Engineers
Client=Jewel Changi Airport Trustee

Athletic Facility

Tokyo Tatsumi International Swimming Center —— 038
1994 Tokyo, Japan
Design=Mitsuru Man Senda and
Environment Design Institute
Client=Bureau of Port and Harbor, Tokyo
Metropolitan Government

Odate Jukai Dome Park —— 098
1997 Akita, Japan
Design=Toyo Ito & Associates, Architects
Joint Engineering Design=Takenaka
Client=Odate City

Sapporo Dome —— 150
2001 Hokkaido, Japan
Design=Hiroshi Hara + Atelier ϕ, Atelier BNK
Client=Sapporo City

Hotel and Guest House

Hotel Poluinya —— 022
Current: HOTEL KIYOSATO
1992 Hokkaido, Japan
Design=Toyo Ito & Associates, Architects
Client=Nexus

W Seoul Walkerhill —— 192
2004 Seoul, Korea
Design=RAD, Studio GAIA
Client=SK Networks Walkerhill
Operator=Starwood Hotels & Resorts

The Tokyo Club —— 206
2005 Tokyo, Japan
Design=Taniguchi and Associates
Client=The Tokyo Club

Kyoto State Guest House —— 212
2005 Kyoto, Japan
Design=Nikken Sekkei
Client=Cabinet Office, Government of Japan

The Chedi Chiang Mai —— 236
Current: Anantara Chiang Mai Resort & Spa
2005 Chiang Mai, Thailand
Design=Kerry Hill Architects
Client=Suriyawong Holding
Operator=GHM

Banyan Tree Phuket, Doublepool Villas —— 268
2007 Phuket, Thailand
Design=Laguna Resorts & Hotels Public
Client=Laguna Banyan Tree
Operator=Banyan Tree Hotels & Resorts

Hilton Niseko Village —— 274
2008 Hokkaido, Japan
Design=Hashimoto Yukio Design Studio, Tanseisha
Client=Citigroup Principal Investments (Japan)
Operator =Hilton Hotels & Resorts

W Hong Kong —— 284
2008 Hong Kong
Design=Wong & Ouyang, GLAMOROUS (Interior)
Client=Sun Hung Kai Properties
Operator=Starwood Hotels & Resorts

Alila Villas Uluwatu —— 300
2009 Bali, Indonesia
Design=WOHA, CICADA
Client=Bukit Uluwatu Villa
Operator=Alila Hotels & Resorts

Aman New Delhi —— 304
Current: THE LODHI
2009 New Delhi, India
Design=Kerry Hill Architects
Client=Lodhi Property
Operator=Aman Resorts

St. Regis OSAKA —————————— 322
2010 Osaka, Japan
Architect=Nikken Sekkei, Taisei
Interior Design=GLAMOROUS,
GA Design International
Client=Sekisui House
Operator=Starwood Hotels & Resorts

Waldorf Astoria Shanghai on the Bund —— 334
2011 Shanghai, China
Design=HBA, John Portman & Associates
Client=New Union
Operator=Hilton Hotels & Resorts

PARKROYAL on Pickering —————— 376
2013 Singapore
Design=WOHA, Tierra Design
Client=UOL Group
Operator=PARKROYAL Hotels and Resorts

InterContinental Osaka ——————— 382
2013 Osaka, Japan
Design=NTT Facilities + Ilya,
BILKEY LLINAS DESIGN,
Hashimoto Yukio Design Studio, Ilya
Client=NTT Urban Development,
Mitsubishi Estate, and others
Operator=InterContinental Hotels & Resorts

Aman Tokyo ——————————— 396
2014 Tokyo, Japan
Architect=Taisei Design Planners
Architects & Engineers
Interior Design=Kerry Hill Architects
Enterprising Body=Tokyo Tatemono
Operator=Aman Resorts

Residence and Condominium

ACTY Shiodome ——————————— 201
2004 Tokyo, Japan
Design=Urban Renaissance Agency,
TOHATA ARCHITECTS & ENGINEERS,
HEADS, PAC, Takenaka
Client=Urban Renaissance Agency

Reflections at Keppel Bay —————— 330
2011 Singapore
Design=Studio Daniel Libeskind, DCA Architects
Client=Keppel Land

The Interlace ———————————— 380
2013 Singapore
Design=OMA / Ole Scheeren,
RSP Architects Planners & Engineers
Client=CapitaLand Singapore,
Hotel Properties and a third shareholder

d'Leedon —————————————— 400
2014 Singapore
Design=Zaha Hadid Architects,
RSP Architects Planners & Engineers
Client=CapitaLand Residential Singapore, Morganite
(A consortium led by CapitaLand Singapore, together
with Hotel Properties and two other shareholders)

Large Scale Complex

Osaka World Trade Center ——————— 056
Current: Osaka Prefectual Government Sakishima
Building
1995 Osaka, Japan
Design=Nikken Sekkei, Mancini Duffy Associates
Client=Osaka World Trade Center Building

Tokyo International Forum ——————— 074
1996 Tokyo, Japan
Design=Rafael Vinoly Architects
Client=Tokyo Metropolitan Government

Roppongi Hills ——————————— 178
2003 Tokyo, Japan
Design=Kohn Pedersen Fox Associates,
THE JERDE PARTNERSHIP, Mori Building
First Class Registered Architect Office,
Maki and Associates, Ohtori Consultants
Environmental Design Institute, and others
Client=Roppongi 6-chome Area
Redevelopment Association

Toki Messe Niigata Convention Center
Toki Messe Bandaijima Building ————— 186
2003 Niigata, Japan
Design=Maki and Associates, KAJIMA DESIGN
Client=Niigata Prefecture,
Niigata Bandaijima Building

International Commerce Centre ————— 276
2008 Hong Kong
Design=Kohn Pedersen Fox Associates,
Wong & Ouyang
Client=Sun Hung Kai Properties

The Star ——————————————— 362
2012 Singapore
Design=Andrew Bromberg of Aedas,
ICN Design International (Landscape)
Client=Rock Productions (Cultural Complex) /
CapitaLand (Retail Complex)

Ping An Financial Centre ——————— 412
Ongoing Shenzgen, China
Design=Kohn Pedersen Fox Associates,
AECOM (Landscape)
Client=Ping An Insurance (Group)

Urban and Environmental Planning

Waterfront City Symbol Promenade ———— 082
1996 Tokyo, Japan
Design=Nikken Sekkei
Client=Tokyo Waterfront Sub-center Construction

one-north Master Plan ————————— 158
2002 Singapore
Design=Zaha Hadid Architects
Client=JTC Corporation

Lighting Masterplan for Singapore's City Centre — 246
2006 Singapore
Client=Urban Redevelopment Authority

OSAKA "City of Light" ————————— 310
2010 Osaka, Japan
Client=OSAKA "City of Light"
Planning & Promotion Committee

Proposal for A New Nightscape
for Sumidagawa River ————————— 388
2013 Tokyo, Japan
Client=Tokyo Metropolitan Government

Plaza and Park

Beppu Park ————————————— 042
1994 Oita, Japan
Client=Beppu City

Fuji-Q Highland FUJIYAMA ——————— 104
1997 Yamanashi, Japan
Design=Kitayama & Company
Clent=Fujikyu Highland

Keyaki Hiroba ———————————— 128
2000 Saitama, Japan
Design=Ohtori Consultants Environmental
Design Institute, NTT Urban Development,
Peter Walker and Partners (Design Collaboration)
Client=Saitama Prefecture

OASIS 21 —————————————— 132
2002 Aichi, Japan
Design=Obayashi
Client=Nagoya Urban Development Public,
Sakae Park Promotion

Moerenuma Park Glass Pyramid ————— 176
2003 Hokkaido, Japan
Design=Architect 5 Partnership
Client=Sapporo City

Alexandra Arch, Singapore ——————— 282
2008 Singapore
Design=Look Architects
Client=Urban Redevelopment Authority

Gardens by the Bay, Bay South ————— 368
2012 Singapore
Design=Grant Associates,
Wilkinson Eyre Architects, CPG Consultants
Client=National Parks Board

Exhibition and Temporary Event

World City Expo Tokyo '96 ——————— 062
1995 Tokyo, Japan
Design=Toyo Ito & Associates, Architects,
Akira Kuryu Architect & Associates,
Kazuhiro Ishii Architect & Associates,
Riken Yamamoto & FIELDSHOP, and others
Client=Tokyo Frontier Committee

Kaoru Mende + LPA Exhibition
"A Manner in Architectural Lighting Design" — 118
1999 Tokyo, Japan
Organizer=TOTO GALLERY - MA

The 39th Tokyo Motor Show 2005
Nissan Booth ————————————— 220
2005 Chiba, Japan
Design=Curiosity
Client=Nissan Motor

OMOTESANDO akarium ————————— 260
2006 Tokyo, Japan
Client=Meiji Jingu,
Harajuku Omotesando Keyaki Organization

Commemorating the 50th Anniversary of the
Reconstruction of MEIJI JINGU [akarium] —— 296
2008 Tokyo, Japan
Client=Commemorating the 50th Anniversary of the
Restoration of Meiji Jingu Committee

Lighting Units
lx=Lux (Illuminance)
cd=Candela (Luminous Intensity)
cd/m²=Candela per square meter (Luminance)
K=Kelvin (Color Temperature)

Photography Credits

Satoshi Asakawa
pp074-075, p076 top, p080 bottom, pp086-087,
p089 below, pp092-093, pp114-116, p117 top

CapitaLand
pp406-407

Hideki Casai
pp132-133, p134 top

Casappo & Associates
p207 bottom

Mitsumasa Fujitsuka
pp118-119, p120 top left and middle left, p121

Katsuaki Furudate
pp048-049, pp050-051 top, p051 bottom

Edward Hendricks
p391

Hiroyuki Hirai
pp404-405

ION Orchard
pp288-289

Kajima Overseas Asia
p229, p230 top, p231 above right

Toshio Kaneko
pp016-017, p022, p023 top, pp024-025, p026,
pp029-031, p034 bottom, pp035-040, p041 bottom,
p042, p044, p045 top and center, p052,
p053 below left, p055, p056, pp058-059,
p060 above right, top left, and above left, p061 bottom,
pp077-079, pp081-083, p085, p088, p089 top, p100,
p145, p146 bottom left, pp152-155,
p156 top and bottom right, p157, p165, p167,
p168 above left, below left and below right,
p169 bottom, pp170-171, pp174-184, pp188-189,
p190 top, p191, pp196-197, p199, p201 bottom,
pp202-206, p207 top, pp208-216, p218 bottom,
p219, p241 below left, pp242-243, pp256-259,
pp262-264, p265 top, pp274-275, p277, pp284-287,
pp296-297, p298 top and bottom left, pp299-307,
pp318-325, pp338-342, pp352-353, pp355-358 above,
p360, p361 bottom right, pp366-375, pp382-383,
pp392-399

Keppel Land
p349

Kyoto State Guest House
p217

Albert Lim
p240

Mitsubishi Electric Lighting
p097

Nacása & Partners
pp032-033, pp104-105, pp124-127, p134 bottom,
p146 top right, p147 bottom left, pp278-279,
p280 top, p281

Tomio Ohashi
pp150-151

Koji Okumura
pp128-129

Panasonic
p046, p135

Philips Electronics Japan
p101, p103

Shinkenchiku-sha
p164, pp186-187

Shokokusha Photographers
pp098-099

Takenaka Corporation
pp244-245

Toyo Ito & Associates, Architects
p147 bottom right

Yamagiwa
pp110-113, p117 bottom

Nigel Young, Foster and Partners
p232, p235

Lighting Planners Associates
Cover, pp018-021, p023 below (both), p027, p028,
p034 above, p041 top, p043, p045 bottom, p047,
p050 bottom, p053 top and below right, p054, p057,
p060 bottom left, p061 above right,
top left and above left, p062, p064, pp066-067,
p076 bottom, p080 top and center, p084, pp090-091,
pp094-096, p102, p106-109,
p120 middle right and bottom right, pp122-123,
pp130-131, pp142-143, p147 top right, pp148-149,
p156 bottom left, p168 above right, p169 top, p173,
p190 below, pp192-195, p198, p200, p201 top,
p218 top and center, pp220-221, p230 bottom,
p231 bottom, p234, pp236-239,
p241 top and below right, pp248-249, pp252-254,
pp260-261, p265 center and bottom right,
pp266-273, p276, p280 bottom, pp282-283,
p298 bottom right, pp308-309, p314, pp316-317,
pp326-337, p343, pp346-347, pp350-351,
pp355-358 bottom, pp362-365, pp376-381,
pp384-388, p390, pp400-403
(in alphabetical order)

※ Except for all images and drawings above mentioned belong to LPA.
※ All photo credits in Chronology are included in Chronology.

The descriptions of projects in this book are as of the time of
completion and their current condition may be different in some cases.

Kaoru Mende

Lighting Designer

Born in Tokyo in 1950, he earned a bachelors and master's degree from Tokyo University of Art in the field of industrial and environmental design. In 1990, he founded Lighting Planners Associates Inc. The scope of his design and planning activities ranges widely from residential and architectural lighting design to urban and environmental lighting. He is also the acting chief of the "Lighting Detectives," a citizens' group that specializes in the study of the culture of lighting.

He has been involved in such superb projects as Tower of Winds, Tokyo International Forum, Kyoto Station Building, Sendai Mediatheque, Roppongi Hills, Nagasaki National Peace Memorial Hall for the Atomic Bomb Victims, Kyoto State Guest House, Chino Cultural Complex, National Museum of Singapore, Lighting Masterplan for Singapore's City Centre, Alila Villas Uluwatu, Gardens by the Bay, Bay South and Façade Lighting for Tokyo Station Marunouchi Building.

His numerous awards include the Illuminating Engineering Society (IES) International Illuminating Design Award of Distinction, International Association of Lighting Designers (IALD) Radiance Award, Illuminating Engineering Institute of Japan (IEIJ) Japan Culture Design Award, Mainichi Design Award, President's Design Award in Singapore and others.

He is a visiting professor at Musashino Art University and a part-time lecturer at Tokyo University, Tokyo University of Art, and other institutions.

He is a member of the following associations, Architectural Institute of Japan (AIJ), Japan Urban Design Institute (JUDI), Illuminating Engineering Society of North America (IES), International Association of Lighting Designers (IALD), and Japan Design Committee (JDC).

He has authored, *Science of Illumination and Lighting* (Shokokusha), *Welcome to Lighting Detective* (Nikkei BP), *Transnational Lighting Detectives* (Kajima Publishing), *LIGHTING DESIGN for Urban Environments and Architecture* (Rikuyosha), *Designing with Shadow* (Rikuyosha), *The Light Seminar* (Kajima Publishing), *A Manner in Architectural Lighting Design* (TOTO Publishing), and many other publications on lighting.

Lighting Planners Associates

LPA is an organization of lighting specialists established in 1990 by six lighting designers led by Kaoru Mende. The goal of LPA is to design and build outstanding lighting environments that enrich our architectural and lighting culture. Today LPA has a total of 57 unique lighting specialists at its offices in Tokyo, Singapore and Hong Kong.

While the majority of LPA projects are in the area of architectural lighting design, in recent years its many outstanding design accomplishments have reached to residential, hotel, office, commercial, public space, and landscape lighting as well as full-scale urban lighting projects. LPA has become a leading lighting consultancy in the world.

LPA is also the guiding force behind Lighting Detectives, established in 1990 dedicated to the study of lighting culture. Lighting Detectives promotes greater awareness through activities such as Lighting Detectives City Walks and the society's Salon Series, the activities of Transnational Lighting Detectives — an international network dedicated to lighting culture, and field surveys of urban lighting environments.

Tokyo
Lighting Planners Associates Inc.
5-28-10, Jingumae, Shibuya-ku, Tokyo 150-0001, Japan
Tel: +81 3 5469 1022
Fax: +81 3 5469 1023
E-mail: lpa@lighting.co.jp
www.lighting.co.jp

Singapore
Lighting Planners Associates (S) Pte. Ltd.
51B Neil Road, Singapore 088829
Tel: +65 6734 3086
Fax: +65 6734 2786
E-mail: singapore@lighting.co.jp

Hong Kong
Lighting Planners Associates (HK) Ltd.
Unit D 16/F, Wah Ha Factory Building, No.8 Shipyard Lane, Quarry Bay, Hong Kong
Tel: +852 2578 9007
Fax: +852 2578 9116
E-mail: hongkong@lighting.co.jp